PELICAN BOOKS

MUSIC IN ENGLAND

by Eric Blom

(A107)

Owing to production difficulties it is impossible to maintain large stocks of our publications, and the titles available change so rapidly that the complete catalogue is of little value as a means of knowing what books are in print. If you are not already on our mailing list and would like to know when new books or reprints are added, please send in your name and address on a post card.

Suggestions for new additions are welcomed.

PELICAN BOOKS

Music in England

BY

ERIC BLOM

PUBLISHED BY
PENGUIN BOOKS
WEST DRAYTON MIDDLESEX ENGLAND
245 FIFTH AVENUE NEW YORK U.S.A.

Published in Pelican Books OCTOBER 1942
Reprinted JUNE 1943
Reprinted JANUARY 1945
Revised Edition 1947

MADE AND PRINTED IN GREAT BRITAIN
FOR PENGUIN BOOKS LIMITED BY WYMAN AND SONS, LTD.,
LONDON, FAKENHAM AND READING

Contents

Contents

Preface

This book is not what scholars call a well-documented work. The reader will find in it no footnote references, no names of authorities and no bibliography. But this does not mean that its contents are not based on a great deal of reading and referring to the work of others, nor that the lack of detailed acknowledgment should be taken to indicate a want of gratitude for the information offered by them. These omissions are due solely to the necessity of saving space for the treatment of a vast subject in a small volume. In spite of the astonishing facts disclosed by a well-known limerick about the pelican's capacity, a "Pelican" is capable of accommodating no more than a certain specified amount, and it will be only too evident that I needed every line of space for my actual text.

My thanks must thus perforce be addressed to innumerable authors collectively. Having gone to true scholars only for my sources, however, I feel assured that they will be content to remain anonymous. After all, any author who gives us new information or ideas, or usefully summarizes facts for us, adds something to common intellectual property, and it is the glory of scholarship that this should be its own reward. I am, however, particularly and personally indebted to two authorities to whom I am anxious to express my thanks here: Professor Edward J. Dent, who read the MS. of the first six chapters, and Mr. A. H. Fox Strangways, who looked over chapter XI. They have both made useful corrections and invaluable suggestions. Professor Dent, indeed, has raised so many interesting points that I can only regret my inability to incorporate more than a fraction of them in my work. The temptation to use more of them was almost irresistible, but had I done so I could no longer have claimed the book as my own. Instead of a pelican it would have become something more like a magpie.

It may be asked why a title indicating that it deals with music in England, not with music in Britain, should have been chosen. The answer may be suggested by another question. Would a book on music in Britain have been materially different? Scotland, Wales and Ireland have had, if we come to think of it, few musical activities independent of those of England. There are endless mutual influences, and England was often the debtor; but where this is so, as in the case of folksong, Scottish, Welsh and Irish aspects of the story will be found to enter into the discussion as a matter of course, even if it is kept mainly to the English scene. True, such phenomena as the early Welsh Bardic music and the more recent Eisteddfod movement in Wales, which have never affected English music in the least, had of necessity to be dismissed briefly; but on the whole little that was of equal significance anywhere in Great Britain has been wilfully ignored, because musical England could not ignore it in its time. The Scottish and Irish influences which affected musical Europe during the nineteenth century, though mainly in a literary way, had of course to be duly noticed in a discussion of English musical life.

I say "English musical life" rather than "English music" because this little book was not written with the intention of furnishing simply a history of English composers and their work. That would have been too much a matter for specialists, or at any rate for a specifically musical public, whose needs in this direction are amply supplied by at least two books on the subject: Ernest Walker's *History of Music in England* and Henry Davey's *History of English Music*, both of them works the reader who wishes to study English composition in greater detail may be recommended to look up. All that is attempted here is to set the English scene in which musical life throughout the centuries unfolded itself, not only through the activities of composers, but also those of performers, scholars and institutions. To provide that scene with an elaborately detailed background, however, would have been impossible in the small space at my disposal. Thus, while doing my best to show something of the social as well as the artistic conditions of each period, I have been compelled to take a broad knowledge of English history for granted in the reader. I have also assumed some slight acquaintance with musical terms, mainly because it is more offensive to those who know to be offered elementary instruction than annoying to those who do not to find one or two technicalities they do not understand. Popular musical literature has made it easy in recent times to acquire such an understanding, and those who are sufficiently interested in a musical subject will not hesitate to do so; but I do not think that I have made my tale unreadable for those who wish to take a more superficial view of my subject.

It may be said, perhaps, that if my title is quite properly not "Music in Britain," it ought almost to have been "Music in London". But that cannot be helped. The reason is that music in this country has always been largely centralized in the capital, though not to so great an extent as French music has been in Paris. The large provincial festivals and the activities at the universities of Oxford and Cambridge are exceptions (duly taken into account), but on the whole it is true that musical conditions in London reflect those throughout the country, just as those prevailing all over England, properly discussed, are bound to throw light on certain aspects of musical life elsewhere in Great Britain. Many Italian and German towns, whether their music was supported by courts, as at Mantua, Ferrara, Dresden or Mannheim, or by the municipality, as at Venice, Hamburg or Leipzig, have almost watertight little musical histories of their own; England has a single big one—how big the deficiencies of this small volume are only too likely to show

—and its focal point is London. If our scene is laid there for the most part, the reason is that the most picturesque and fruitful episodes in English musical life were enacted there.

Dates of birth and death are not given in the text after the names of the personages discussed, but they will be found in the index. No attempt has been made to be consistent in quoting titles of old works. Where faulty or obsolete spelling seemed to add a touch of colour to the picture, it has been reproduced; elsewhere the wording has been modernized to avoid tiresome quaintness.

In conclusion, I affectionately dedicate this little book to all those who feel that they have been unjustly omitted from it. Among them are, in particular, the contemporary singers and instrumentalists, the inclusion of some of whom would have been more offensive than the omission of all.

ERIC BLOM

May, 1947

CHAPTER I

The Beginnings (. . . —1485)

We do not know when music became a consciously cultivated art in England, or indeed anywhere else, nor can we
tell how it first shaped itself. What is certain is that remarkable developments must have gone on far beyond the reach
of history. From immemorial times the people must have
danced and sung, from its establishment in Britain the
Christian church must have chanted at least part of its liturgy,
and sculptural and pictorial representations of musical
instruments date from far earlier times than any extant
music we know to have been played on them. Unfortunately for history music was for centuries transmitted merely
by ear and by tradition, and even when some system of
notation was in use, it long remained so inexact as to serve
merely as a rough reminder of what was already known to
the performers from aural teaching.

It is very uncertain at what period harmony, even of a
crude sort, first occurred to musicians. The view has been
asserted again and again that plainsong, which is not harmonized, represents all earlier music as a higher development of
purely single-line melodic music preceding the "discovery"
of harmony. It is just thinkable, of course, that such a
simple fact as the pleasing effect of a coincidence of two or
more notes did not strike anybody for centuries, just as the
possibility of representing an eye otherwise than as seen from
the front in a portrait shown in profile did not occur to the
Egyptians. Incredible as it seems, it is a fact that the Egyptians painted not what they saw, but what they knew was
there; and with a similar sort of preconception early musicians
may have refused to notice what it was actually possible to

hear, even if only by accident, but what was not recognized
as legitimate.   Any coincidental sound of two notes, indeed,
may have been regarded, not as harmony, but as intolerable
discord.   Yet it seems unbelievable that harps, dulcimers,
psalteries and other instruments capable of producing several
notes at once should have existed so long without ever
bringing it home to their players that the sound of several
strings together could be pleasant.   On the whole it seems
more likely that some sort of harmonized music was current
long before plainsong was consolidated by St. Ambrose in
the fourth century and by St. Gregory, the first Pope of that
name, in the sixth.   Plainsong may have been merely a
special means of maintaining a sort of ecclesiastical tradition
of purity opposed to a secular influence.   Monody (i.e.
pure melody) may have been the exclusive property of the
church, harmonized melody the "impure" luxury of the
world.   We have no direct evidence, but early pictures are
preserved which appear to show the concerted playing on
groups of varied instruments amounting almost to orchestras
of a kind.   A miniature in an eighth-century codex in the
British Museum, for instance, shows King David playing
on a rotta (a generic link between the lyre and the harp),
surrounded by four cornett players and four other people
apparently producing various percussive noises, including
hand-clapping.   The cornetts, being of different sizes and
therefore producing notes of different pitch, suggest some
kind of harmony, and percussion is unimaginable without
regular rhythmic patterns.   Moreover, dancing, which
reaches back into the dimmest beginnings of history, is as
inconceivable without such rhythmic patterns as it is without
music itself.   We should thus beware of taking it for granted
that all early music resembled that of the church, merely
because the church alone, having a monopoly of learning,
had the means of preserving its musical traditions by written
records.

Plainsong was introduced into England by St. Augustine, who was sent on his mission by Gregory I and landed in Thanet in 597, hospitably received by Æthelbert, king of Kent, who offered the guests a dwelling-place at Canterbury, where Augustine became the first archbishop. Specialists affirm that the English plainsong tradition is the next best after the Roman, because from the first the Britons sang much better than the French and the Germans, the latter of whom were notoriously bad.

According to the Venerable Bede, Roman liturgy remained confined to Kent for a long time: in his *Ecclesiastical History of England* he does not refer to its spread northwards until he reaches the year 669. He sang at the monasteries of Wearmouth and Jarrow, however, according to the practice of St. Peter's of Rome, as a boy of seven or eight in 680, he tells us, and he was later in charge of the music there. Bede, who shows great concern lest the music in church should deteriorate, as it continually threatened to do through excessive familiarity with some of its elements and through neglect of others, as well as through ever-intrusive secular influences, was clearly a considerable musician. So was Alfred the Great, who translated Bede's history from the Latin at the end of the ninth century and near the end of his own reign. It is tantalizing to be unable to form any definite conception of the music cultivated by such men outside the church and of the influence such cultivation must have exercised on society. We know, however, that music did play an important part in social life, and since dancing did so too, we may be sure that metrical music co-existed with the measureless plainsong of the church, the former being, so to speak, the counterpart of verse, the latter of prose. That some sort of harmony, too, was a feature at any rate of instrumental music has already been tentatively suggested.

In the church no harmony, even of the most primitive

kind, appeared until about the tenth century, when plainsong
began to be sung by higher and lower voices at a distance
of a fourth or fifth instead of in unison, at first probably by
a sort of carelessness, merely because the voices habitually
inclined to be used at different pitches. This led to the
discovery that at certain points, especially in cadences, thirds
and sixths, formerly regarded as more discordant than
fourths and fifths, were actually more satisfying and melli-
fluous, and so gradually harmony became more pliable and
was accepted by the church for certain purposes, though
plainsong has maintained itself as a special tradition to the
present day.

These developments do not belong to English musical
history in particular, but they had to be briefly discussed as
part of it. This applies also to the modes—the musical
scales which preceded our modern major and minor scales.
They are often called church or ecclesiastical modes, but this
is misleading, as all music (including folksong, which still
retains its modal character: see Chapter XI) was based on
them. The modes can be quite easily determined on the
keyboard of the piano if the following scales are played on
the white keys only:

Starting from D for the Dorian mode;
     ,,   ,,   E   ,,   ,, Phrygian mode;
     ,,   ,,   F   ,,   ,, Lydian mode;
     ,,   ,,   G   ,,   ,, Mixolydian mode.

To these four main tonalities were added what may be
described as four "pseudo-modes" (actually called "plagal"
as distinct from "authentic" modes), distinguished by the
addition of the prefix "hypo-" ("Hypo-Dorian," etc.) to
the names given above. They did not differ in their succession of notes from the authentic modes, but were used in
such a way that the final (tonic) note was felt to be shifted
away from the keynote to the fourth below. In the sixteenth
century, moreover, two more modes were added: the Æolian

(starting from A) and the Ionian (starting from C). It will be seen at once that the latter is our present major scale and that the Æolian mode differs from one form of our minor scale only in containing a minor seventh instead of the major seventh which became the "leading note"—the most distinctive feature not only of the new scale but of our normal procedures in harmony and modulation. The need for a sharpened note to lead naturally to the tonic with a conclusive cadential effect made itself felt to musicians long before the modal system became obsolete, and although composers continued to write strictly modally, performers often sharpened the sevenths as they sang and played—probably more often than we dare to suppose without the authority of conclusive evidence. This manner of performance with modified intervals was called *musica ficta* (see p. 25).

The tenth-century procedure of singing in parallel fourths and fifths, known as *organum* or "diaphony," gradually developed into a more and more independent handling of the separate vocal parts, much as about the eighth and ninth centuries plainsong had already developed by the interpolation of ornamental melodic passages into the liturgy, known as "tropes," English examples of which are preserved in a tenth-century collection used at Winchester Cathedral. By the early twelfth century we know that there was, again at Winchester so far as the English records show, a kind of polyphonic music the parts of which, anything from two to four, proceeded by a kind of free imitation which produced harmonic effects that were far from primitive. The words were Latin metrical poems used on solemn occasions and for processional purposes both in the church and out of it, and the name under which this species of music is known is the Latin one of *conductus*. It differed from plainsong not only in admitting more than one melodic line at a time, but in being measured: a modern transcription of it can, unlike plainsong, be divided into regular periods by bar-lines, though originally these periods were determined only by the words.

Primitive as such music appears to us, we are not entitled to suppose that to its contemporaries it was anything but intensely alive. The parallel chords of the *organum* must have been as eagerly taken up by progressive musicians and as hotly disputed by conservatives as any innovation of the present day; we may in fact guess something of their startling effect—as modernisms, not as archaisms—if we recollect how greatly delighted or shocked people were a quarter of a century ago by Debussy's new application of them in such a piece as "La Cathédrale engloutie." We must not imagine that this music, even in church, was sung in the tame devotional manner we now deem alone appropriate to worship. It should be remembered that the medieval cathedrals and churches, with the great bare floor of their nave, were meeting-places where people walked, talked and dropped into and out of the service as they pleased; that their miracle plays were the origin of the theatre, and at that time a substitute for it; that the Mass itself had cast the sacrament of the Eucharist into a dramatic form, because it was in such a form that it was most likely to strike the imagination of the populace. In spite of periodical papal or episcopal disciplinary edicts the church continually tended to admit secular elements calculated to attract worshippers by an appeal to their human interests. The music too must have been vigorously human. One can imagine it only as being roared lustily at the top of the singers' voices, and where it was accompanied by the organ, the process was exceedingly rough and cumbersome. Each pipe had at first its own bellows, requiring incredible numbers of blowers; the keys were large and unwieldy; the instrument was not so much played as struck or smitten; the tone was raucous in the extreme. But it was all full of vitality and doubtless engendered a wild excitement of faith and enthusiasm.

The parts in a *conductus* rarely proceeded by parallel motion, as those of the *organum* did, though examples of passages in consecutive thirds and even consecutive common chords have been found. The third, which we regard as the most suave interval for the purpose of parallel motion, was then still exceptional and discordant. Even in the thirteenth-century Scottish hymn to St. Magnus, which has been preserved as a unique specimen, the singing by two voices almost entirely in thirds was abnormal, so far as we know. In the twelfth century, at any rate, the lower voice had as a rule to fall whenever the upper one rose, so that the intervals constantly changed.

According to Giraldus Cambrensis the Northumbrians sang in two parts while the Welsh sang in many. Whether singing in thirds was common in Northumberland is not clear; more probably the second voice provided only a kind of drone, since it left the enunciation of the words to the first. Part-singing was no doubt common in other regions of Britain—if we only knew. What we do know is that an elaborately polyphonic vocal piece was composed by somebody or other, but not by John of Fornsete of Reading Abbey and possibly not as early as about 1240, as musical historians have asserted until recently, for Dr. Manfred Bukofzer has lately attempted to show that the piece cannot have been written before 1280 at the earliest. It is a "rota" or round in the Wessex dialect, "Sumer is icumen in," and like the St. Magnus hymn a solitary thirteenth-century example of a particular type of work, differing from it by its lay-out in six parts, four of them singing a long tune of no less than forty-seven bars in canon, the voices entering at distances of four bars, the two remaining parts adding a kind of "ground" of eight bars persistently repeated and forming itself a perpetual canon.

Scotland, then, shares with England the distinction of having left the world just one thirteenth-century musical relic that throws light on the state of music in that century as no other documents have done. Not light only on the state of music in Britain, however. It is no exaggeration to say that the "Reading rota," as it is called from its provenance, makes a revolutionary difference to musical history, but by no means English history alone, for we must beware of jumping to the conclusion that the accidental preservation of an English document of the greatest imaginable importance necessarily suggests that other countries did not possess similar music. After all, England itself must have had a multiplicity of specimens which have vanished as completely as their foreign counterparts. What we may conclude is that Europe probably and England certainly had developed a remarkably complex polyphonic music by the second half of the thirteenth century.

Of instrumental music we have no such early records. We can form little idea of what it was like, though the practice which persisted as late as Queen Elizabeth's time of playing vocal music on instruments indicates that it must as a rule have closely resembled sung music until the fashion of playing to audiences and with it the vanities of virtuosity arose. One exception, however, was dance music, which, although sometimes joined into by singers, was of course essentially instrumental. We have no contemporary documents to judge by, but the later survival of obviously early tunes indicates that early dance music differed from other kinds in at least two points apart from the fact that it was for instruments: (1) it was metrically measured and (2) it anticipated the modern major scale by frequently making a sort of premature use of the Ionian mode. In addition it may have been more fully harmonized than vocal music, and have made use of its harmony vertically, in block chords, rather than by the polyphonic combination of melodic lines.

Much of this is, admittedly, conjectural, but it is curious

to find, for instance, that Welsh harp music, which had a long enough tradition in the twelfth century to become subject to official regulation, and was derived from Irish models that were even older, is neither modal nor unharmonized, so far as is shown by the extant specimens which, though not very ancient in themselves, clearly perpetuate an ancient tradition. No less remarkable is it that we find orchestral assemblies of instruments shown in such early relics as the eighth-century codex already described, the eleventh-century codex in the Cambridge University Library where David with the harp is supported by a miscellaneous band, or the glorious fifteenth-century minstrels' gallery in Exeter Cathedral, where twelve angels play as many different instruments. The twelfth-century " Speculum Caritatis " by the abbot Ailred (or Ethelred) of Rievaulx asks in dismayed concern for those who, "under the show of religion, doe obpalliate the business of pleasure" (William Prynne's translation) :

"Whence hath the Church so many Organs and Musicall Instruments ? To what purpose, I pray you, is that terrible blowing of Belloes, expressing rather the crakes of Thunder, than the sweetnesse of a voyce ?"

And, after inveighing against the dreadful habits of singers, who by that time seem to have pushed sheer uproarious joy in performance to the length of imitating "a horse's neighings," "the shrilnesse of a woman's voyce" and the "agonies of a dying man," he goes on to say that :

"in the meantime, the common people standing by, trembling and astonished, admire the sound of the Organs, the noyse of the Cymballs and Musicall Instruments, the harmony of the Pipes and Cornetts."

Returning to vocal music, we find later examples of polyphony, more developed and assured, in the gymels and faburdens (to use the English term rather than the French *faux bourdon*) which reached their perfection in the fourteenth century. The artistic principle of both was to add fresh melodic material to a given melody by letting it second the tune in the treble part, and the main difference between the two was that the gymel added two parts (*gemellus*=twin), which, being both for high voices, lay very close together and frequently overlapped, while the faburden added only one, very much like its present-day descendant, the descant. Unfortunately the modern descant is too often degenerate, and even its best examples sometimes resemble nothing so much as over-ornate icing on a cake that would be quite good enough in itself; but the old gymel and faburden were a legitimate means of admirable and highly characteristic artistic expression. Both have been claimed, by no means only by English scholars, to have originated in England; but for the discussion of so highly controversial a matter this is not the place. One thing, however, is certain, and important from our point of view: the English faburden was much admired on the Continent and cultivated there according to the English example.

Thus began that intermittent influence of English musicians on those abroad, particularly in the Netherlands, Northern France and Germany, that was to be often interrupted and more often reciprocated, but did not cease until the seventeenth century. It was towards the end of the fourteenth that the first English master was born who was destined to teach much to his younger contemporaries abroad. He was John Dunstable, the earliest great English composer we know by name. Not very much of his work is available, and of his life next to nothing is known; but the preserved manuscripts are numerous enough to show that he possessed a new mastery of counterpoint equal to his great Franco-

Flemish contemporaries, Dufay and Binchois, and that he fruitfully influenced the next generation of the school of the southern Netherlands (or Northern France) and Burgundy, besides proving that he must have travelled or even lived abroad, probably as far away as Italy, since these manuscripts were discovered at Modena, Bologna and Rome as well as at Dijon.

Dunstable died in 1453, during the reign of Henry VI, who may himself have been a composer, unless we accept the recent conjecture that a Gloria and Sanctus for three voices, marked "Roy Henry" in the Old Hall Manuscript (c. 1440) are by Henry V. With Henry VI were associated, among others, Lionel Power, a composer scarcely less distinguished than Dunstable and an excellent theorist, and Henry Abyngdon, who after being succentor at Wells Cathedral became the first Master of the Children in the Chapel Royal in 1455. Another learned musician was John Hothby, a Carmelite friar, who about 1468 went to Italy to teach grammar, arithmetic and music (the last being then a branch of those sciences) at Lucca. In 1469 Henry granted a charter to a newly formed Musicians' Guild, thus showing his interest in the welfare of musicians even outside his own chapel, of which he took the greatest care, as is shown by the fact that in 1471 the chapelmaster to Galeazzo Sforza, Duke of Milan, came to London to choose singers from those in the royal establishment. Two younger men destined for outstanding musical careers became Gentlemen of the Chapel Royal in the 1470's: Gilbert Banestre and William Newark, the former soon succeeding Abyngdon as Master; and the fact that Robert Fayrfax entered the chapel at the age of about fourteen in 1479, when his voice must have been about to break, shows that it was not merely a place to draw singers into the royal service, but a school for gifted musicians.

Edward IV's reign was marked by much the same interest in music, and so was even the short-lived and lawlessly entered one of Richard III, who commissioned one of his Gentlemen, John Melynek, to ransack the cathedrals and collegiate churches of the country for the best singers. Richard was slain in the Battle of Bosworth the following year (1485), and when the houses of Lancaster and York were united by the marriage of Henry VII and the Plantagenet dynasty gave place to the Tudors at his accession, music in England was in a flourishing state and ready for greater glories.

CHAPTER II

Tudor Music before Elizabeth
(1485–1558)

With the advent of the Tudors in the person of Henry VII we come upon the English dynasty that cultivated music most assiduously, for personal pleasure as much as for reasons of state. Henry was keenly interested in it. The solemnities of his marriage to Elizabeth of York, on January 17th 1486, were celebrated with great splendour, not least in the matter of music. Thomas Ashwell, a youthful composer who afterwards became master of the choristers at Lincoln Cathedral, wrote a five-part anthem, "God save King Harry," for the occasion, and Gilbert Banestre, who had been appointed Master of the Children in the Chapel Royal during Edward IV's reign, supplied another for the same combination of voices, "O Maria et Elizabeth," especially addressed to the queen.

Henry surrounded himself from the first with the best musicians he could lay hands on, determined that the Tudor court should compare favourably with that of the Plantagenets in musical distinction. It was to be a musically erudite court, not one bent merely on entertainment. Scholarship was welcomed by the new king; more than that, it was sought out by him. When Banestre was taken ill soon after the royal marriage, the priest-musician Laurence Squire was temporarily appointed to his place in the Chapel Royal, succeeding formally even before Banestre's death at an early age—almost certainly before his fortieth year—in 1487. Moreover, John Hothby had been summoned back from Italy, where he had been teaching music, grammar and arithmetic for the last twenty years or so.

But if in the most exalted circles music was taught as one of the exact sciences rather than purely as an art, it could get along without science, after a fashion, among the common people. They sang their ditties in unison or in crude parallel harmonies and danced their clodhopping measures to the primitive pipe and tabor, or some such bucolic accompaniment. The tunes of the songs and dances were full of vitality and as highly organized in a new rhythmic way as the old plainsong, from which they still retained the modal scales, had been in its own free declamatory way. But these old tunes, whose inventors had already fallen into obscurity, for all that they must often have been great artists, though probably untrained and unconscious ones in most cases, did not lend themselves to delivery in harmony. The more enterprising singers may have tried to put "seconds" to them by the old uncouth *organum* device of simply reproducing the tune a fourth or fifth lower, with occasional adjustments to a third where a cadence would obstinately refuse to make sense; and a crwth or rebec or bass viol player may have indulged boldly in a double stop supplying a bass note here and there to give a semblance of perspective to the melody. But on the whole modal melody, stuck fast in the tradition of unaccompanied plainsong still, except in the matter of rhythm, lent itself but unwillingly to harmonic treatment. For reasons already explained in the first chapter, that treatment was found so difficult that only musicians who viewed their profession as a scientific pursuit could hope to solve it.

To accustom their ears to vertical hearing, i.e. listening to the chordal incidence of parts rather than to their separate horizontal flow, was not the only problem. Indeed the masters who had worked under Henry VII had already very largely solved it; but they had not yet fully realized that the modal scales, which do not allow of modulation, are not readily adaptable to polyphony, where contrasts of key are the underlying principle of fugal statement and answer. More than another century was to elapse before this truth could be grasped, and meanwhile it was only half comprehendingly acknowledged by a compromise. That compromise is known as *musica ficta*, a system—if anything so indeterminately applied may be so called—whereby the penultimate note of the ascending scale in any mode but the Lydian and the Ionian could be so changed that by sharpening it the distance between it and the final became a semitone instead of a whole tone. There were other such changes, sharpening or flattening, on different degrees of the scale, intended to soften harmonic solecisms in part-writing, such as the tritone (augmented fourth), but that of the minor seventh to the major (leading note) was the most important and frequent, especially in final cadences. Unfortunately the principle of *musica ficta* was never consistently carried out by composers in writing, but left to the discretion of singers, or at any rate of choirmasters, who in those days were trained in the art of applying it according to rules about which we have now regrettably little definite information, with the result that we cannot be at all sure how far we ought to go in making these semitonic alterations in modal polyphonic music if we wish to interpret it exactly as it was performed in its own time.

England very early had what more "musical" countries, and countries that have since put greater value on musical scholarship, have never had: specific musical university degrees, including that of Doctor of Music. The earliest Cambridge doctorate on record ante-dates this chapter, going back to 1463 at the latest; but it is attached to a name now obscure: Thomas Saintwix. Oxford followed much later, in 1511, but on the other hand with a name of the greatest distinction: Robert Fayrfax. A Cambridge doctor already, organist and choirmaster at St. Albans Cathedral and a Gentleman of the Chapel Royal, Fayrfax was then somewhere in his middle forties. He had been one of the great men under Henry VII, at whose funeral he sang in 1509, as well as at the coronation of Henry VIII, who granted him an annuity of £9 2s. 6d.—little enough in all conscience, if it had not implied the continuance of royal service.

Fayrfax's most gifted colleague was William Cornyshe, who entered the royal household about 1492, probably aged something under thirty; at any rate he appears in the records for the following year: "to one Cornyshe for a prophecy in reward, 13s. 4d." Cornyshe only resembled many later musicians attached to courts in rendering other services. He seems to have been a versatile artist. In 1504, when he was confined in the Fleet prison, apparently for some satirical writing that gave offence, he wrote a poem entitled: "A Treatise between Truth and Information," which suggests that he considered himself ill-used for having been courage-ously honest, and later he acted in plays at Court, where he does not appear to have fallen out of favour, and was placed in charge of the music played at pageants, banquets and other functions. In 1509 he became Master of the Children in the Chapel Royal on the death of William Newark, who, like Avery Burton, also cut something of a figure in Henry VII's time. Cornyshe set poems by John Skelton, thus beginning that collaboration of musicians with the great poets of their time which again and again arrests the attention of students of English music down to the present day. Corn-yshe again had his fee of two-thirds of a pound in 1502, this time for "setting a caralle on Christmas Day." A carol, it seems, was as good as a prophecy. A song of another sort was worth a whole pound, for that is what Newark received for such a piece on January 1st 1493; but a Mass was valued at no more, for Burton was paid another £1 for such a composition from the privy purse the next year. The same was given to Fayrfax by the queen in 1502 for a mere anthem, however.

Not all the best composers of the day were in royal service. Richard Davy, a priest and composer, for instance, who was appointed organist and choirmaster at Magdalen College, Oxford, in 1490, was one of the early musicians who, like so many up to the end of the eighteenth century at least, submitted to private patronage. He became chaplain to Sir William Boleyn, Anne Boleyn's grandfather, in 1501, and remained in the service of his son, Sir Thomas, in 1507, the very year usually assigned to the birth of the future queen and mother of Queen Elizabeth. And some ten years later a younger master, Richard Pygott, who can hardly have reached his later twenties at that time, was in charge of the choirboys in Cardinal Wolsey's private chapel, an establishment ostentatiously designed to rival the royal household itself, in whose service Cornyshe and Fayrfax were now growing elderly.

These two masters, with other musicians of the royal retinue, followed Henry VIII to France in the summer of 1513. The Chapel Royal sang its services at Thérouanne and Tournai, and at the former place they would have met their distinguished French colleague Jean Mouton, if the war had not forced him to fly to Saint-Quentin. There is little doubt that these musicians would have come together quite amicably, for it is improbable that there was much civilian hatred between French and English people. Wars were the affairs of kings and statesmen, too involved for others to understand or meddle with. Indeed one may doubt whether even those who unchained them always knew what they were about, which of course did not prevent them from meddling. Be that as it may, we know that in 1520, when the war in France still dragged on, Henry again took the Chapel Royal with him, and that at the Field of the Cloth of Gold it combined with the Chapelle de Musique du Roi, the two choirs actually singing together before François I and the English king with a professional detachment suggesting that music formed a link between nations quite capable of withstanding the dissensions of statecraft.

It was a truly international art. Differences between the music of this and that country, which were later to make the varied manifestations of the art so interesting, but also subjected them to endless prejudices and jealousies, it simply did not occur to anybody to consider. Each country pursued its musical cultivation as best it could, and if there was anything to be learnt elsewhere, its musicians welcomed the opportunity. Thus the eleventh-century French troubadours influenced the German Minnesinger of the twelfth and thirteenth centuries, and altogether the amazing early florescence of French song had its effect on the rest of Europe. The first Englishman to impress the Continent, Dunstable, left his mark on the Flemish polyphonists of the fifteenth century, who in turn repaid those of the sixteenth century in England with interest. The English madrigal and later the masque owed much to Italian models; but then again the Elizabethans sent their musicians abroad, influencing church music in Flanders through John Bull and Peter Philips, and song through the lutenists John Dowland, William Brade and others in Scandinavia and Germany. The French school was curiously inert during the great polyphonic period, but awoke again to song when the lute came to the fore, and French masters of that instrument had something to teach both Italy and England. Conversely, the English virginalists and Italian clavicembalists anticipated the French clavecinists. English ballad opera crept into Germany by the back door and served as the direct model for the German *Singspiel* while Handel was busy with his conquest of England all along the front. And so on and on, until national schools began to form themselves deliberately towards the end of the nineteenth century.

To return to the period under discussion: Benedictus Ducis, one of the outstanding Flemish composers, attached to the cathedral of Antwerp, is said to have come to England in 1515, but if he did he does not appear to have stayed long, perhaps because the time had not yet come for foreign musicians to find a ready outlet for their genius here. Such exchanges as took place between the English and continental intellectuals were by no means mainly musical. In 1521 John Dygon, another clerical musician some twenty years younger than Fayrfax and Cornyshe, but already a sub-prior of St. Augustine's Abbey at Canterbury, was sent to Louvain for further study under the Spanish humanist Juan Luis Vives, then only twenty-nine years of age. He returned to England two years later accompanied by Vives, who was appointed lecturer at Oxford at Wolsey's instigation. Erasmus of Rotterdam paid several visits to England, not only because of his friendship with Sir Thomas More, but also because he was attracted by the scholarship at the universities. What did not please him, however, was the excess of musical cultivation in England, or at any rate in the English church:

"They have so much of it in England that the monks attend to nothing else. A set of creatures who ought to be lamenting their sins fancy they can please God by gurgling in their throats. Boys are kept in the English Benedictine colleges solely and simply to sing hymns to the Virgin."

The great man was not a musician, and we may thus take some pride in his complaint: it is not often that foreign scholars have objected to an excess of music in this country.

The reader may ask what the earliest Tudor music was like. No description unaided by quotation in music-type can do much to give him a perception of a kind of music that is supposed to be no longer alive, though it is certainly not incapable of revival under suitable conditions and given

the right choice, as for instance of the wonderful Mass:
"O quam suavis" attributed to Fayrfax. But an attempt
must be made to show the stage at which music had arrived
during the reign of Henry VII.

In the first place it may be said that, as the Flemish theorist
Joannes de Tinctoris pointed out, the English school which
followed Dunstable, who had been progressive and whose
new notions had been readily absorbed by his continental
disciples, now became conservative. However, the con-
servatism was that of assured, consolidated mastery, comparable, *mutatis mutandis*, to that of Bach or Brahms, to choose
familiar examples of similar phenomena.

Church music—which is what mattered chiefly and what
we are able to study conclusively with the aid of a manuscript choir-book of the time preserved at Eton College—
was quite elaborately polyphonic, and motets at any rate,
as distinct from Masses, had begun to free themselves from
the convention of using a plainsong theme in one of the
lower parts, usually the tenor, a convention that could fetter
a composer's invention unduly, though it was also capable
of exercising a stimulating discipline upon him, as in the
case of Palestrina, who a good deal later on still retained this
practice.

The polyphony of Fayrfax and Cornyshe, of Davy, Pygott,
Banestre and the rest, was not disciplined in the sense that
Palestrina's was to be; but only the sort of criticism which
holds that art is engaged in a constant process of "improvement" and moves towards some kind of ultimate perfection
that is wholly illusory would dare to assert that Henry VII's
composers are any the less valuable in themselves for lacking
certain developments in which they could not possibly have
had any share. Their music was not only highly polished,
civilized and learned by comparison with the crude singing
in parallel parts once cultivated by the old *organum* and
probably still followed in the singing of folksongs; it still

shows qualities of fluency and euphony which, although they differ from what later traditions have led us to expect, are perfectly capable of moving a modern audience profoundly, provided the work exhibiting them happens to be a vital masterpiece like "O quam suavis." For artistic value is not a matter of period; it is a matter of personal creative force.

Considered from the point of view of those later traditions, the earliest Tudor music lacks organization, not only in form, but also in texture. The parts mingle with a good grace, but do not defer to each other in the matter of shape. Each takes its own course and leaves the composer free to wander at will, without reconciling voices imitating each other in similar formations.

The great virtue of polyphonic writing as we now conceive it is the art of combining parts that follow the same melodic outline at different distances, both of pitch and of time, in such a way that the result produces a rich web of interlaced tunes so beautiful and natural in its total effect that the hearer nowhere feels the strain of the composer's great mental effort, yet is able to watch its results with pleasure in every ingenious detail. Henry VII's composers were on the whole content if the total effect was good, and though the best of them were quite capable of seeing to it that details were so too, in the matter of a singable melodic flow of each part they were unaware, except in fleeting moments, that the interweaving of similar parts was a problem worth solving for the sake both of its technical fascination and its value as a structural expedient.

This device, which was later to lead to the development of fugal writing as one of the chief musical procedures, seems so obvious to us that we find it hard to imagine a school of highly accomplished musicians to whom it did not occur as a matter of course. But it was then obvious only in the sense that, for example, electricity or the circulation of the blood had always been before it became inevitable for someone to "discover" them. Still, if the masters of Henry VII's time did not make the discovery, they may nevertheless be said to have led to it unconsciously by occasionally introducing into their part-writing passages of imitation or near-imitation that gave the next generation a hint of what could be done more deliberately and artfully in that direction. What is more important, however, is that their non-imitative music had special virtues of its own: a marvellous fertility of pure melodic invention and of extraordinarily long-drawn phrases.

Netherland masters like Obrecht, Okeghem, Isaac and Josquin des Prés were at that time already performing polyphonic feats requiring the peculiar mentality of those who devise intricate riddles and mathematical problems; but we have seen that the English school was conservative. Moreover, there is no evidence that it knew much about the Flemings, who do not seem to have visited England, until their work began to be published early in the sixteenth century. By that time English musicians must have begun to see for themselves that imitation between one vocal part and another was going to be a stimulating means of musical development, even though it may at first have suggested itself to them, as indeed to the Flemings too, simply by the fact that the repetition of the same words at the entry of each voice must surely always have called for the use of the same melodic formation. What it is surprising to find in a hymn to the Blessed Virgin by Cornyshe in the Eton book, for instance, is that the entries of three voices on the words: "Salve Regina Mater misericordiae" all take a different course.

If the "modern" influence did not come through visits of foreign masters—for even that of Ducis is after all unconfirmed—English musicians, who continued to go abroad, could not fail to pick up new expedients of value, even if in the first place they went to teach their own old-established traditions. Thus Richard Sampson, an ecclesiastic, afterwards Dean of the Chapel Royal and still later Bishop of Chichester, who was appointed proctor at Tournai in 1517, but seems to have been in Flanders earlier, contributed two motets in the new manner to a volume dated 1516.

A generation slightly younger than Henry VII's great musicians, especially the group we may call the "three great T's", John Taverner, Christopher Tye and Thomas Tallis, who all grew to manhood in the early years of Henry VIII's reign, began to take to the new ways of achieving a more convincing construction by means of a closer texture of parts imitating each other in canon and tending towards fugue; and it may be said here that the tendency shown by canon to grow into fugue, with its imitation at different pitches, had sooner or later inevitably to affect vocal music, where altos and basses can be more easily made to reproduce melodies a fourth or fifth below the sopranos and tenors than at the same pitch or an octave lower.

Soon after the death of Fayrfax in 1521, of Hugh Aston (an early pioneer of virginal music) in 1522 and of Cornyshe in 1523, the newer school began to assert itself. Taverner, who up to the age of about thirty had been in the obscure position of a lay-clerk at Tattershall in Lincolnshire, was in 1526 recommended by the Bishop of Lincoln to Wolsey, who appointed him Master of the Children at his newly founded Oxford college—Cardinal (later Christ Church) College—with an allowance of £10 a year for livery and commons. Tallis, some time in the 1530's, and his own early thirties, became organist and choirmaster at Waltham Abbey and a Gentleman of the Chapel Royal. Tye, a few years later, when he was some forty years old, was made choirmaster at Ely Cathedral. Other outstanding musicians at that time were John Merbecke, lay-clerk and organist at St. George's Chapel, Windsor, and John Shepherd, organist and instructor of the choristers at Magdalen College, Oxford.

B

At least one great work must be mentioned as characteristic of the music of this period: Taverner's Mass "The Western Wind," so called because the whole composition is based on a folksong of that name which does not survive in its original secular form and the original words of which remain unknown. Continental masters had long indulged in the practice of using folksongs as a *cantus firmus* round which they built the elaborate polyphonic textures of their Masses, and one of the reforms insisted on by the Council of Trent (1545–63) was the proscription of tunes often associated with ribald words in people's minds. However, these basic melodies were usually reproduced in such long notes that it was quite impossible for the ear to catch them among the surrounding complexity of parts. Taverner's technique, however, is entirely different: so far from concealing the tune, he uses a variety of devices to make it conspicuous and not only keeps it at a pace in which it remains always recognizable, but assigns it for the most part to the treble or so lightens the texture when it is in the tenor or bass (it never appears in the alto) that it can be heard with ease.

Like everybody else, the musicians under Henry VIII were vexingly and variously affected by the shifting uncertainties of the English Reformation. The movement in its early stages was anything but a simple, drastic change from Roman Catholicism to Protestantism, being not nearly so much a unanimous expression of the people's will as a series of complicated chessboard moves dictated by Henry's matrimonial affairs and Wolsey's over-ambitious foreign policy, both of which the course of events involved in extraordinary vicissitudes. Thus, after the Augsburg Confession of 1530 had consolidated Protestantism in Germany and Henry had already denied the authority of the Pope, who would not countenance his divorce from Catherine of Aragon, Lutheran heretics were still condemned to death in England,

and the first independent national church established in 1534 remained Catholic in every particular save obedience to the authority of Rome. Henry, not so long before a papal "Defender of the Faith," now styled himself head of the English church, a church on which the reformatory writings of More, Luther and Erasmus had had some influence, but so vacillating in its tenets that as late as 1540 it was possible for three members of the Lutheran clergy to be burnt and three Roman Catholics to be beheaded for nonconformity.

Taverner seems to have come under the influence of Lutheranism at Cardinal College, where it was cultivated from the first. He was in fact imprisoned for heresy, though "the Cardinal for his musick excused him, saying that he was but a musitian, and so he escaped"; and "he repented him very muche that he had made Songes to Popish Ditties in the time of his blindness." Pygott lost his appointment at Wolsey's private chapel on the cardinal's fall in 1529, but passed into the Chapel Royal, as Hampton Court had passed into the king's hands. But he seems to have been only nominally a member, for he entered the monastery of Coggeshall in Essex.

Less than ten years later, alas! it turned out that monasteries were far from safe refuges from life's instabilities. During their dissolution, ordered by Henry as a policy of plunder conveniently excused to himself and others as a desirable religious purge, Pygott was expelled. Dygon at Canterbury also lost his office of prior at St. Augustine's Abbey. Henry, however, perhaps because he himself dabbled in composition (the music attributed to him may or may not have been written with professional help), was lenient towards clerical musicians; the value of Pygott's confiscated property was converted into a pension. Tallis, too, received a pension when the greater abbeys followed the monasteries into dissolution in 1540, and withdrew to London, where he was allowed to remain a Gentleman of the Chapel Royal. So

were others, provided they proved pliable enough to conform
to the new service.

Taverner, who in 1530 had left Oxford and returned to
his native Lincolnshire, where he remained until his death
at the stately Boston church of St. Botolph, became a religious
fanatic and acted as paid agent to Thomas Cromwell.
Whether he took a special pleasure in persecuting those of
his fellow-musicians who held posts at religious institutions,
or whether he tempered the storm of royal displeasure to
them, we do not know. But we have seen in Pygott's
case that the storm did not blow too hard upon musicians,
and when Merbecke was condemned to death for heresy
in 1544, together with three other courtiers, he alone was
pardoned. Before he was allowed to take up his post at
Windsor again, he may have had to modify his views. On
the other hand, the church may have once more modified its
own doctrines. It is impossible to disentangle the complex
interplay of changing faith and changing opinions at that
time. Shepherd resigned his appointment at Magdalen
College for some reason in 1543, resumed it—for some
other reason?—two years later, only to give it up finally in
1547.

In this confusion at the early stages of the English Reformation, church music received no unequivocal guidance towards any definite new regulations, as it had done in Germany
by the introduction of congregational singing, which Luther
and his associates had encouraged by providing hymns in
the vernacular, the new words of which were as a rule set
to four-part adaptations of folksongs, not only German, but
Dutch, French and others, and in a few cases of ancient
plainsong melodies which were strait-jacketed into regular
rhythmic patterns. Much the same was done, not only in
Germany but in other countries affected by the Reformation,
with metrical and rhymed versions of the Psalter, made firstly
because it was poetry and therefore always the favourite

book of the Bible and secondly because the psalms could thus be sung to simple square-cut tunes plainly harmonized in four parts with one note to each syllable and without any polyphonic treatment.   Musically speaking this was the first great result of the Reformation.

In England the musical contribution to the church service continued to be made by the appointed professional choir, consisting of boys trained by the choirmaster for the treble parts and of lay-clerks for the altos, tenors and basses.   Composers went on writing in the strictly polyphonic manner which, so new and outlandish in Henry VII's time, was now in turn becoming conventional.   The liturgical requirements, however, remained uncertain.   Shepherd, for instance, set both Latin and English texts to music with apparent impartiality, though the rapid changes in the occupancy of the throne after the death of Henry VIII may have had something to do with that, as indeed it had with the repeated revisions of the prescribed service between the extremes of Roman Catholicism and Calvinism.

It was towards the latter that Edward VI tended after his accession in 1547 at the age of ten, or rather was made to tend by those who influenced him.   It is possible that Tye may have been partly responsible for this, for as organist at Ely he was probably appointed music master to the young prince in 1544, when the Bishop of Ely, Richard Cox, became his tutor.   It was Merbecke, though, to whom fell the task of making the first musical setting of the Anglican liturgy, in English, when Edward's first prayer-book came out in 1549 under the title of "The Booke of Common Praier Noted" (i.e. furnished with notes=set to music). Merbecke was given a pension for his services at Windsor the following year, and it is significant of the new doctrine that he was now able to publish his *Concordance*, which had been among the papers that had nearly cost him his life only a few years earlier, with a dedication to the young king.

"Common Praier Noted" was superseded in 1552 by
Edward's second prayer-book, which is still the basis of the
present Anglican service, a service based by Cranmer on the
Catholic monastic offices, independently alike of the Mass
and of the Lutheran example. Matins and Evensong were
purposely designed to offer plenty of opportunities for music.
Hymns, which Luther thought so important, were thus not
required—they are a later growth of the end of the seventeenth
century. But from the first—that is from 1549—private
services in the many domestic chapels of the great families
had an equivalent for them in the metrical psalms, which
there took the place of the Latin prose psalmody sung in
plainsong by the Roman church, whereas in the official
Anglican church the prayer-book psalter was taken directly
from the English Bible. Two books of verse paraphrases
appeared that year. They were not the first attempts of the
kind, for some sort of endeavour to introduce that form of
musical worship seems to date back to the tentative reforms
of Wycliffe and the Lollards. One of these books was

> "Certayne Psalmes chosen out of the Psalter of David
> and drawn into Englishe Metre by Thomas Sternhold,
> Grome of ye Kynges Maiesties Robes."

This is the better-known of the two, for it maintained itself
in the Anglican service up to the early nineteenth century;
but it contains no music. The other book gives tunes in
four-part harmony set to a melody derived from plainsong
which appears in the tenor voice. It is entitled

> "The Psalter of David newely translated into English
> metre in such sort that it maye the more decently, and wyth
> more delyte of the mynde, be read and songe of al men.
> Whereunto is added a note of four partes, with other
> thynges, as shall appeare in the Epistle to the Readar.

Translated and Imprinted by Robert Crowley in the yere of our Lorde MDXLIX the XX daye of September. And are to be sold in Eley rentes in Holbourne. Cum privilegio ad Imprimendum solum."

If this metrical psalm-singing at family prayers was the forerunner of the Anglican hymn, a precursor to the Anglican chant also arose in the reign of Edward VI. This was Merbecke's adaptation of the Roman plainsong psalmody, which remained in use in some form until the eighteenth century (not counting recent revivals), though not for long in its first form, which was simply an unaccompanied render- ing of the original tune with English instead of Latin words. It soon began to be harmonized, probably at first only on the organ by way of accompaniment, and afterwards for a four-part choir. Even in the harmonized version, however, the rhythm retained the non-metrical delivery of plainsong, to which indeed the Anglican chant still keeps to-day, as in fact it cannot help doing so long as the psalms are sung in their original prose and metrical paraphrases are relegated to the hymn-book.

Another rhymed version, of stories from the Bible, entitled "The Acts of the Apostles," was set by Tye in 1553 and dedicated to Edward, with a clear indication that it was for domestic use, not for the church service. But the boy-king died on July 6th of that year, and Jane Seymour's son was succeeded by his half-sister Mary, Catherine's daughter, who had come of age the year he was born. She was an ardent Catholic, not only because she wished to honour her mother's faith, but perhaps chiefly because it was only with the support of the Pope and of her kinsman, the Emperor Charles V, that she was able to uphold her claims and even to defend her legitimacy, which her father had disputed by a quibble, the absurdity of which none had realized better than himself. Shepherd entered the Chapel Royal under Mary, but whether he had been openly or secretly a Catholic all the time or was merely a turncoat is uncertain. At any rate he set Latin liturgical texts to music for the new queen, including the magnificent "French Mass" for four voices in 1554, so called because it was in the Flemish (i.e. northern French) style which had by this time begun to depart from the old use of a plainsong theme in the tenor part and instead introduced short plainsong motifs by polyphonic entries in all the voices. The same year England was visited by the greatest of the Flemings of that time, Orlande de Lassus (with little reason usually called by the Italianized form of his name, Orlando di Lasso, since he did not live much in Italy). He came in the company of an Italian nobleman, Giulio Cesare Brancaccio, and during his stay composed some Latin verses in honour of Cardinal Pole, whom the Reformation had driven into exile in Italy, but who was recalled by Mary. In 1554 Pole formally absolved England from the "sin of Protestantism" and two years later succeeded Cranmer, a few days after his execution, as a Catholic Archbishop of Canterbury.

Cranmer, Rogers, Hooper, Ridley and Latimer were only the most distinguished victims of Mary, or rather of her reign, for it is extremely unlikely that she would have countenanced so savage a persecution of Protestants had not her advisers succeeded in persuading her that it was unavoidable. She was surprisingly lenient towards the Duke of Suffolk, who had tried to grasp the throne for his daughter, Lady Jane Grey, and did not unduly revenge herself upon her rather spiteful half-sister Elizabeth, whose mother, Anne Boleyn, had done her utmost to make her girlhood miserable. Her musicians she seems to have treated handsomely. Warrants for new liveries abound in the records of her short reign, and in 1556 she granted Tallis and Richard Bowyer, Master of the Children in the Chapel Royal, a joint lease for twenty-one years in the Manor of Minster in the Isle of

Thanet, thus augmenting their incomes by the rents accruing therefrom. In April 1558 was issued a

"Warrant to deliver to John Grene, coffer-maker, as much grene velvett as will suffice for the covering of one pair of virgynalls and as much grene satten as shall serve to lyne the same, with passamayne lace of silver for the garnishing and edginge of the same. And that ye paie until the said John Grene as well for two cases of tymber covered with lether and lyned, th' one being for the aforesaid virgynalls.

"Payment also to be made for a newe key for the aforesaid virgynalls, also for mendynge the iron worke and gildinge of eight squyers to the same. Item for one locke, a pair of hendges, two handles, two hooks, with nailes for the case of the same virgynalls"

No doubt these virginals were for herself. She played the instrument uncommonly well, and had apparently done so as long as she could herself remember, for the story goes that she entertained some visitors with it before she was five years old. But in 1558 she can have played very little. Her always precarious health had broken down completely, and she died in November, aged forty-two. With her death opened the Elizabethan era and England's most glorious musical period.

CHAPTER III

The Elizabethans (1558–1603)

When the eager, energetic daughter of Henry VIII and Anne Boleyn ascended the throne at the age of twenty-five, England was ready to enter upon an era of literary and political florescence such as Elizabeth's shrewd head and shrewish temperament could direct with a self-possession that would brook no interference, though she was ready to take advice when it pleased her. The coveted reign might easily have slipped through her fingers; but she was well prepared for it. Her upbringing, coupled with the strange hardships and perplexities of her youth, had bred an imperious disposition, and she had been educated with extreme care. Her literary attainments were those of a scholar. She could bandy words as readily in Latin or Italian as in French with an ambassador who had no English. She knew early how to surround herself with learned and famous men, whose company she enjoyed at least as much as that of sycophants. Subject to moods and passions as she was, she had no favours to bestow with any promise of permanence, either on those who professed to admire her or on those she was forced to admire; yet her court was always frequented by some who were truly great as well as by many who hoped to have greatness thrust upon them.

Elizabeth was skilled in music as in many things besides. Whether she played the harpsichord as well as Mary had done we do not know, for although tradition has it that she did, one courtier's report qualified rumours of her skill by saying that she played "for a queen, very well," and on one occasion she was furious to discover that she had been overheard practising. What is certain is that she cultivated music assiduously at her court, supported musicians from inclination as much as from a sense of duty and patronized them as generously as her capricious nature would allow. The greatest of her time, William Byrd, she favoured regardless of public opinion, in spite of his dogged adherence to the Roman faith, which went to the length of obstinate recusancy while it was tempered by an artistic detachment that allowed him to write for the Anglican church as well as for his own, and indeed to become organist at Lincoln Cathedral in 1563, the very year Elizabeth consolidated Anglican Protestantism by the publication of her Thirty-nine Articles.

Byrd was only fifteen when the Protestant queen entered upon her reign. Since the rest of the school associated with her consisted of even younger people, we must not think of Elizabethan composers as strictly contemporary with her. Only two musicians of outstanding genius as composers, Richard Farrant of the Chapel Royal and Robert Whyte, belonged to her generation. Whyte, a considerable church composer, succeeded Tye as choirmaster at Ely in 1561, and later he was probably at Chester Cathedral and at Westminster Abbey in the same capacity. Of the "three T's" Taverner had died in 1545; Tallis and Tye were now in their fifties, Merbecke and Shepherd in their forties. Robert Johnson, the first Scottish composer of importance, who had fled from his native country "lang before the Reformation ... for accusation of heresy" and is said to have been chaplain to Anne Boleyn, was getting on for his seventieth year. (We must bear in mind that the Reformation came to Scotland later than to England: John Knox's Confession of Faith dates from 1560.)

There was a kind of interregnum in English music, as far as composition was concerned, as though new forces were being gathered. Some signs of these are to be seen in the work of Thomas Whythorne, a third close contemporary of Elizabeth's, but an artist of that dashing enterprise often found in amateurs rather than those of great professional skill. What makes Whythorne important, up to a point, is that he had travelled in various countries, including Italy, and studied the new music there and that his "Songes, for three, fower, and fiue voyces . . . of sundry sortes, that is to say, some long, some short, some hard, some easie to be songe . . ." etc., etc. (the title amounts almost to a preface) are the first printed book of English secular vocal compositions after the earliest of all, published by Wynkyn de Worde in 1530, that they anticipate in style the lutenist songs of thirty years later and that they include the first English solo song with instrumental (viols) accompaniment.

Innovation, of course, must not in itself be regarded as the equivalent of creation. Composition as a great, consolidated art hung back in the early days of Elizabeth's reign. But this *reculer pour mieux sauter* showed itself also in Italy, where great new forces were preparing to appear, but ripe mastery was not conspicuous, at any rate among native musicians. Of the few masters of other countries destined to influence the Italian school or at least to form part of it, Lassus in Flanders was still young and Victoria in Spain even younger. Palestrina himself was only just over thirty, and he was not a "modernist" even then. True, in Venice new influences stirred in Andrea Gabrieli, but his nephew, Giovanni, and others who were to bring about new developments— Marenzio and Gesualdo, Prince of Venosa, in the madrigal, Cavalieri in oratorio (shooting off into opera) and Orazio Vecchi in a curious type of madrigal-opera—were then mere children. Even the Flemings who greatly influenced the madrigal in Italy, which in turn fertilized that of England, the most characteristic product of the Elizabethan age in vocal music, were only in middle age, with the exception of Willaert, who was well over seventy. Verdelot, if still alive, was nearly sixty, Arcadelt, Philippe de Monte and Cyprien de Rore were somewhere in the early forties.

In other than musical ways Italian influence did much to mould Elizabeth's court from the first. Her retinue was composed of nobles for whom travel in Italy in early manhood was part of a genteel education, and Baldassare Castiglione's book on manners, *Il cortegiano*, first published in 1528, was a standard work for well-read people even before its translation into English by Thomas Hoby in 1561. Castiglione laid much stress on the value of musical attainments in courtiers and gentlemen, and by the time his book had become naturalized Englishmen of that standing were disposed to take his recommendations to heart, the more readily because they included suggestions which at once flattered their vanity and encouraged dilettantish indolence:

"I would not our Courtier should doe as many doe, that as soone as they come to any place, and also in the presence of the great men with whome they have no acquaintance at all, without much entreating set out them selves to shew as much as they know, yea and many times that they know not, so that a man would weene they came purposely to shew themselves for that, and that it is their principall profession.

"Therefore let our Courtier come to showe his musick as a thing to passe the time withall, and as he were enforced to doe it, and not in the presence of noble men, nor of any great multitude.

"And for all hee be skilfull and doth well understand it, yet will I have him to dissemble the studie and paines that a man must needes take in all things that are well done. And let him make semblance that he esteemeth but little of him selfe that qualitie, but in doing it excellently well, make it much esteemed of other men."

Italian dances, and their music with them, were in vogue at Whitehall, St. James's and Hampton Court, whence no doubt they were soon exported to the country houses of the great—to Arundel, to Kenilworth, to Ludlow. The *padovana* became the pavan, the *allemande* the almain; and if not many people would "go to church in a galliard and come home in a *coranto*," no doubt they often did so humming the Italian tunes, so much more easily remembered than polyphonic services and anthems. For nothing was as yet provided in the Anglican church in which the congregation could take part vocally. Although Elizabeth had at once made provision for "a hymn or such like song" in her prayer-book, it was the anthem that took the place of the old Catholic office hymn, and like that hymn it was sung by the professional choir.

In spite of foreign influences, the English habit of engaging the services of continental musicians, which lasted well into the nineteenth century, cannot be said to have been begun by the great Tudor queen. It was rather a peculiarity of the Stuarts in the next century, though one of that dynasty cultivated it earlier, with disastrous results. For when Mary Stuart landed in Scotland in 1561 and seized the throne, she was followed by the Italian musician Davidde Rizzio, whom she retained at her court at Holyrood Palace as a bass singer. He seems to have been her favourite already before she married Darnley at the age of twenty-three, for she had made him her Foreign Secretary the preceding year, and he was murdered in 1566, by Darnley and others who fancied themselves his rivals, for political and perhaps more than political reasons.

Elizabeth too had a young Italian at her court quite early: Alfonso Ferrabosco, the founder of what was to be a distinguished English family of musicians. But compared with the literary, political and fashionable influences that came from abroad, few foreign musicians were as yet allowed to have much say in the developments of English music. One of the causes that stemmed their incursion in Elizabeth's early days lay in the church, for the church was not open to many suggestions from outside. It had gone through reforms that were anything but thorough-going and clear-cut, and it was content with the compromise. The much more sweeping Lutheran conversions had hardly touched it musically. Much less could the austerely plain services of the Huguenots do so, for all the English queen's support of them. Italy, on the other hand, retained the old Roman Catholic liturgy in Latin, which in its own way was just as unsuited to adoption by the new Anglican service in the vernacular. Other southern nations who had remained faithful to Rome, if only because as Latins they were able to laugh at abuses which had aroused the militant indignation of more staid races, did not perceptibly stimulate England; nor did the milder reforms diplomatically introduced into the Roman liturgy by the Council of Trent, with the intention of forestalling possible challenges to papal authority on the part of Catholics in countries turned Protestant, affect the Anglican church, where the turning of the service into English had already done away with certain undesirable practices in the setting of Latin to music.

Musical service-books began to appear in print early in Elizabeth's reign, even before the Thirty-nine Articles. In 1560 the London printer and publisher John Day issued

"Certaine notes set forth in foure and three parts to be song at the morning, Communion and evening praier, very necessary for the Church of Christe to be frequented and used: & unto them added divers godly praiers & Psalmes into the like forme to the honor & praise of God."

Robert Stone, Master of the Chapel Royal, one of the Gentlemen of the Chapel named Okeland and William Whitbroke, sub-dean of St. Paul's Cathedral, were among the contributors, Stone appearing with a setting of the Lord's Prayer.

In the year of the Articles (1563) Day brought out a psalter containing "The Whole Psalmes in foure parts," together with prayers, including one for which Tye appears to have written the words set to music by Shepherd, who died that year. Four years later appeared Archbishop Matthew Parker's new metrical version of the psalms with nine tunes by Tallis, one of which has been perpetuated for modern hearers by Vaughan Williams in his "Fantasia on a Theme by Tallis" for string orchestra. The volume contains a curious example of that attribution of different emotional influences to the modes which is as old as Plato:

> "The first is meeke: deuout to see,
> The second sad: in maiesty.
> The third doth rage: and roughly brayth,
> The fourth doth fawne: and flattry playth.
> The fyfth delight: and laugheth the more,
> The sixth bewayleth: it weepeth full sore.
> The seuenth tredeth stoute: in froward race,
> The eyghte goeth milde: in modest pace."

The modes, it may here be said, though they were to persist in folksong, could not much longer maintain themselves in the work of composers, who may have found the principle of *musica ficta* (see p. 25) too vague for their purpose and could not fail to discover a feeling for major and minor tonalities interchangeable by means of modulation; and modulation gradually established itself as a device indispensable to polyphonic writing, where successive fugal entries in various voices take the most plastic and satisfying form if they occur in at least two different keys—e.g. the first and third entry in the soprano and tenor in the key of the tonic, the second and fourth in the alto and bass in that of the dominant. Both theory and practice, however, fluctuated up to the end of the sixteenth century and even beyond, practice, as usual, taking the initiative in bold new developments and theory limping behind, disputing the innovations of creative musicians until it saw fit to explain them as though it had been the first to make their discovery.

The Italian literary influence included the stage, needless to say. The university plays the queen went to see at Cambridge in 1564 and at Oxford in 1566 and 1592 were based on Italian Renascence models, which meant that their subjects were taken from classical mythology or history and that their manner was at any rate pseudo-classical. It is obvious that such plays were early literary ancestors of the eighteenth-century opera libretti of Apostolo Zeno and Metastasio, and there can be no doubt that the plays themselves, Italian and English alike, were to some extent operatic, nearly half a century before opera proper was to come to light. Consorts of music were certainly played between the acts on the occasion of royal visits, if they did not indeed accompany certain scenes in the manner of incidental music, and we know that the introduction of songs into plays was a common practice with Elizabethan playwrights. The great examples of another species of Italian play—the pastoral—which affected the development of opera, Tasso's "Aminta" and Guarini's "Pastor fido," did not appear in their own country until the 1580's; yet something in the nature of an English opera was given before Elizabeth as early as the 1560's, although we are supposed not to come upon the first English opera until 1656. Richard Edwards, Master of the Chapel Royal children, produced his play with music, "Damon and Pythias," at Candlemas, 1565. It is as a poet that he is mainly connected with this entertainment, in which other composers collaborated; but after all he was chiefly a musician, or he could not have held one of the most important musical posts in the country, and since his choristers acted in the piece, there was a good deal of singing as well as instrumental scenic music. In September 1566 Edwards took those choristers to Oxford, where they gave a second play of his, "Palamon and Arcite," before the queen at Christ Church (formerly Cardinal) College. Elizabeth sent for him and promised him a reward, but if it was not paid more quickly than such remunerations usually were at court, he never received it, for he died that same year, aged probably not much more than forty. Had he lived longer and founded a school, he might, as Purcell nearly did later on, have established a tradition of English opera, and England instead of Italy would have been opera's native country.

The term "consort of music" has just been used. "Consort" is the old form of "concert," to which it is etymologically related in the sense that both mean "union" (as in marriage), "agreement" (as in corporate action) or "harmony" (as in human relationships or indeed in music). In sixteenth-century England consorts were most commonly played on sets of viols ranging from treble to bass instruments, but we also hear of "broken consorts," which meant a mixed team of bowed string and other instruments. Recorders (early flutes), hautboys and curtalls (bassoons) would most often take part, in fact literally take parts— parts written out for instruments producing single melodic lines in a polyphonic work; but if keyboard instruments such as regals (portable organs) and virginals or instruments of the lute type capable of producing chords were available, they could join in, playing not tunes so much as harmonic fillings based on the incidental chords arising from the coincidence of contrapuntal parts. These harmonic instruments thus began casually to take on the function they or their descendants assumed quite regularly in the next two centuries under the name of *continuo* (see p. 161).

This kind of performance was mainly domestic. It had no place in the Anglican church for the first century after its establishment, and in public life it had no function anywhere but in the theatre, which itself was allowed no popular following to speak of until towards the end of the century. There was no such thing as going to consorts, as nowadays we go to concerts. Nothing that could be called a public taste for music had the chance of showing itself. On the other hand a great deal of individual and family cultivation of the art developed as the enlightened reign of Elizabeth progressed and music, like poetry and drama, counted among the great English conquests of the age. It was made possible by social conditions enabling people to live comfortably in their houses without daily fear of enemy raids, as in the middle ages. Not only aristocratic families, but countless others of good standing, had chests of viols which they handed down to their children as heirlooms treasured with the best of the plate and furniture. To sing at sight and to play at least one instrument with ease was an accomplishment causing less surprise than the lack of it would call for censure, though we need not suppose that the average standard of performance was such that a madrigal sung at a nobleman's house after dinner or a fancy for viols played at a friendly gathering of city merchants often had the finish of a modern concert performance. No doubt some of this domestic music-making was execrable. What matters, however, is that it was a recognized home entertainment with which we cannot unblushingly compare the modern equivalents of bridge and cocktail parties, and that it was genuinely enjoyed, since there was in it no particularly fashionable or intellectual element to tempt people to cultivate it snobbishly. If proof of this is needed, all we have to do is to remember that as often as not servants were engaged who could sing or play (more likely both, for any player would be able to take a voice-part in a madrigal tolerably) and that they would be called in to join the musical party whenever their talents were required.

The popular solo instrument of the time was the cittern, a relative of the lute whose strings were tuned in odd intervals, like those of the modern ukelele. The fact that it was to be found in every barber's shop, for people to play on while they waited to be shaved, indicates how widely it was used.

The "fancy" or fantasy, more often called by the Italian name of *fantasia*, was the current form of music for assorted string instruments or broken consorts. It was a sectionally-organized structure the different episodes of which were loosely related to each other by relevance of style rather than by any sort of thematic connection, each being at the same time a self-contained piece of admirable consistency giving the composer unlimited scope for the display of polyphonic skill. The fugue had not then developed into a form, but neither had it settled into stereotyped formulas, so that a master's "fancy" could wander as it pleased, though it could not shape itself into a satisfactory work of art unless it did so by adhering to a logic of its own. The fantasies by the great Elizabethan masters, with William Byrd at their head, did this in a way unsurpassed by later users of the form, which still remained an admirable vehicle for such mid-seventeenth-century composers as the enterprising Matthew Locke and the duller Christopher Simpson, and did not finally expire until it had been briefly but gloriously revived by Purcell towards the end of that century.

A curious instrumental species akin to the fantasy, but more in the nature of an exercise in counterpoint, always based on the same plainsong theme, was the "In Nomine," which we find in the work of various composers from Taverner to Byrd. The name has never been satisfactorily explained; but it does not much matter whether it originally came from some sort of instrumental use of vocal phrases from the "Benedictus" in the Mass (". . . qui venit in nomine Domini") or from a pious habit of inscribing the words "In nomine Domini" at the head of a work, much as later composers would set "Laus Deo," "Dei gratia" or some other such sigh of relief at the end of a finished manuscript.

Instruments would also take part in madrigals, for although these were primarily vocal compositions, they were as often as not intended to be "apt for voyces or viols." The instruments could either double the voice-parts for greater safety if not merely for pleasure, or fill in the remaining parts if only one or two were taken by a voice, or even play the whole work as an instrumental and wordless piece, much as we nowadays play an opera on the pianoforte with a good deal of pleasure, provided we know at least some of the words or have an idea of what the plot is about. The words of Elizabethan madrigals were, of course, well known to their contemporaries, and they were often among the great poetry of the day.

The same is true of the lute song, at any rate of the later specimens of their great florescence towards the end of the century, when Dowland, Campion, Rosseter, Pilkington, Cavendish, Robert Johnson and others wrote exquisite tunes perfectly matched with no less exquisite words, both sometimes written by the same artist. Campion, indeed, ranks at least as high among Elizabethan poets as he does among musicians. His words could be as intimately "apt" to the instrument as his tunes were to the voice:

> "When to her lute Corinna sings,
>   Her voice revives the leaden strings,
>   And doth in highest notes appear,
>   As any challeng'd echo clear.
>   But when she doth of mourning speak,
>   E'en with her sighs the strings do break."

The serious cultivation of the lute began when these great exponents were still children or not yet born—about the middle of the century. It came from France and may be

said to have consolidated itself by 1568, when a minor lutenist,
John Alford, published a translation of Adrien Le Roy's
work on the lute under the title of "A Briefe and Easye
Instruction to learne the tableture, to conduct and dispose
the hande unto the Lute."

If the chief influence on lute music and on the song to the
lute was French, that on the madrigal was Flemish and
Italian. But long before any of these things became naturalized in England a domestic instrument producing a wholly
home-grown kind of music had established itself. It was
the virginal, the direct ancestor of the harpsichord, from
which it does not differ in its method of tone-production
and did not at first differ even in shape. Not all virginals
were made in England: some came from Flanders; but virginal music was purely of English origin. Cabezon may
have brought a Spanish element into it when he came to
Queen Mary's court with Philip II (1554–5), but it is at least
as old as Hugh Aston, who was dead by the time Queen
Elizabeth was born.

The novelty introduced by sixteenth-century English
composers through the virginal was the variation form.
This appeared in a primitive way in an anonymous piece
called "My Lady Carey's Dompe" early in the century, but
was anything but primitive by the time masters like Byrd,
John Bull and Orlando Gibbons came to handle it. They
seem to have understood at once that the principle of musical
variation is a twofold one. Some of their pieces varied a
given tune by increasing complexities of ornamentation,
while others based their developments on progressive changes
in the texture of the accompanying harmony, the skeleton-
form of which remained unaltered throughout. Both these
principles have since maintained themselves, for although
the latter, upheld during the seventeenth century by the ever-
growing importance given to the bass, gradually yielded to
ornate melodic variation in the eighteenth, it still appears in

Beethoven's thirty-two Variations in C minor, and even as late as Brahms's variation works on themes by Handel and Haydn.

Gibbons favoured the contrapuntal fantasy form on the virginal, but he too used the modish dances of the time and varied some of the popular songs (e.g. "The wood so wild"), as Byrd and Bull did more frequently, the former in "Go from my window," for instance, and the latter in "The King's Hunt," to name examples of tunes still known as part of the nation's heritage.

In all this activity the queen was keenly interested. She watched personally over the musicians' appointments and saw to it that the best of them should be kept in her own service. To Ferrabosco she granted a pension of £100 a year on condition that he should remain in her service all his life. He was some years younger than she, but it did not occur to her that anyone would presume to imagine outliving her. However, Ferrabosco did, for he had the temerity to request that a clause should be added to his contract to the effect that the pension should continue under her successor.

This was in 1569, the year in which Elizabeth called the young Lincoln organist, William Byrd, to her court by making him a Gentleman of the Chapel Royal and asking him to share the organist's duties there with Tallis, his senior by more than forty years. But Byrd did not resign the Lincoln appointment until three years later, when he was twenty-nine, so that until then one of his posts must have been in the nature of a sinecure, since clearly the journey between London and Lincoln could not in those days be frequently made. The queen learnt to admire and respect Byrd, who as time went on developed into one of those universal geniuses capable of handling with sovereign ease any species of their art current in their time and passing them on enriched to future generations. That Byrd, no less than Purcell and Mozart, was such a genius is shown by the fact that he was equally great in cultivating the Roman Mass and motet, the Anglican service and anthem, the madrigal and the solo song, the fantasy for strings and the virginal piece. What is more, he was one of those detached artists we find only among the greatest: that is why, although a devout Catholic, he could without loss of dignity serve the Protestant queen he admired, and she in turn was great enough to understand that the truest art is not a matter of personal feelings, and thus not only to tolerate a recusant who could so gloriously serve a church he refused to recognize, but to mitigate as far as she could the troubles in which that refusal frequently involved him and his family. In 1575 she granted Byrd and Tallis jointly a licence to print music and sell music-paper, and two years later she acceded to their petition for an annuity.

Music printing, though it developed later than on the Continent, flourished greatly under Elizabeth. But the systematic manufacture and sale of music-paper is no less important in its influence on musical cultivation. While printed music-books did much to encourage music-making in private houses, easy access to paper ruled for music, and indeed to any paper at all, which was then rare and costly, could not fail to stimulate composition.

In 1571 John Bull, aged nine, entered the Chapel Royal as a chorister, and although William Blitheman was Master of the Children, Bull must have learnt something from Byrd, who two years later accepted Thomas Morley as a pupil. In another three years, at the age of nineteen, Morley wrote a motet for five voices—a curious beginning for a master who was to excel, not in church music, but in the lighter forms of vocal composition: ayres and fa-las, balletts and canzonets, not to mention his setting of a song, or songs, in Shakespeare's "As You Like It" towards the close of his life, which ended with the queen's death in 1603.

If Byrd found the future author of *A Plain and Easy*

Introduction to Practical Music (1597) ready enough to conform to rules and regulations, he may have thought the young Bull less easy to tame. Bull, who was to become organist at Hereford Cathedral at the age of twenty, at the Chapel Royal eight years later and Professor of Music at Gresham College at thirty-four, was from the first a "modernist" and a virtuoso-composer of a type more frequently encountered in the eighteenth and nineteenth centuries than in the sixteenth. He wrote mainly for his own instrument, the virginal, and there is something at once enterprising and superficial about his music that makes him more interesting as a pioneer at the keyboard than impressive as a creator of work capable of holding the attention by something more than its quality as a landmark in musical history.

After the death in 1585 of Tallis, the last of the "three T's," church music would have languished for a time but for the presence of the even greater Byrd, whose serving of two creeds, whatever may be thought of it as evidence of a lack of personal conviction or moral courage, can only be counted as the greatest artistic good fortune, since it benefited the two great Christian denominations. The next English church composer of outstanding genius, Orlando Gibbons, and the only one who was destined to approach Byrd in versatility, was then but two years old. Bull, we have seen, tended towards a more worldly career, the later stages of which were to take him abroad, and the only other young musician who was going to devote himself mainly to the church was Peter Philips, then about a quarter of a century old. But Philips, a stricter Catholic than Byrd, like Bull spent his later life in the Netherlands, where he won great esteem as organist of Antwerp Cathedral and as one of the important ecclesiastical composers of his day, ranking with Hassler in Germany, with the Anerios and Naninis in Italy and with Sweelinck in his adopted country.

Byrd, however, is in the company of the very greatest of

his time.   He is for England what Palestrina is for Italy,
Lassus for the Netherlands and Victoria for Spain; or if we
take these three to stand for the church of Rome he, perversely
but gloriously, stands both for Rome and England.   Moreover, he gave some peculiar qualities to church music which
they denied it, not only because he could set the vernacular
as readily as Latin, but because he was an uncommonly
assertive musical personality.   His work, even that for the
Roman liturgy, has the strong rhythmic incisiveness of
accented English speech (as distinct from quantitative Latin).
His counterpoint can be ruthlessly logical in letting each part
pursue a declamatory course ideally suited to the words
rather than accommodating it to harmonize suavely with
the others.   He often deliberately seeks the expressive harmonic clashes of harsh discords and false relations (semitonal
incongruities appearing closely together in two different
parts).   His polyphonic skill in writing such things as canons
interlaced in several parts, invertible counterpoint, and so on,
is as great as that of any master who ever existed; but he
never exploits it for its own sake.   He could doubtless have
emulated and surpassed Tallis in writing a motet in forty
parts—real parts none of which merely doubles another—
but there is no mere *tour de force* anywhere in his work; the
dizziest feats that make the fan-tracery at Westminster,
Windsor or Cambridge look like simple brickwork by comparison were always performed to some definite expressive
purpose by this great musical architect.

Other Elizabethan church composers were highly skilled
and could write sumptuous and eloquent services and anthems,
or Masses and motets, as their religious case might be.   But,
as we have seen, they were not numerous; nor was there
much surpassing genius among them.   The diligent Merbecke
died about the same time as Tallis, and the young men and
children who were then growing to artistic maturity, though
trained in the church and quite capable of writing for it later

on, were nearly all destined to develop along one of the two lines—or both in some cases—music was ready to pursue towards the end of Elizabeth's reign. One of those lines followed the development of the song, the other that of the madrigal, and both these species are more significantly characteristic of the age than its church music, for it was pre-eminently the age of domestic musical art.

There was no very clear distinction between the song and the madrigal, it must be said. Even a solo song originally accompanied by the lute could be arranged in parts for instruments or a group of singers; even a madrigal in five or more vocal parts could be reduced to a single sung treble part with the rest arranged for the lute, the polyphony of the parts transcribed in tablature into the kind of fake counter-point the instrument could suggest successfully enough. Neither was sacred music strictly segregated from secular. Byrd's five-part *Psalms, Sonnets and Songs of Sadness and Piety*, published in 1588, and his *Songs of Sundry Natures*, issued the following year, contain, as their titles indicate, contemplative religious pieces side by side with secular compositions that must be regarded as the first English madrigals of any note. But they were first intended as songs for a solo voice accompanied by a quartet of viols. It is this which makes his madrigal form different from the Italian forms.

It is significant that the first of these books coincided with —and therefore actually anticipated, since no music can be published that has not previously taken a certain time to compose—the important collection of fifty-seven Italian madrigals published by one Nicholas Yonge under the title of *Musica transalpina*. It has been said, and repeated over and over again, that it was this collection which gave the first impulse to English composers to take to the madrigal; but one might equally well claim that this impulse was given by Byrd. However, there is no point in trying to deny that without the Italian madrigal (not always written by Italians) the brief but glorious English florescence of the species would have been impossible, just as without the Italian sonnet we should never have had the wonderful sonnets of Sidney, Spenser and Shakespeare. But much as the English sonnet differed radically in form from the Petrarchian model, the English madrigal became something very different from its Italianate forerunners, not so much in form as in spirit and character. Indeed, this English manifestation of a particular form of art improved upon its foreign patterns by the peculiar national genius for character, human understanding, humour, or whatever we like to call it, just as Chaucer had improved on Boccaccio's stories within a story and the Elizabethan dramatists were even then improving on the Senecan play—those dramatists the greatest of whom was later to be misunderstood by people like Voltaire, who could not see character because they were looking for a style conforming to their own traditions.

The kind of poetry we find in Italian madrigals, mainly pastoral and amorous, we find again in the words of their English counterparts; the same sort of complexity of loose polyphonic part-writing cultivated by the Flemish masters of the madrigal and their Italian disciples strikes the eye in the score of any English madrigal. The ear, however, catches a new note, a new accent, something that is bolder and more modern than the common run of the "transalpine" madrigals (though less so than the freak works of Gesualdo), and at the same time more assured in the way of achieving striking declamation of every single sentence in even the most complex musical textures, in poetical aptness and in human insight.

Byrd, here as elsewhere, was the leader, and it is significant that two madrigals of his were included in *Musica transalpina* and another two in a second collection of foreign pieces, including twenty-three by Marenzio, entitled: *The first Sett*

*of Italian Madrigalls Englished, not to the sense of the originall
dittie, but after the affection of the Noate* and published in 1590
by Thomas Watson, who appears to have been a lawyer
and an amateur poet.　The first book to consist exclusively
of madrigals by an English composer was Morley's *Madrigalls
to Four Voyces* of 1594.　With this a brief but copious spate
of publication began to which some fifty composers contributed and which did not cease until two decades or so
after the death of Elizabeth.　Only the greatest members
of the school can be named here, and one of them, Gibbons,
published no madrigals during the period covered by this
chapter.　The first book by Thomas Weelkes appeared in
1597, the first by John Wilbye in 1598.　Both these men are
among the supreme masters of the species.　They had the
kind of genius for combining atmosphere and characterization
with unfailing technical and formal mastery which Mozart
was later to display in opera.　If the English stage had not
been occupied at the time by an incomparable school of
playwrights, Weelkes and Wilbye might have produced
great works for the theatre and secured for England the
discovery of opera.

There were distinct tendencies towards musical development on the stage, as indeed there could not fail to be in an
age that was equally under the spell of music and of the
drama.　We hear of an example of that typically seventeenth-
century phenomenon, the masque, as early as 1572, when
Ferrabosco took part, either as performer or composer, if
not both, in such an entertainment given before the queen
and the French ambassador, and the following year Byrd,
always ready for a new experiment, contributed a three-
part song to a Latin play, "Ricardus III," by one of the
university begetters of the English drama, Thomas Legge,
given at St. John's College, Cambridge.　Again, in 1575,
John Johnson, lutenist to the queen, took part in a dramatic
entertainment got up for her by the Earl of Leicester at

Kenilworth Castle. In 1591, on a similar occasion at Elvetham, the residence of the Earl of Hertford, she took so much pleasure in Morley's music that she herself suggested a new name for one of his pavans.

All this was in the nature of incidental music, and incidental music, once it has wormed its way into the theatre, is always apt to turn a play into an opera, if a composer of compelling genius happens to be present. At any rate it tended in the sixteenth century to turn it into a masque, which was what nearly happened even to Shakespeare in so early a play as "A Midsummer Night's Dream" and so late a one as "The Tempest"; and the later stages of the masque are indistinguishable from the earliest attempts at opera, so far as England is concerned. Shakespeare was much attached to music, and it would be rash to conclude from the mere evidence of printed texts that he contented himself in his plays with a few songs and an occasional tucket (*toccata*) or sennet (*sonata*) for trumpets behind the scenes. Most of the early English plays dating from before him and Marlowe contained many episodes in dumb-show, which were always accompanied by music; and the tradition of using groups of instruments in the theatre was not to be broken by the mere discontinuance of these pantomimic incidents. Still, Shakespeare was after all a great poetic playwright first and foremost. Had he been only a little less, and but a little closer in touch with musicians, he might have become the musical world's first and greatest librettist instead. That he was in touch with Morley, though perhaps not personally, we have already seen.

Morley might have been the operatic Shakespeare's composer, though Weelkes and Wilbye had greater dramatic potentialities. As things were, opera was to be Italy's conquest, not England's. But English composers filled the madrigal with the same kind of character their contemporaries on the stage gave to plays, and it was Morley who in 1601 glorified this great Elizabethan musical achievement, and the

great queen with it, by assembling for publication a collection
of pieces to which twenty-six master madrigalists contributed.
It was entitled *The Triumphs of Oriana*, the queen being
named after the heroine in "Amadis of Gaul," and it was
modelled on a similar Italian miscellany called "Il trionfo di
Dori." Each composer wrote what music he pleased, but
the words of the collection, though by different hands, are
closely connected by the refrain with which each poem
ends:

> "Thus sang the shepherds and nymphs of Diana:
>   Long live fair Oriana."

But the fiery daughter of Henry VIII, who had never
been particularly fair, did not comply with this adulatory
exhortation. She had enjoyed many triumphs, but was not
to see the publication of Oriana's, which, although it was
dated 1601 by the printer, Thomas East, did not occur until
after the last Tudor monarch's death on March 24th 1603.

CHAPTER IV

The Earlier Seventeenth Century
(1603–1660)

Although Elizabeth was no more, and Morley did not long survive her, the Elizabethan school was to survive and flourish for some time to come. None of the composers who had achieved distinction during her reign had as yet reached any great age at her death. Dowland was forty, and only Philips and Bull were just over. Orlando Gibbons, the youngest, was about to come of age. Even Byrd, now a veteran of sixty, was to survive another twenty years. He was the leader of a great school, and it could endure in all its vigour as long as he, at least. During the whole of the first Stuart reign, which ended with the first quarter of the century, there was little sign that England as a music-making country was no longer what it had been under the great Tudor queen. Many composers were about to yield to the Italian example of emancipation in some departments of their art, but others remained wholly conservative, and the healthy traditions of musical practice in general, established by the ageing generation and its predecessors, was not soon to be wiped out.

The court, which remained the focus of organized musical activity, was not so far affected by new fashions. James I did nothing to encourage change. As good a classic as Elizabeth had been and more of a scholar in the strict, pedantic sense of the term, he was only conventionally interested in music, though more so than the Stuarts who followed him, among whom only Charles II showed a taste for the art, not backed however by either the love or the knowledge that had distinguished the Tudors, more or less. Like his successors, of course, James kept musicians about him at court; but that was largely a matter of usage and fashion. It would have been inadvisable for him to make drastic changes in the established constitution of a court to which he had come, so to speak, by accident—the accidents of Elizabeth's spinsterhood, of Mary's childlessness and of Edward VI's death as a boy.

So musical life, at court as well as outside, went on in the early years of the seventeenth century much as it had done at the end of the sixteenth. That was good enough—more than good enough, since the English school then outshone in numbers and importance all others. In France old Costeley was the outstanding figure, and he may have been of Scottish or Irish descent. In Germany Hans Leo Hassler stood almost alone as a man of the first importance, the "three S's," Scheidt, Schein and Schütz, being as yet in their teens. Sweelinck stood for the Netherlands and Victoria for Spain with great but almost isolated distinction. Only Italy was something like a match for England, though not her superior except in new enterprise. After the passing of the old order with the death of Palestrina, men like Monteverdi and Gabrieli, and even such a half-amateur as Caccini, were ahead as innovators of the proud conservatives encouraged by Elizabeth and now left behind by her.

While musical practice in England went on much as before, however, composition did not stand still in the early Stuart days. The changes were not nearly as drastic as those we observe in the Italian music of the time, and those that did come about were less conspicuous because they were not wrought on the stage, as they were by the Florentine group of amateurs engaged in the first years of the century in bringing opera to birth, not without pangs, difficulties and clumsinesses. Still, even in England only the composers established by virtue of the solid Elizabethan traditions

c

thought these changes, if not alarmingly subversive, at least
contemptibly experimental. The first madrigal, "The Silver
Swan," in Gibbons's set of 1612, ends significantly with the
words:

> "More geese than swans now live,
> More fools than wise."

Gibbons, though still a young man then, was a classic
who adhered to the passing school and scorned newfangled
notions, not always without reason. But with aged Byrd's
Psalms, Songs and Sonnets of 1611 and Gibbons's own single
volume the great madrigalian era was over, although several
books, the contents of which we still value as an enrichment
of its repertory, if not as positively great examples, were
yet to appear up to 1630. But many were no longer madrigalian by name, though some at least remained so by nature.
Indeed, Byrd's work just mentioned was itself originally
devised for solo voices and strings. Thomas Bateson's
second set of madrigals of 1618 was the last important one
to be so called; Francis Pilkington's second of 1624 contained
Madrigals and Pastorals. Thomas Vautor's set of 1619, containing the pretty "Sweet Suffolk Owl," was entitled *Songs
of Divers Airs and Natures*, Thomas Tomkins's of 1622
simply *Airs or Fa-Las*, and Martin Peerson published a book
entitled *Motets, or Grave Chamber Music* in 1630, indicating
great changes. "Songs" and "airs" implied tunes for a
single dominating voice, and indeed some of these later
pieces nominally set for several voices now tended to sound
like solo songs the lute accompaniments of which had been
arranged for supporting lower voices. Even the old madrigal, we must remember, was not in its own time thought of
as so purely a vocal form as it is in modern times; but the
late examples were not so much polyphonic compositions
"fit for voices or viols" as homophonic tunes with chordal
accompaniments.

The influence of the lute song, in fact, had encroached upon the madrigal; and the lute song, indeed, now flourished exceedingly in the hands of several highly skilled masters. We are inclined to think of it as belonging to a rather later period than it actually does because we see so much of the lute in the delightful mid-seventeenth-century domestic scenes by the great school of Dutch painters. But we hear of no corresponding school of Dutch lutenist song masters, and if we bear in mind how much John Dowland had been esteemed on the Continent and how greatly musical publication flourished in the Netherlands at a time when composition did not, we may imagine that what we see the minstrels and topers and burghers sing so lustily in Dutch pictures of high and low and especially middle-class life must often have been translations of English songs, though not as often, perhaps, as they may have been of French origin. Dowland, of course, was sung in Germany with the respect English singers now give to Schubert, Brahms and Wolf, with the only difference that there was no snobbish inhibition about translations into the vernacular, and instrumental adaptations of his tunes were played.

Dowland was born in 1562. The lute song, then, it is worth repeating, is older than we are apt to imagine. But even this greatest of the lutenist song-writers, as also the great poet-composer who comes nearest to him in perfection, Thomas Campion, published only a third book of songs in the year of Elizabeth's death, and they did not complete their issues until 1613 and about 1617 respectively. Among the others only Michael Cavendish, Morley and Philip Rosseter had finished their output before that time. Robert Jones had published two books in 1601, but he tenaciously continued after 1608, although the title of his third book then, *Ultimum vale*, had hinted that it would be the last. Indeed he went on with evident gusto, for the later books were called *A Musical Dream* (1609) and *The*

Muses' Garden for Delight (1611). All the others, Thomas Greaves, Francis Pilkington, Tobias Hume, John Bartlet, John Cooper (*alias* Giovanni Coperario), John Danyel, Thomas Ford, the younger (English-born) Alfonso Ferrabosco, William Corkine, John Maynard and John Attey all published only in the reign of James I.

The lute and its allied instruments, such as the cittern and the theorbo, found many friends, now that instrumental music tended to become popular by its own merits, and not merely as the medium for the dance that had always been the opposite of song among the people's natural attempts at artistic expression. It was much liked, especially among the middle classes. Its portability made it more convenient than the keyboard instruments and it had the advantage of full harmonic resources over the bowed string instruments, than which it may also have been easier to play with striking effect, once its principles had been mastered. Its music was not written down in ordinary notation, but in tablature, a sort of lettered diagram which conveys no musical shapes to the eye, as notes do to the practised reader, but had the advantage of allowing the player to produce the music with an almost automatic correctness as soon as he had learnt to stop the strings according to its indications. Unfortunately the tablature was an obstacle to composition, for no musician could hope to write effectively for the lute family of instruments at all if he had not been trained in the art of playing them and of reading their special notation. It was not only a matter of knowing which strings had to be stopped by which fingers to produce which notes, but of allowing for the continued sound of each string struck until it was stopped by the next finger producing the next note. Merely to strum chords on such instruments was easy enough, no doubt, but to make a web of interesting patterns of that spuriously polyphonic kind so characteristic of its best music was a matter for specialists. The art of lute composition declined as soon as it had attained its height of virtuosity, not because the instrument was particularly difficult, but because composition was necessarily a performer's pursuit. It was precisely when the lute's cult was at its ripest that composition and performance began to be practised by different classes of musicians. Arabella Hunt, a lutenist-singer but not a composer, who died in 1705 and who was celebrated in song by Purcell and Blow as well as in poetry by Congreve, was already something of an antiquarian, rather like the members of the Dolmetsch family to-day.

This split between composition and performance as a musical avocation was to take centuries yet to become very pronounced (great later composers like Mozart and Brahms were still their own performers; great instrumentalists like Paganini and Liszt still their own composers), and it never became complete. All the same, the early seventeenth century began to produce singers and players as classes by themselves to an extent we never hear about in earlier musical history. Italy did more to establish these classes than any other country, because Italy was first in the field with opera, which necessitated a large number of vocalists and instrumentalists who did not compose, as the singers in the Vatican choir, for instance, had very often done before, or in England the Gentlemen of the Chapel Royal. In a list of the court musicians as constituted at the death of James I, containing over a hundred and twenty names, we find only one among the "Musitions for Violins" designated specifically as "composer," and the rest show less than half a dozen now known to have been composers of any standing, though they include men of such eminence as Nicholas Lanier (as singer among the "Consorte"), Nathaniel Giles, the Master of the Children in the Chapel Royal, and Orlando Gibbons, then both "privy organ" in the Chapel and organist at Westminster Abbey. This stands in significant contrast to the many distinguished composers who had surrounded Elizabeth in the capacity of executive musicians.

The influx of foreign musicians, engaged simply for their skill in performance, also begins to become outstandingly noticeable about this time. The girl-queen Henrietta Maria, already married to Charles I by proxy in Paris, brought eleven French musicians over with her among a retinue of servants who were "to have black cloth for liveries," or more if the "3 little singing boys to each of them 5 yards" were also among the foreigners. James I's queen, Anne of Denmark, had already had Danes in her service, who seem to have been sent by her brother Christian IV in exchange for Dowland, William Brade and Thomas Cutting, who were all at the court in Copenhagen at various times. And—to anticipate a later chapter—the queens of Charles II and James II, Catharine of Braganza and Mary of Modena, were equally anxious to have their countries' music represented at the English court by Portuguese and Italian artists.

Looking back from the year 1625, which saw the sudden death of Orlando Gibbons, almost the last of the great Elizabethans except Bull and Wilbye, a few days before the reception of the young queen at Canterbury, we see as great a change coming over musical composition—as distinct from musical life—as had come into the royal dynasty. Tudors and Stuarts differed hardly more strikingly as human characters than Tudor and Stuart music now began to differ in the stress it laid on various artistic values. True, the lute song acted as a link between them at first and church music kept for some time yet to the honoured polyphonic traditions; but the former was to die out before long while the latter now lacked a great leading figure after the death of Byrd in 1623 and Gibbons two years later. Even church music was destined to become subject to vicissitudes, political at first and artistic afterwards, from which it was never to recover its ancient character. Its Gothic period, so to speak, was

over by 1650 as surely as Gothic architecture had been by
1550. Later revivals of the style in both arts have been
endlessly numerous, but they have never at the best risen to
the value of more than good imitation. As for the gracious
artificiality of English baroque, one master of music was to
stand out in it in a greater splendour of isolation than Wren
did among architects. But Purcell and the age of baroque
belong to the next chapter of our story.

The greatest changes came about in secular vocal music,
so far as it went in England, which was not as far as the
firm establishment of opera, the new art that was now
exciting Italy. A series of historical accidents peculiar to
the eventful period we have now approached, as well as
various peculiarities of English social conditions, such as the
scarcity of professional singers, frustrated all attempts to
make opera an indigenous form of art, in spite of the fact
that gifted composers were ready to handle it and one
great master—Purcell again—actually did handle it with a
genius equalling Monteverdi's in Italy and excelling Lully's
in France.

The first operatic experiments in Italy, however, did influence English music, particularly in its new dealings with the
solo song. We have seen that this did not detach itself from
the madrigal and its allied forms for several voices such as
the canzonet and the ballett for several voices as irrevocably
as in Italy, because the lute song was already an independent
solo art in England before opera made solo singing a dominating preoccupation for the Italians. The English lute song
was unique, for it proceeded from literature—the great
Elizabethan heritage of lyric verse, which it adapted to itself
because a fine feeling for poetry and for music at their best
so often went hand in hand in one artist, even if he were not
actually and gloriously productive in both, like Campion,
who was also a physician, a classical scholar and something
of a lawyer.

There had been light songs in Italy long before 1600, such as the *frottola*, the *villanella* and the *canzone*, the last of which became subject to instrumental adaptation in a freely fugal manner. France, of course, had had a vast treasury of song for centuries past, but its most current examples were shapely tunes of a less highly organized nature than the English lute songs, which were matched in complexity only by the *airs de cour*. England itself had long had many folksongs (Shakespeare mentions "Heart's Ease," "Greensleeves" and "Light o' Love," for instance), but they were either artlessly sung unaccompanied or artfully arranged in parts. The instrumentally accompanied art-song—to use a convenient if abhorrent term—was new to the turn of the sixteenth century and found a peculiarly mature early expression in the English lutenist composers' work. The mock-polyphonic accompaniments these masters so ingeniously contrived on an instrument constitutionally unsuited to part-writing were a compromise with tradition on the one hand and the exercise of a skill natural to artists who could not have been content with a musical texture consisting merely of a tune with a primitive series of thrummed chords beneath it. Nevertheless, the tune was very important, and owing to the character of a particularly weak instrument it could not fail to stand out much more prominently than any part in a madrigal, however richly melodic, had ever done before. Thomas Ford's "When first I saw your face"—to choose a very familiar example—is now thought of as one of the great English tunes of all time, and probably many people are under the impression that it is a folksong. That is a great tribute indeed, but it is historically wrong: we have here a piece of music we can only most decidedly if regrettably call an art-song.

The Italian solo song, the first printed examples of which, by Caccini, appeared in 1601, was quite different. It was in the declamatory, recitative-like manner that found its finest early expression in Monteverdi. Its influence, if not that of the Monteverdian opera—but then it almost certainly came by way of that opera—reached England during the earlier Stuart reigns and is quite plainly noticeable in many composers of that time. But, being in the nature of vocal declamation rather than organized vocal melody based on regular musical patterns, and being in that nature because it pays a great deal of attention to the reproduction of the cadences and inflections of speech, music of that kind set to English words inevitably turned out to be different in some respects from music set to Italian, even where the English composers— as some of the less independent ones certainly did—aimed at imitating the Italians as closely as possible. The influence may have come directly from Monteverdi through Walter Porter, who is said to have been a pupil of the Italian master and who did publish, in 1632, a book of vocal pieces in which he directly copied one of Monteverdi's most startling innovations, the trick of setting a single syllable to several semiquavers on the same note, so that it was sung as a kind of bleat, in a quivering manner probably not unlike the modern "wobble," which however nobody has ever endeavoured to use purposely to artistic ends. This volume was entitled:

"Madrigales and Ayres. Of two, three, foure, and five Voyces, with the continued Base, with Toccatos, Sinfonias and Rittornellos to them. After the Manner of Consort Musique. To be performed with the Harpsechord, Lutes, Theorbos, Base Violl, two Violins, or two Viols."

Nothing could be more revealing of the many changes which this century of subversion wrought in music, as in other spheres. In the 1630's madrigals are no longer published alone: there are airs with them, and airs are essentially tunes confined to a single voice, whatever other parts may be added; there is a *basso continuo*, or thorough-bass, to be

amplified with chords by harmonic instruments of the keyboard or lute families; there are sections about to develop
into the purely instrumental species of the symphony (in
the old sense of introductions and interludes) and the toccata
(literally "a thing to play"); and the violin, though still
disliked by many people for the nagging tone by which it
seeks to assert itself above the viols, is coming to the fore.

The now old-fashioned consorts of viols, to be sure, were
still played, and indeed composed for. Even so late and so
aggressively modern a composer as Matthew Locke, who was
born about 1630, still wrote fantasies for the old instruments,
although Roger North, forgetting Purcell, said in 1728 that
they were "the last of the kind that hath been made," and
although they were followed in each case by a courante,
an air and a saraband, so that these sets must be classed as
suites. Families who treasured their chests of viols as precious
heirlooms naturally went on using them, and the age was
not one to cultivate the "classics" as exclusively as chamber
musicians do as a rule to-day, if only because they were
not easily accessible in print, if indeed they were published
at all. What passed from house to house in manuscript
copies was chiefly the contemporary output.

Publication, all the same, if still casual and dependent on
the caprice of opportunity, began to make great strides early
in the century. Indeed Thomas East had begun to print
madrigals and other music, including Byrd's earlier "Psalms,
Sonnets and Songs," some dozen years back in the past
century. Thomas Snodham, Peter Short and Humfrey
Lownes were other early London printers who issued music,
especially madrigals printed in part-books (there were
never any scores). It is significant of the eminence of the
English school at that time, too, that some of the foremost
music publishers on the Continent, among whom were
Vincenti of Venice and Phalèse of Antwerp, brought out
specimens of it. That the latter was Peter Philips's publisher

is not surprising, since Philips was on the spot as Antwerp's cathedral organist, and Dowland's foreign fame accounts amply for his being represented in Zacharias Füllsack's "Auserlesene Paduanen" issued at Hamburg in 1607 as well as in Georg Leopold Fuhrmann's "Testudo Gallo-Germanica" (Nuremberg, 1615). But at Lübeck in 1617 William Brade, an English musician as well known at the Danish court as Dowland and just then in the service of the Margrave of Brandenburg, brought out a book of "Neue auserlesene Branden," among which were some by Robert Johnson, one of the "King's Musicians for the Lute." In 1621 Dowland and Johnson again appeared in the "Taffel Consort allerhand lustiger Lieder" edited by Thomas Simpson, an English violist at the court of the Prince of Holstein-Schaumburg. And just in time, less than a year before the execution of Charles I, Paul Matthijss of Amsterdam printed a collection of "royal" fantasies for viols "and other play-things" by Thomas Lupo, Giovanni Coperario, William Daman and especially Orlando Gibbons, all of them long dead and by that time regarded as classics.

The fantasy (or fantasia or fancy), which, like the Italian *ricercare*, opened conventionally with a fugal exposition and went on in a freer but always essentially polyphonic style which, in the hands of a master, could be as intricate as Tudor fan-tracery, was not the only music to cling to old traditions. Church music did so too, the more so, doubtless, because in its Anglican form, which had settled down in its own traditions, it remained impervious to foreign influences, just as for the same reason it was the one English musical species disregarded by the rest of musical Europe. At any rate it clung to tradition until the Commonwealth brought it to a standstill, and we may be reasonably certain that it would have continued without the drastic changes the Restoration brought to it but for that artificial historical interruption. In this it was unlike the fantasy, which came to an end for

purely artistic reasons: the decline of the playing in consort
at home, the gradual supersession of the viols by the violin
and its family and the harmonic as distinct from polyphonic
element brought into music by the thorough-bass.

This newly-imported Italian device did manage to creep
even into the church while music for worship still remained
untouched by political disturbances. In 1639 William Child
published "The first set of Psalmes of iii. voyces, fitt for
private chappells, or other private meetings with continuall
Base, either for the Organ or Theorbo, newly composed
after the Italian way." The Italian way, indeed! What was
it doing in the Anglican church? But perhaps private
chapels were different. They could permit themselves a little
modishness that would never have done where the common
people worshipped, and also they may have needed a rich
instrumental support for very small, weak and amateurish
choirs. It is not that a modern note, particularly, insisted
on intruding into church music as a whole, and Henry
Lawes's settings of "A Paraphrase upon the Psalms of David"
by George Sandys "for voice and thorough-bass" (1637)
were sacred songs in the new manner, not ecclesiastical
music. As late as 1641 a minor canon of St. Paul's, John
Barnard, calmly surveyed the past in "The First Book of
Selected Church Musick, consisting of Services and Anthems,
such as are now used in the Cathedrall, and Collegiat Churches
in this Kingdome," which, though he could add to his title
that the whole of its contents were "never before printed,"
consisted exclusively of music by deceased masters.

"This kingdom," as a kingdom, was in a very sorry state
by this time, the year of the execution of Strafford, the Irish
massacre and the Grand Remonstrance. Civil war was
imminent. Benjamin Rogers was obliged to flee from
Dublin, where he had been organist of Christ Church
Cathedral, and to take refuge as a lay-clerk at St. George's
Chapel, Windsor, and Arthur Phillips, professor of music

at Oxford and organist at Magdalen College, composed a work with the significant title of "The Requiem, or Liberty of an Imprisoned Royalist." Many other composers were Royalists, naturally enough, since they were attached to the court more or less closely. John Wilson, now the best lutenist left in England, moved to Oxford with the court in 1643 as one of the "King's Musicians"—indeed Charles's favourite musician; Henry Cooke enlisted in the king's army, to be known thereafter as "Captain Cooke" for the rest of his life; William Lawes, though he was by that time over forty years of age, also joined up on the royal side and took an active part in the fighting, for all that Lord Gerrard had made him a commissionary to keep him out of danger, and he was to succumb to a stray shot at the siege of Chester in 1645. Christopher Simpson joined the Royalists under the Duke of Newcastle and suffered great hardships. Christopher Gibbons, Orlando's son, did likewise, perhaps from sheer necessity rather than loyalty, for he was compelled in 1644 to relinquish his post of organist at Winchester Cathedral. Cromwell was busy at that time suppressing the organ in the church service and indeed the choirs too, being anxious to reduce the music in church to hymns sung by the congregation.

Thus not only the musicians at court, but those in the churches all over the country suffered under the Cromwellian purge, which was not intended by him to affect music as such, but could not fail to do so where music was connected with the Anglican church service that was now intended to undergo reforms of a Calvinistic severity. Cromwell himself was fond of music, and as Lord Protector he did not scorn to have the Magdalen College organ, where of course it could no longer be used, moved to Hampton Court, where he saw no reason for not using it; and he had his daughters instructed in the art. He also took the new Magdalen organist, John Hingston, with him, who pleased him particularly by his frequent performance of Dering's Latin motets, of all things—a purely aesthetic enjoyment, one must suppose.   However, Cromwell's Puritan zeal went so much farther than his musical enthusiasm that when the two interests clashed, as they were bound to do in church matters, music had to yield.   Moreover, he had to depute the execution of his wishes all over the country to countless others, and it was inevitable that many of them were more thorough-going and ruthless than he would have been himself.   An organ reduced by stringent regulations to the duty of mere hymn-tune accompaniment would have been enough for him; for too many of them nothing less than its destruction would do.

We hear of endless changes in musicians' lives between the outbreak of the Civil War and the execution of Charles I on January 30th 1649, two years to the day after his surrender to Parliament by the Scots.   Child, though only thirty-seven, was forced to retire, perhaps to a farm, when the royal musicians were disbanded and to devote himself to composition alone, with the poorest material rewards, no doubt. The elder John Milton, who was a musician of good repute and a composer, left Reading when the town was taken by the Earl of Essex and went to live with his son, the poet. John Hilton lost his appointment at St. Margaret's, Westminster, in 1644, and in the same year the Master of the Choristers at Westminster Abbey, Porter (the alleged Monteverdi pupil), as well as the organist, Richard Portman, was dismissed.   Rogers's place at Windsor became vacant after only three years.   After the second siege of Worcester in 1646, when the cathedral services were suspended, Tomkins retired from the organist's post at the age of seventy-three, forced by circumstances rather than by age.   Some, as Wilson did after the surrender of the Oxford garrison, luckily enough found shelter in the houses of noble or wealthy patrons. Others tried their best to support themselves by teaching, but Playford's list of the London music teachers who sought to make a living during the Commonwealth was alarmingly long. Many suffered poverty and want.

Composers turned their thoughts to serious things. Among these were the elegies on the death of William Lawes written by such masters as Hilton, Jenkins and Wilson, and by minor men like Simon Ive, formerly a vicar-choral at St. Paul's, and John Cobb, who had been organist of the Chapel Royal. Portman in 1645 published "The Soules Life, exercising itself in the sweet Fields of Divine Meditation, collected for the comfort thereof, in these sad days of distraction." The sad days had their effect on the courtly musicians as well as on those on the parliamentary side. Music sobered down all round, not merely in the church, where it did so by compulsion. The "distractions" of the times were not those of canzonets, fancies, fa-las and masques.

The masque had flourished sumptuously and extravagantly under Stuart patronage and that of the great houses of the nobility. It was a kind of hybrid offspring of the earlier Italian operas, which were classical in subject and already lavishly spectacular, and of the French masquerades, *ballets comiques* and *ballets de cour*, types of mythological pieces in which spectacle and dance bore the major share, but which from about 1600 onward had replaced what had previously been explanatory passages in prose by songs interlarded with the action, by way of elucidation or didactic commentary. (The operatic aria long continued to sum up some sentiment or other expressed in the preceding dialogue or recitative, a practice parodied in a neatly epigrammatic way by John Gay in the eighteenth-century "Beggar's Opera," where the songs often begin in some such way as "Thus when a good housewife sees a rat," "The turtle thus," etc.)

The English masque favoured the song as much as the dance, and it was here that composers found their widest scope in developing a type of declamatory or dramatic song

that was akin to the later accompanied recitative in opera.
There were formal, lyrical songs, too, corresponding to the
later aria, though smaller and less highly organized. Settings,
dresses and what would nowadays be called "production"
were of the utmost importance—far more so than the music
in fact, for had the composer's share in the work been at all
comparable with that of the designer, or even with that of
the "stage manager," the English early seventeenth-century
masques would have grown unawares into full-dress operas
similar to the most elaborate examples of baroque opera
known to musical history—the Venetian opera of the second
half of the century.

Inigo Jones began his career as a stage artist and designed
settings for masques. Indeed this was very much an architect's rather than a graphic artist's task, for the new delight in
stage perspective demanded that the action of a masque
should take place as often as possible in settings reproducing
the interiors of vast palaces where massive columns formed
the wings and lost themselves in a backcloth actually only a
few yards distant, but apparently half-way down a long vista
which it seemed to continue to infinity. Even when a
landscape was imperatively required, trees or rocks would
imitate rows of columns as closely as nature would allow, or
a good deal more so. Spectacular effects like thunderstorms,
fires and earthquakes were obligatory, and at the end gods
would as a matter of course descend from heaven with
messages of delivery or reconciliation in machines hung
from stout ropes, but pleasingly disguised as clouds, chariots,
suns or dragons.

Dance music and instrumental interludes as well as songs
formed part of what the masque required of composers,
and the task was often divided between two or more
musicians according to their particular aptitude for this or
that species. For one of the more primitive May-Day
entertainments—that day was then celebrated by royalty!

—held at Highgate in 1604, possibly on the village green that still exists, Martin Peerson as a young man had set an ode by Ben Jonson, who was then only thirty-one himself. But the following year Jonson provided a real masque for the court, "The Masque of Blackness," for which the younger Ferrabosco wrote the music. Other distinguished literary men followed suit. In 1607 Campion wrote the words for a masque performed at the marriage of Sir James Hay and set two of the songs himself. He wrote four more masques and composed songs for them, in 1613, for the marriage of Princess Elizabeth to the Elector Palatine, Frederic V; for the marriage of the Earl of Somerset; a piece performed before the queen on her way to Bath at Caversham House near Reading, the residence of Lord Knowles; and "The Masque of Flowers" presented by the Gentlemen of Gray's Inn at the Banqueting House in Whitehall. Nicholas Lanier, another versatile man, who became art adviser to the court and was sent to Italy to buy pictures for the royal collection, not only set two Ben Jonson masques to music in 1617, but sang in them and painted the scenery.

James Shirley wrote a masque, "The Triumph of Peace," in 1633, by which time Jonson's example had made the species more interesting to literary men. Shirley's composers were the Lawes brothers and Simon Ive. Henry Lawes, again, set a masque by Thomas Carew, "Coelum Britannicum," performed by the Gentlemen of the four Inns of Court before Charles I the following year. Two of the Earl of Bridgewater's sons performed in it, and the younger Lawes became their music master, with the result that he had the honour of supplying the music for and to produce a masque by no other than Milton; for now, in 1634, this form of entertainment had attracted the greatest poet of the age. Lawes, who did not then realize his eminence, seems to have dealt with him rather high-handedly, but the young genius saw to it that it should be an entertainment pure and simple no longer,

and "Comus"—for this was the piece done at Michaelmas
in the great hall of Ludlow Castle, the Bridgewater residence
—became in his hands the vehicle for moral allegory.
"Comus" was certainly pure, but it was not simple as the
masque had been in treating mythological subjects merely
for their picturesque, heroic or miraculous qualities. It is,
in fact, not a typical example, and quite exceptional in its
form. Less than a year later Davenant joined the ranks of
literary men who devoted themselves to the masque, and his
"Triumph of the Prince d'Amour" was set by the Lawes
brothers.

There had been a Puritan emigration to New England as
early as 1630, nearly twenty years before the execution of
Charles I. There had also, we know, been much Puritan
opposition to all the court stood for in politics and religion;
nor did the arts go free of censure from those who reacted
with rigid austerity against real or fancied laxity at court and
lavish ceremony in church. But the masque as a form of art
was not opposed by all Puritans, for its classical subjects
could give no offence to reasonable men, though we may
be sure that fanatics thought them reprehensibly heathenish.
"Comus" was a masque by a Puritan for Puritans and showed
a great and respected member of their ranks sanctioning the
species. Still, the theatre was looked at askance by many
quite early in the century. In 1615 already, the year before
Shakespeare's death, Robert Jones and Philip Rosseter, with
two others, were made to feel the censorious spirit that was
about to oppose the stage, guilty or not of immorality,
blasphemy, irreverence and whatever else the current re-
proaches were. These four obtained a patent for the erection
of a theatre on the site of Jones's house at Blackfriars, for the
use—innocent enough, one would think—of the "Children
of the Revels to the Queen"; but the Lord Mayor and city
aldermen forbade it.

Even during the Commonwealth the masque was not

altogether discredited, partly perhaps because it had always
been a private rather than a public entertainment—and it
was public morality that Cromwell was concerned about,
being wise enough to know how useless and therefore ridiculous it would be to interfere with the aristocracy at home, if
indeed it could afford extravagant festivities. But it was not
only that: the masque, as we have seen, could be a vehicle
for noble ideas and sentiments. If the public theatre was
proscribed it was because plays were, or were thought,
much more profane.

And here we come upon a curious and engagingly ironic
fact. Or shall we say, for safety, a curious notion? But it
does look as though the Puritans were responsible for the
beginning of English opera, and they are certainly not
accountable for its almost immediate extinction, which is
due to the Restoration and its brilliant, cynical and licentious
comedy. The Puritans, if they allowed anything on the
stage at all, could tolerate only elevated subjects and would
have nothing in the nature of frivolous comedy. Such
subjects had already appeared in the masque, accompanied by music: they seemed therefore to demand music,
which as one of the major arts could not fail one day to over-
rule the minor ones of the dance, of scene-painting and of
stage display, claiming equality with drama and poetry.
The masques by Shirley which actually succeeded in getting
themselves produced (privately, of course) during the
Commonwealth—"The Contention of Ajax and Ulysses"
and "Cupid and Death" (both in 1653)—were akin to serious
drama rather than to spectacular and choreographic diversion,
and their music—by Edward Coleman, a teacher of the lute,
viol and singing, for the former and by Christopher Gibbons
and young Matthew Locke for the latter—is exactly what
one would expect that of a small-scale opera between
Monteverdi's "Orfeo" and Purcell's "Dido and Aeneas"
to be.

But a real opera, or at any rate a so-called opera, was to appear three years later. It was "The Siege of Rhodes," written by Davenant for his Entertainment at Rutland House, a barn-like place in Charterhouse Yard, Aldersgate Street. The music was by Henry Lawes, Captain Cooke, George Hudson and Charles Coleman (the father of Edward, who sang in the piece with his wife, with the elder Henry Purcell, Cooke and Locke). Locke may also have contributed with his pen, but all the music of the work is lost, and we neither know how it was shared nor what it was like. What it was like in detail, that is. Its style in general is quite easy to imagine from what we know of the composers and the musical manners of the period. The instrumental interludes and the dances, if any, probably had much in common with the string fantasies and the keyboard suites of dances which had formed themselves gradually ever since Morley had advocated the contrasting of pavans and galliards side by side. As for the vocal portions, which must have enormously predominated, they can only have been in the new declamatory style of which Henry Lawes was a master. It was to him that Milton, in 1646, addressed the sonnet beginning, not quite truthfully:

"Harry, whose tuneful and well-measured song
　　First taught our English music how to span
　　Words with just note and accent";

and it was he, now an experienced composer of sixty-one, who must have been the outstanding contributor to this first English opera.

"The Siege of Rhodes" was also pretty well the last English opera for some time to come; and the fact that the species could not begin to flourish healthily in England may just as easily be due to the Restoration as its first flowering may be attributable to the conditions affecting the stage during the Commonwealth. For the Restoration not only re-admitted comedy, the more flippant the better, but happened to produce a galaxy of writers who could handle it with a wit as great as and a polish greater than Molière's, though neither with his human insight nor with his moral purpose.

With Cromwell's death in 1658 a great period came to an end. Compared with him his son Richard was a mere shadow that made the dramatic flash of Charles II's seizure of the throne two years later the more dazzling. Music in England had gone through transformations almost as astounding during that time. It was not its greatest phase, but certainly its most convulsively evolutionary. Only a fraction of its crowded scene has been surveyed here: much had perforce to be left out of the picture. The cultivation of music by amateurs, for one thing, and its encouragement by great families. There was Tobias Hume, for instance, an army officer and viola da gamba player, who published— and showed the English amateur's taste for foreign things in doing so—"The First Part of Ayres, French, Polish, and others together" in 1605; there was the Earl of Derby, who in 1624 contributed a Fancy for viols and a Pavan for orpharion, a freak instrument of the lute type, to Pilkington's second book of madrigals; there was Sir Hamon L'Estrange taking John Jenkins, aged eighteen, into his Norfolk country house; there were other East Anglian families, such as the Kytsons at Bury St. Edmunds, who made a home for Wilbye, the last of the great madrigalists; there was Sir Christopher Hatton, Orlando Gibbons's patron and friend; Sir Robert Bolles offering a refuge to Simpson in Lincolnshire during the Commonwealth; Lady Villiers, mother of the vainglorious and politically reckless Duke of Buckingham, Vautor's patroness in Leicestershire; and there had been young Henry, the Prince of Wales, himself, whose very promising musicianship was carefully fostered by John Bull (? virginal and

composition) and Thomas Ford (? lute and singing) until
he died at the age of eighteen in 1612.

Publication of music went forward vigorously. A surprising number of collected works of the greatest value,
landmarks in the history of English music, appeared during
the first half of the century, often as beautifully produced as
the state of the early printing-presses would permit. In
1605, to begin with, Byrd finished the first book of his
"Gradualia," a collection of motets for the whole ecclesiastical
year of the Roman church, for he still enjoyed the com-
parative religious tolerance Elizabeth had shown him for the
sake of his genius; and in the same year Dowland published
his "Lachrymae, or Seven Tears, figured in seven passionate
Pavans," an early example of purely instrumental concerted
music, though madrigals had long been played on viols of
different sizes or on "broken consorts" at will. Six years
later, in 1611, appeared:

"Parthenia/or/The Maydenhead/ of the first musicke
that/euer was printed for the Virginalls./Composed/By
three famous Masters William Byrd, Dr. John Bull &
Orlando Gibbons./Gentilmen of his Maties most Illustrious
Chappell. Ingrauen/by William Hole/Lond: print: for
M. Dor. Euans./Cum/priuilegio.

Also Byrd's "Psalmes, Songs and Sonnets," curiously and
significantly described as "for voice or viols" and dedicated
to the Earl of Cumberland. There were also rounds and
catches published in Ravenscroft's "Melismata" that year,
and though that form of canon-singing was to be cultivated
more thoroughly in the later seventeenth century and onwards, we know that it had delighted people ever since the
"Sumer" rota, and it is shown as a fine, lusty carousers'
pastime in "Twelfth Night." Shakespeare's last play but
one, "The Tempest," by the way, also came out in 1611,

with the songs set by Robert Johnson, who probably wrote some incidental music as well. Orlando Gibbons, already something of a reactionary at twenty-nine, issued in 1612 a book of madrigals which shows the fine poetic taste of the day, including as it does settings of Spenser and Donne. In 1614 another famous collection, this time of sacred songs and anthems, owed its publication to an amateur, Sir William Leighton. It was "Tears and Lamentations of a Sorrowful Soul" and contained contributions by almost all the eminent composers of the day, not by any means all church musicians, it may be mentioned, since it is worth observing that composition for the church was not then the speciality of organists and choirmasters, who may possess no real creative gifts beyond that of mere technical facility.

In 1618, two years before his death, Campion showed that he was a theorist as well as everything else by bringing out a treatise entitled "A New Way of Making Four Parts in Counterpoint, by a most familiar and infallible Rule." Ravenscroft's "Whole Book of Psalms" of 1621, containing a hundred four-part tunes by various composers, continued the fashion of metrical and rhymed paraphrases of the Psalms which converted them musically from chants into something like hymn-tunes. Among publications a treatise, "Sylva Sylvarum," left by Bacon at his death in 1626, must be mentioned because it deals with the phenomenon of sympathetic vibrations in stringed instruments and shows that in those days men of learning as well as great writers and poets were interested in music.

That was the Elizabethan tradition, however, and the Elizabethans were vanishing one by one. As the second quarter of the century dawned musical publication showed new trends. The "Ayres, or Fa-La's, for Three Voyces" by John Hilton, one of the newer lutenists, more famous for his "Catch that catch can" of 1652, showed already in 1627 that the madrigal tended more and more towards the light

glee type that was to flourish in the eighteenth century, and
to which even some lightly polyphonic pieces as late as
Sullivan belong—for whatever Gilbert will say about a
"merry madrigawl," the quartet "Brightly dawns our
wedding-day" in "The Mikado" is not a madrigal at all,
but a perfectly written and very pretty glee.

After about 1630 no publication comparable in importance
with those just enumerated appeared for some time, but in
1648 Henry Lawes brought out his "Choice Psalms put into
Music for Three Voices," containing settings by himself
and his late brother William, the elegies on whose death
were also published, as well as a set of canons—another
pointer towards the glee school—by Henry.

What is curious, considering the trend of those days, is
that in 1650 the bookseller and publisher John Playford was
allowed to bring out, as his first musical work, "The English
Dancing-Master." It looks as though the Puritans of the
Commonwealth were not after all quite as eager to repress
all public enjoyment as is too often supposed, although
Playford goes out of his way to say of the dance in his preface
that "these Times and the Nature of it do not agree." But
after all, the Playford book contained popular country-dance
tunes, not sophisticated ballroom dances, and there was a
good deal of innocently sportive dancing on village greens
and round the maypole going on in Cromwell's time. If
he looked with a less benevolent eye upon the introduction
of these tunes and dances into fashionable houses, which is
what happened with Playford's help, that was beyond his
control; but we must remember that the Cromwellian
conception of the Commonwealth was not communistic or
proletarian. He had no notion that a "gentleman's" accomplishments could possibly be incompatible with it, and he
encouraged such accomplishments.

Again, the fact that the very next year Lawes published
settings of poems by and songs in the plays of William

Cartwright shows that stage pieces were not banned if no attempt was made to perform them, even if they were by a zealous Royalist like Cartwright. But then he was also a cleric, and his theatrical writings were blameless.

In 1656 William Child re-issued his Psalms of 1639, now entitled "Choice Musick to the Psalmes of Dauid." Nothing was said now about private chapels; if they still existed, they were not acknowledged. The year before Cromwell's death old Wilson, thinking of the good past times—as they seemed to him now, at any rate—was surprisingly allowed to publish a "Psalterium Carolinum. The Devotions of his Sacred Majestie in his Solitude and Sufferings, Rendered in Verse," for three voices with organ and that now very old-fashioned instrument, the theorbo. Scarcely less curious was Simpson's publication of a treatise on viola da gamba playing, "The Division Violist" at John Playford's. For divisions were purely decorative variations on a ground bass of a kind that was now going out of fashion, and this was the year 1659, the very year a great composer was born who was to do away with the sort of music the viol stood for—Henry Purcell.

CHAPTER V

The Age of Purcell (1660–1710)

The dates given in this heading are not Purcell's own. He was born in 1659 and died in 1695, not so much as a year older than another master was at his death whom he almost matched in fertility and approached in genius— Mozart. The limits of time set to this chapter are those of the Stuart dynasty's restoration at one end and what may, without too much exaggeration, be called a revolution at the other, with the difference that the former event was political, though it affected the art of music very considerably, whereas the latter was wholly artistic; nor did it come so suddenly in 1710 as to make that date anything more significant in itself than a chronicler's landmark. Still, the appearance of Handel in England that year marks off a division between two distinct eras that is useful enough for practical purposes, though the far-reaching changes in musical habits and fashions for which Handel was to stand had begun to show themselves from the death of Purcell at the latest, as we shall see presently.

When Charles II boldly seized the vacant English throne in 1660 musical England, though not moribund, was in a morose state. Many of the Puritans, to be sure, had cared for music well enough as an innocent diversion, according to their light, but it had to behave to suit their conceptions of life, which were necessarily narrow. They were incapable of viewing art as a thing standing above and detached from morality and saw it as only too apt to sacrifice its innocence to worldly vanities of all kinds, vanities that threatened perpetually to creep even into the church.

Charles's reign seemed to justify their scruples amply.

By way of reaction the court, and many of those who came closely or remotely within its influence, now plunged into a riot of extravagance. Music not only emancipated itself, as it should quite properly have done, from the inhibitions of Puritan morality; it began at once to be pressed into the service of courtly laxity. The new king cared little for it as an art, but as a dabbler who had enjoyed only too much leisure during his foreign exile to cultivate a superficial taste he knew its value as an adjunct to the regal splendours he at once strove to display in emulation of Louis XIV's dazzling household, though funds were by no means adequate and he can have had no very clear idea of where they were to come from.

Louis having his *vingt-quatre violons du roi*, Charles had as a matter of course to have his "twenty-four violins"—which did not mean violins only, but a complete string orchestra in which the modern violins and the obsolescent viols met together. But this was merely a nucleus. The records show an endless succession of musicians' appointments during the year 1660, appointments for all sorts of instrumentalists as well as singers, and as endless a series of changes thereafter. The list of extant documents is headed by "Captain Cooke appointed a base in Mons. Du Vall's place," for Cooke was not only deemed to deserve a reward for his military services to the Royalist cause, but was an excellent singer, more than fit to grace the re-established Chapel Royal, in which indeed he was soon afterwards appointed Master of the Children. What "Mons. Du Vall" may have done in the Chapel, and why his place fell vacant almost as soon as the Chapel was reopened, nobody knows. He may have come to England with Charles, who as the son of a French mother and with years of residence abroad just behind him, was the very man to set going the amiable English tradition that no native musician will do if his place can possibly be given to a foreigner. However, even Charles may have recognized that Cooke, a man of great gifts, would be better than a Frenchman at singing in the Anglican service, which for political reasons had now to be resumed with a good deal of pomp, although the king was at heart a Roman Catholic.

For the moment, indeed, although four Dutchmen were trumpeters in ordinary, a good many Englishmen were drawn into the service of the court, and among the "Musitians of the private Musick" appeared men of the greatest distinction, such as Henry Lawes as "composer in the private musick for lutes and voices" and Matthew Locke as plain "composer in the private musick." A harper, a "Master of the organs and virginalls," more than one lutenist, "flutes, hoboys and cornetts in ordinary," all found their places apart from the twenty-four violins and the Chapel Royal singers. In addition there were military elements which could be drawn into the private music on festive occasions. We read of an "Appointment of Gervace Price as yeoman of the bowes and gunnes and sergeant trumpeter" and of "John Mawgridg appointed drum-major." The sackbut (trombone) as well as trumpets and drums formed part of these extras.

All this cost a great deal of money, but as extreme laxity in the matter of honouring pecuniary obligations at once became one of the guiding principles of an otherwise unprincipled court, this did not matter to anybody but the defenceless victims whose talents could be exploited the more easily because no musician once attached to the court had any desire to detach himself. Private teaching was even more precarious than royal service, and there was as yet no public music-making that could be expected to prove in the least lucrative; at any rate not until John Banister, driven from his office of leader of the "twenty-four," sought to repair his ill-fortune by giving daily afternoon concerts of "musick performed by excellent masters" at his house, "now called the Musick-school, over against the George Tavern in White Friars."

This was not till 1672. Meanwhile the court lived merrily on a basis of unscrupulous extravagance. The records abound in warrants for this, that and the other, with reckless regularity: "1s. 8d. per diem, and £16 2s. 6d. yearly as livery"; "£60 per annum, and £20 per annum for strings. Also £24 per annum for breeding a boy for vocall musick. . . ." (for Captain Cooke); "To each of them £40 per annum, which with all payments above mentioned to be paid quarterly" (for ten vocalists, theorbists and violists appointed on one and the same day); "Bill of £147 4s. for 64 surplices for the gentlemen of the Chappell";

"Fourteen yards of chamblett for a gowne, 3 yards of black velvet to gare the same gown, one furre of Budge for the same price £4, 8 yards of damask for a jaquet and three yards of velvet for a doublet.

"The above to be delivered to him yearly at every Feast of St. Andrew during his life; the making also to be paid for out of the Great Wardrobe."

And so on and on. It was easy enough to undertake on paper to pay quarterly or to pay out of the Great Wardrobe, from which came also the fine feathers worn by Charles and his queen, as well as, doubtless, the brocades and silks that so lavishly clad his mistresses. There was no way open to the court's underlings to enforce these obligations. After a great deal of humble petitioning a royal creditor was lucky if he could extort from the exchequer an instalment on account of arrears, a favour for which he was expected to render thanks in suitably deferential terms. Even tragedy, such as that which befell Charles Evans, the harper who had been one of the very first musicians to be appointed by the merry monarch, did not mend matters. On December 19th 1666 Pepys writes in his diary:

"Talked of the King's family with Mr. Hingston, the organist. He says many of the musique are ready to starve, they being five years behindhand for their wages; nay, Evans, the famous man upon the harp, having not his equal in the world, did the other day die for mere want, and was fain to be buried at the alms of the parish, and carried to his grave in the dark at night without one link, but that Mr. Hingston met it by chance, and did give 12d. to buy two or three links."

That was not long after a far greater tragedy—the dreadful fire of London, with which Charles dealt splendidly; but if the king's band could fiddle (on twenty-four fiddles) while London was burning, who was to turn a hair at court because one of its musicians had died from want and neglect? So long as outwardly the music made a brave show, all was well enough. It did make a brave show. At the Chapel Royal, under the energetic direction of Cooke, who was not appointed Master of the Children until June 29th 1660, the services presented something of a countenance as early as July 8th, the first of Pepys's "Lord's days" on which, at the age of twenty-seven, he became acquainted with a full-dress Anglican service in the old style. Only five of the old members had reassembled at the resumption of the Chapel Royal services, the boys had of course all been unfamiliar with the order of the service, which even the organists had almost forgotten, and neither music-books nor vestments had been found. Yet on that Sunday Pepys could write:

"To Whitehall chapel, where I got in with ease by going before the Lord Chancellor with Mr. Kipps. Here I heard very good musique, the first time that ever I remember to have heard the organs and singing-men in surplices in my life."

The gallant captain soon set matters to rights by a reorganization based on the principles of military discipline, and he pressed for the revival of the old method of requisitioning good voices from any cathedral or parish church up and down the country if he judged them suited to his purpose. He looked for more than voices in his pupils, however, and so he had among them at least half a dozen who showed promise as composers, including one at least of outstanding genius, Henry Purcell, who joined the choir at the age of nine or so, about 1669, both his father, Thomas Purcell, and his uncle Henry (for that, not the reverse, is now believed to have been the family relationship) being then Gentlemen of the Chapel Royal. Before that Cooke had already had Pelham Humfrey, John Blow, William Turner, Thomas Tudway and Michael Wise among his boys, whom he fathered, bullied, occasionally flogged and instructed very soundly in vocal and instrumental music-making, sight-reading (in which Pepys says they had "extraordinary skill"), singing in Latin and Italian as well as in English, and above all in every aspect of musical theory. They could write their own anthems for a change, so that, Tudway said later, "every month they produced something fresh." In 1664, when Humfrey at seventeen was sent to Paris by the king, to be turned, as Pepys disgustedly remarked three years later, "into an absolute Monsieur, as full of form, and confidence, and vanity," he, with Blow, who was only sixteen but had already published anthems in Clifford's "Divine Services," and Turner, who was thirteen, wrote an anthem: "I will always give thanks," to commemorate their friendship—the so-called club anthem.

So far as the order of the services went the church was reinstated on its old lines; but church music now became a very different thing, for all that it was set to the same words as before, when great and pure polyphonists like Tallis and

Byrd and Gibbons had set them. The old school was, of course, still respected and some of its music was sung as a pious tribute to a past still recognized as a glorious memory; but in an inventory "of severall Services and Anthems that have been transcribed into the books of his Majesty's Chappell Royall since anno 1670 to Midsummer, 1676," we find Farrant's High Service alone as an archaic example among the nineteen services, the rest of which are by Mr. This and Dr. That—all of them contemporaries. Much the same is true of the far more numerous anthems catalogued, among which Byrd's "O God, the proud" looks almost like an isolated curiosity.

The humbler churches, no doubt more conservative in their use of anthems, contented themselves with simpler fare in the matter of psalms and hymns, very much like the material that had been allowed, if not approved, by the Puritans. In 1671 Playford published a book of "Psalms and Hymns in Solemn Music of four parts on the Common Tunes to the Psalms in Metre: used in Parish Churches." But wherever the necessary material was obtainable, the service was now allowed to be orchestrally accompanied, and this in turn encouraged the use of the new harmonic style, in which blocks of chords supported contrapuntal parts, if they did not wholly predominate even in the voices, a style admirably suited to the orchestra, and for that matter to the organ too, which is not an essentially polyphonic instrument any more than any other capable of producing chords. This style, of course, had already been cultivated in the masque and in opera, so far as the latter had gone in England, and the church tradition, broken by the interregnum of the Commonwealth, was in no condition to impose a more suitable new style of its own upon the new fashion. The fashion as such had the upper hand, and it was not to be expected that the church, influenced on the one side by the frivolity at court and on the other by an inevitable reaction against Puritan stringency, should override it with any great show of severity.

The music for Charles's coronation (April 23rd 1661) composed by Cooke and Lawes, who wrote the anthem "Zadok the Priest" (reset by Handel for George II), set the tone. "Anthems, and rare music, with lutes, viols, trumpets, organs, and voices, were then heard," wrote John Evelyn in his diary on that day; and on December 21st 1662 he says that after a sermon delivered by one of the king's chaplains

"instead of the ancient, grave, and solemn wind musique accompanying the organ, was introduced a concert of twenty-four violins between every pause, after the French fantastical light way, better suiting a tavern, or playhouse, than a church."

Taverns, then, it seems, had their music, though it may be doubted whether Evelyn's suggestion that it resembled a royal concert should be taken literally. It was simply that the violin as such was still thought a vulgar instrument, at any rate by so conservative a man as Evelyn had become at the age of forty-two or by Anthony Wood, who wrote priggishly in his "History and Antiquities of the University of Oxford" (1669) that some musical Oxford gentlemen

"esteemed a Violin to be an Instrument only belonging to a common Fidler, and could not endure that it should come among them, for feare of making their Meetings to be vaine and fidling."

As for the playhouse, theatrical performances ran riot after the Puritan suppression, both in private and in public. Theatres were open once more; plays were done at the Cockpit and at the Salisbury Court playhouse; the Duke's Theatre,

D

the new playhouse in Lincoln's Inn Fields, opened in 1661, and the new Theatre Royal in Drury Lane, built in 1663, all flourished exceedingly. Old plays were revived, especially those by Beaumont and Fletcher; Ben Jonson's "Volpone" was done at court, and some of Shakespeare's works were tried again in their original form, though people seemed to be "ill-pleased" with most of them. The spectacular masque had changed the taste. Pepys could tolerate "Macbeth" for a change, strangely enough, but had no use for "Twelfth Night"; Evelyn says after a performance of "Hamlet" that "now the old plays began to disgust this refined age." Presently Shakespeare was to be "adapted" to this alleged refinement in the manner of the masque, not to say that of the modern pantomime, with plenty of opportunities for song, dance and stage-display. Purcell's "Fairy Queen," for instance, is such an adaptation, by an unknown author, of "A Midsummer Night's Dream," which of course contains in itself most of the elements that were to degenerate into the features of pantomime: this adaptation introduces country yokels and wenches, a drunken poet, monkeys, Chinese dancers, allegorical figures of the four seasons, and so on. Shadwell's conversion of "The Tempest" into an "opera" for the same master makes Caliban into a comic figure with an equally comic female counterpart—a kind of loutish pair of ancestors for Mozart's Papageno and Papagena.

But the time for this was not yet. Meanwhile new plays were coming forward in abundance, Dryden, Davenant, Shirley, Sir Robert Howard, William Rowley, Lord Orrery, the Duke of Buckingham, Mrs. Philips and others all wrote for the stage during the very first years of the new reign. Betterton was the great actor, but the chief attraction was the women, now for the first time allowed to replace boys on the stage, much to Pepys's delight, who thought the artistic gain very considerable, while Evelyn deplored the moral loss to "several young noblemen and gallants . . . and another greater person than any of them, who fell into their snares." This "in a time of such judgments and calamities" as the plague of 1665 and the fire of 1666. By then Nell Gwyn, though only sixteen, had already given up selling oranges in the pit and stepped on the stage, if not yet climbed the royal backstairs.

A couple of paragraphs of theatrical history have their relevance to the story of mid-seventeenth-century English musical life. We have already seen that the new vogue of frivolous and risky plays—Evelyn's word is "lewd"—which at their best could of course be polished and witty, led the English stage away from a channel in which music was about to overwhelm the libretto and turn the masque into opera. It was the serious masque approved by the Puritans that had prepared the field for opera, and how nearly that species succeeded may be judged by the fact that "The Siege of Rhodes" became something of a stock piece at Davenant's new theatre in Lincoln's Inn, which Pepys actually calls "The Opera" more than a dozen times in the diary. Even the Restoration would not have nipped English opera in the bud—on the contrary, its lavish musical resources could easily have encouraged it—if the Restoration had not found its fullest satisfaction in the quick repartee and equivocal dialogue of a type of comedy whose artificial brilliance did not require the glamour of music.

Still, Restoration comedy did have some use for music, for it became a convention that such pieces should contain songs, to be sung by actors whose vocal attainments, usually very modest, no doubt, it seemed desirable to show off. Composers were thus required to set these songs to new tunes, and when an orchestra was to be had at the theatre, if it were only a string band, as it certainly was at any rate at "The Opera," it was perfectly natural for the composer to furnish some instrumental pieces as well to entertain the public before the opening and between the acts. Thus overtures and interludes, called "act tunes," became the fashion. During the last fifteen years of his life Purcell was to supply songs and incidental music for nearly fifty plays.

It is to Purcell that we must now turn our attention more closely. To call him the greatest English composer of the second half of the seventeenth century would be ridiculously obvious, so immeasurably did he out-top even the best of his compatriots. To speak of him, on the other hand, as almost the only great composer of that age is scarcely an exaggeration, surprising though the statement may seem. We have only to survey musical Europe from 1650 to 1700 to find that at any rate he stands isolated among the great as a master of all-round versatility. There are some seventeenth-century figures—astonishingly few—who must be regarded as his peers in one domain of music or another, and indeed as to some extent his models, as Lully was in opera and Corelli in the chamber sonata; but look where we may, there is no composer anywhere within his lifetime and some years beyond on either side who is his match in every field of creation then cultivated by composers. Indeed no other great man attempted to till anything like so many fields. Alessandro Scarlatti, who was also born in 1659, excelled only in opera and in the chamber cantata, Schütz only in vocal music, sacred and secular, and Carissimi only in oratorio and early forms of the sacred cantata; and anyway the last two were dead by the time Purcell was fifteen. Bach and Handel were only ten when he in turn died. Rameau was then twelve. Couperin, though but nine years younger than Purcell, belongs to the eighteenth rather than the seventeenth century, and so does Lotti. No others with whose lives his overlapped need be regarded as at all comparable, for Purcell was supreme in all sorts of ways except in the handling of the largest formal schemes: a daring harmonist, a contrapuntist of unlimited skill, a superb inventor of great tunes and an enterprising innovator in rhythm.

Purcell wrote an opera and several masque-like semi-operas, a vast amount of incidental music and songs for plays, many odes and songs of welcome in the form of secular cantatas, church music including some sixty anthems, a number of services, psalms, hymns and sacred canons, many sacred songs and duets, about fifty catches, not far from two hundred solo songs, duets and three-part songs, not counting the songs in the plays, fantasies and other works for strings, twenty-two sonatas for two violins and continuo, harpsichord and organ pieces, and some odds and ends.

Historically, his most interesting achievement, if not in every artistic respect his greatest, is undoubtedly the opera "Dido and Aeneas." It seems to have been written, almost by accident, probably in 1689, when a dancing-master, Josias Priest, commissioned it for the boarding-school for young ladies he kept at Chelsea. The words were by the pompous but inferior poet Nahum Tate, who went to Virgil for the subject, but spoilt it by versification that is always flat and at times descends to doggerel of this kind:

"Thus, on the fatal bank of Nile,
    Weeps the deceitful crocodile;
    Thus, hypocrites, that murder act,
    Make Heaven and gods the authors of the fact."

But Tate had a knack of contriving rapid action, emotional climaxes and a variety of *dramatis personae*, all of which was at any rate good enough to give a great dramatic composer his chance of, so to speak, throwing into relief what the libretto merely outlined in two dimensions. And a great dramatic composer Purcell certainly was. His way of writing from beginning to end of this very condensed but superb masterpiece music that is perfectly satisfying by its own form and invention, yet fits every situation, intensifies every emotion and outlines every character with unfailing aptness is not equalled by any other composer of his time. Lully is pallid and monotonous, Scarlatti formal by comparison. We have to look back to Monteverdi for anything to equal "Dido and Aeneas" in all respects and forward to Mozart for anything to surpass it in range and organization. The remarkable fact is that among operas still living in the operatic repertory, as distinct from those revived as curiosities, "Dido and Aeneas" is by far the earliest anywhere in the world, and that we do not come upon the next work of the kind, Gluck's "Orfeo," until 1762.

It is impossible here to discuss every category of Purcell's life-work, though there is not one that fails to repay study. Let us cast a glance at the most characteristic, however. The most curious, perhaps, is that comprising the fantasies for strings written at the age of twenty-one, which revive the old family habit of playing in consort on a chestful of viols. These works have been regarded as exercises in complex polyphony, and indeed they are miraculous structures of musical fan-tracery and may in a sense be looked upon as a wistful contemplation of the vanished "Gothic" manner on the part of one who could just remember the old St. Paul's Cathedral and was even then watching the progress of Wren's vast new Renaissance structure. Wren, too, by the way, had exercised himself in Gothic out of its time—witness the tower of St. Michael's Church in Cornhill. But both Wren and Purcell were modern artists none the less, and the latter's string fantasies have very much a character of their own. Although on paper they may look deceptively like Byrd or Gibbons, in performance they will strike the listener as much more closely akin to Purcell's own anthems, for instance, than to anything written by an Elizabethan or Jacobean master.

The anthems are very much in the new style, certainly the

verse anthems, which predominate vastly in Purcell's list
of sixty works of the kind. Even some of his full anthems,
which in the main cultivate the Elizabethan manner as a
tradition a great church composer could not altogether ignore,
sometimes contain "verses" for solo voices. The verse
anthems—one of the greatest of which is the coronation
anthem for James II, called more politely than prophetically
"My heart is inditing of a good matter"—have alternating
solos and choruses the latter of which are often dramatic
in their use of pungent harmony and the former invariably
operatic, in the sense that they cultivate a declamatory or
arioso style very much as contemporary stage music did.
(In this respect, though not, of course, in its actual style,
Purcell's church music very much resembles Mozart's.)
The florid vocal decorations of certain outstanding verbal
features of the text, frequently in the dotted rhythm that
was so characteristic a novelty at that time, and the often
extravagant repetitions of single words as much for the
sake of purely musical design as of eloquence, have the
same baroque exuberance as the scrolls of the seventeenth-
century monuments which grace our Norman and Gothic
churches with such charming incongruity.

The art with which these solos are contrived, though
different from the polyphonic ingenuity which still lends
life and variety to the choruses that often move impressively
in solid block harmony, is no less astonishing. The verbal
delivery, sometimes too highly artificial, is after all, like
Lyly's euphuism, a matter of deliberate stylistic intention,
more valuable because Purcell was a greater artist than Lyly
and his followers; and one device that calls for the highest
degree of skill he exploited, sometimes mechanically, it is
true, but surprisingly often with the most telling and beautiful
effect, considering the enormous strain its severe limitations
put upon spontaneous invention. That device is the
"ground," a bass consisting of a definite melodic shape

repeated over and over again through a whole piece with constant changes in the treble melody and the harmony above it, which in Purcell's case are often placed at unexpected angles, with a correspondingly more surprising and varied effect.

Musically akin to the anthems were the odes and songs of welcome, most of them addressed to royalty in excessively fulsome terms allied to contemptibly feeble verse. "The summer's absence unconcerned we bear," wrote one poet, sunning himself in the presence of Charles II on his return from Newmarket, where he had built a palace to attend the races without inconvenience; and "Why, why are all the Muses mute?" asks another, when they ought to congratulate James II on the frustration of Monmouth's rebellion. But these adulatory pieces are interesting for their topical character and as artistic vehicles which Purcell was the first to handle with special distinction. They are the direct forerunners of the secular cantatas Bach wrote for various festivities.

After the accession of William and Mary, Purcell wrote a birthday ode for the queen each year until her death in 1694, on which occasion he composed two elegies and a funeral anthem. Not all the odes were for royal occasions, however. Among the exceptions are one for the centenary of Trinity College, Dublin, the Yorkshire Feast Song, and especially the four Odes for St. Cecilia's Day, a great festival in honour of music which England, that unmusical country, celebrated by performances of specially written cantatas on a lavish scale from Purcell's day onward (his 1683 ode was the first) until well into the eighteenth century. Dryden, Shadwell and Congreve were among the poets who supplied words for these odes and Eccles, Clarke and Blow among the first composers to set them, Handel, Boyce and others following later. Oxford, Winchester, Gloucester, Salisbury, Edinburgh, Dublin and other places took up the lead given by London, where these annual celebrations were held on St.

Cecilia's Day, November 22nd, usually in Wren's exquisite
St. Bride's Church, whose spire Henley called "a madrigal
in stone."

One more group of Purcell's work must be briefly mentioned: the sonatas for two violins and continuo. They
show him as a determined modernist. In his preface to the
twelve "Sonatas of III Parts" of 1683 (the ten "Sonatas of
IV Parts" were published by his widow in 1697) he defiantly
announced that he thought the time had come for English
composers to be serious and to attempt "a just imitation of
the most fam'd Italian Masters" (as for instance Legrenzi,
Bassani and Corelli); and he set out to write for the modern
violin, which he preferred to the treble viol, at any rate for
the purpose of these sonatas, which were actually trios for
two violins and a string bass accompanied by a harpsichord
that filled in the harmony from a figured bass, but may also
be regarded as quartets if the continuo is taken to be an
independent part: hence the confusion between the titles,
"of III Parts" and "of IV Parts," for two sets of works
which are to all intents and purposes alike. The greater
decision of phrasing attained by the new overhand bowing
and the fuller if shriller tone of the violin was better suited
to the new style in Purcell's view, and indeed he also favoured
the violoncello as a bass instrument, though he did not
succeed in driving out the old viola da gamba, which remained pretty generally established in England until the
eighteenth century, except perhaps here and there in string
bands. Needless to say, Purcell was too modest in suggesting
that he was merely following the Italians. He did so, it
is true, in outward matters of style, instrumental treatment
and form, but for technical skill and boldness of individual
enterprise his contribution to the chamber sonata of the late
seventeenth century is unique.

Such music, with string and harpsichord continuo that
made use of the now firmly established figured bass, was

played towards the end of the century, both at the rare
public concerts and in private, much more frequently than
the older consorts for viols, which Purcell too dropped after
his wonderful early essays in that medium. Music-making
by amateurs continued in a new way when the amateur's
much-favoured instrument, the lute, also began to fall into
disuse. Some of the gentlefolk who had patronized Banister's
concerts or that strange music club over the shop of Thomas
Britton, the "musical small-coal man," started in 1678, took
to the cultivation of music in their own homes, either by
playing themselves or by engaging musicians. Men about
town like Pepys had music lessons from acknowledged
masters, and some dabbled in composition. Mrs. Pepys
and her maid Mercer too were taught, and nothing pleased
the diarist himself so much as when his setting of Roxolana's
song, "Beauty retire," from "The Siege of Rhodes" was
"mightily cried up." River parties came into fashion when
Charles II discovered the delights of a new pleasure-boat
in 1661 and had two gondolas presented to him by the Doge
of Venice, and "water music" thus became the rage half a
century before Handel conciliated George I with his famous
set—if the picturesque story is true.

Madrigal singing at home was no more and songs to the
lute were becoming quaintly old-fashioned during the reign
of Charles, almost obsolete during that of James II, and
quite so in that of William and Mary. But singing went on,
of course, both by solo voices, "with a Through Bass to
each Song" harmonically filled in on the harpsichord, and
of canons and catches that had now crystallized themselves
into rigid forms of imitation between the parts from the
freer canzonets and fa-las of the early years of the century.
Gentlemen got together in coffee-houses and taverns to
drink, smoke church-wardens and form catch clubs. Between 1660 and 1700 over a hundred and fifty song-books
of various sorts were published, and their popularity is only

emphasized by the fact that many of them were reprints, often amplified by new additions. The first publication of the kind wholly devoted to songs in 1660 was the "most noted" musician's and veteran's

"Cheerfull Ayres/OR/BALLADS/First composed for one single Voice and/since set for three Voices/BY/JOHN WILSON Dᵣ in MVSICK/Professor of the same in the UNIVERSITY OF OXFORD."

The last, in 1700, was the second volume of Durfey's *Wit and Mirth, or Pills to Purge Melancholy*, a large collection of mostly very ribald verses, seldom showing wit and hardly ever producing mirth, written mostly to folksongs, favourite melodies and well-known tunes by various living composers, though some were newly set—an immensely popular work in spite, if not because, of its flagrant indecency that was to be the principal source for the tunes in "The Beggar's Opera" of 1728.

That polished and poisonous satire was also intended by John Gay to ridicule the conventions of Italian opera and the foibles of its singers; and it was towards Italian opera that England began to verge after Purcell's death. He alone, but for that early death, could have kept its vogue in England within bounds by opposing to it a native opera of at least equal perfection and of so entirely different a nature that the two could have flourished happily side by side, each represented at its finest by a great master born in the same year—Purcell and Scarlatti. The English master's genius could have counteracted even the predominating hold the literary men had over the public through the medium of the stage, for the greatest of these, Dryden himself, after first pinning his faith to the ineffectual Louis Grabu, merely because he was a Frenchman, changed his mind in favour of English music by turning to Purcell for a collaborator, "in whose

Person," he wrote in his preface to "Amphitryon," "we have at length found an *English-man*, equal with the best abroad"—a handsome acknowledgement to be made in 1690, when foreign influence had well begun to get the upper hand. The very next year Dryden, more than satisfied with Purcell's contribution to that comedy of his, expressly wrote an "opera" to be set by the English master, "King Arthur, or The British Worthy," and in 1695 another in collaboration with Howard, "The Indian Queen."

These pieces were operas only as an English poet, whose preoccupation was after all mainly literary, understood the term, though quite as much so as, for instance, Weber's "Oberon" is an opera, or even Mozart's "Magic Flute" was intended by its librettist to be one. There is a great deal of dialogue and, worse, a vast amount of significant dramatic action that makes no provision for music. But although Dryden was the more influential man than Purcell, even he was not the composer's equal as a creative artist, and we may be sure that, had Purcell not died at the age of thirty-six, his genius would have overridden that of any dramatist and shaped a species of fully matured opera from which other native composers could have taken their departure into a future full of promise.

Not that opera matters so very much, for it is plainly ridiculous to speak of England as "the land without music" when it is clear that the author of this absurdity can only have meant "the land without opera"; indeed it matters hardly at all if one compares the rest of England's musical activity with that of countries which are "lands with scarcely anything but opera." But the foreign musical invasion that had begun to penetrate England ever since the Restoration and had become a positive flood by the time of Queen Anne affected not only opera but music as a whole, and once Purcell was dead there was no native composer left strong enough to stem the tide by the assertion of a great creative personality. Child was nearly ninety. Aldrich was much occupied as Dean of Christ Church, Oxford, where, an architect as well as a musician, he had built Peckwater Quadrangle. Akeroyde, Turner and Piggott, men in the vigour of middle age, were secondary figures. Eccles, some ten years younger, only cultivated the theatre as composer of songs in plays and retired at a comparatively early age to devote himself to angling, much as Rossini did later to take to cookery. Daniel Purcell was nothing like his elder brother's equal, and probably prospered largely on the great name he bore. William Croft was still in his teens. Jeremiah Clarke was soon to commit suicide for love of a high-born and unattainable lady. Blow, who most nearly approached greatness, was not without dullness and, having resumed the organist's appointment at Westminster Abbey, which he had resigned in favour of Purcell—voluntarily, it is said—he confined his attention almost wholly to church and organ music. His only work for the stage, the masque of "Venus and Adonis" (1681), really a small opera of the kind of "Dido and Aeneas," approached Purcell but had less vitality.

The earliest foreign musician of whom we hear during the period covered by this chapter was Thomas Baltzar, the great German exponent of that new-fangled instrument, the violin, who astonished John Evelyn and Anthony Wood shortly before the Restoration. Charles II appointed him Master of the "twenty-four violins," doubtless to the disgust of the Englishmen among them, a post that passed to Banister only when Baltzar had incapacitated himself by his addiction to drink, and then only because Banister had been sent to France by the king to acquire a foreign veneer. But he soon found himself displaced by Grabu, whose insolence and aptitude for intrigue equalled his musical incompetence, if the judgment of not unbiased witnesses may be trusted. Charles admired Italian as well as French musicians—the more, perhaps, because he was as indifferent to Catherine's Portuguese musical retinue as he was to herself—so much so that in 1665 he welcomed the arrival (with the plague) of Draghi, a minor composer who was to find much success in London. The same year Blow was provoked to make a setting of Herrick's "Go, perjured man!" in imitation of Carissimi's "Dite, o cieli," to show that an English youth of seventeen could do as well as an Italian master of sixty.

In 1672 a Frenchman of real distinction, Cambert, composer of the first full-fledged French opera ("Pomone"), took refuge in London, Paris having been made impossible for him by the influence and the grasping policy of Lully. The following year Draghi wrote instrumental music for Shadwell's "opera," "Psyche" (operas, significantly enough, were things written by poets rather than things created by composers), but English music saved something for itself by the foreigner's refusal or incapacity to set the songs to music, thanks to the Latin's characteristic way of affecting to despise what he cannot learn to do well in matters of language. Matthew Locke thus had his share in this work. In 1674 Evelyn records his astonishment at another great violinist, this time the Italian Nicola Matteis, and there was an Italian lutenist and singer at Oxford, Pietro Reggio, who in 1677 published "A Treatise to sing well any Song whatsoever."

The year 1679 is sinister. We hear for the first time of an Italian male soprano singer in England, Francesco Giovanni Grossi, surnamed Siface. These highly accomplished eunuch singers, for whose sake even such characters as Julius Caesar or Alexander the Great were made to sing soprano in later operas, came to be so powerful in the early eighteenth century that they could almost dictate their music to any composer less self-willed than Handel, and even Handel wrote parts for them so extravagantly difficult and florid that they have remained to some extent unsingable by normal

voices ever since.   Some time during his residence in London
Siface entered the Chapel Royal, where he certainly was in
James II's reign, welcomed no doubt as a Catholic.   The
indignation of the Gentlemen of the Chapel may be im-
agined, for it is more than probable that he was lavishly paid
while they had to sue humbly for every penny that was due
to them.   However, he cannot have been universally disliked, for when he left in 1688 Purcell wrote a harpsichord
piece entitled "Sefauchi's Farewell."

English musicians were still sent abroad by Charles as
late as 1682, when he paid for the alto singer and lutenist
John Abell's visit to Italy.   But with the accession of James
in 1685 even Charles's dilettantish interest in music ceased
at court, though of course the musical establishment remained
and the Chapel Royal had to continue.   Not that James
was perhaps less fond of music than his brother had been,
but his short and troubled reign gave him other things to
think about—things he held nearer his heart, like his religion
that became more and more of an open secret, and others
he would have liked to keep from his mind, like Monmouth's
insurrection and the Anglican clergy's refusal to read the
Declaration of Indulgence from the pulpit.   Foreign musicians continued, however, to enjoy their success in public.
Grabu had been chosen to write the music for Dryden's
"Albion and Albanius" in 1685, and in 1688 Gottfried
Finger, a Moravian who afterwards anglicized his Christian
name into Godfrey, published a set of sonatas for various
instruments, while Matteis brought out two books of pieces
for the violin.

In the early years of William and Mary's reign a German
musician settled in London, Johann Wolfgang Franck, began
to give concerts in collaboration with Robert King, a
member of the royal band, and Margherita de l'Épine, an
Italian or French singer, made her first appearance in England.
About 1698 Johann Christoph Pepusch arrived from Holland,

a refugee who had witnessed an act of barbarity at the Court of Brandenburg—a modern touch. He later married the singer just mentioned, who meanwhile, in 1704, had been the occasion of one of those Hogarthian scenes that must have made the theatre of the time (it was Queen Anne's time now) a more entertaining place now and again than the public had a right to expect. De l'Épine sang for the first time at Drury Lane that year, and at her second appearance an appalling disturbance broke out in the auditorium which a native singer, Catherine Tofts, was suspected of having caused deliberately. Mrs. Tofts was able to clear herself afterwards, and it is probable that an all too devoted servant of hers had caused the riot without her connivance; but the mere fact that such conduct could be imputed to her shows that by this time English artists were considered to have a grievance where foreign rivals were concerned. In vain did Playford try to uphold native musicians at his concerts, held three times a week at a London coffee-room from 1698 and weekly at Oxford from 1701. More and more foreign artists arrived. In 1702, the year of Anne's accession, Francesco Gasparini, an Italian violinist and opera composer, came to London, and in 1705 the Flemish flute-player and composer Jean Baptiste Lœillet settled there as a teacher and member of the opera orchestra, at the new Queen's Theatre in the Haymarket built by Vanbrugh, where a German, Jakob Greber, produced a pastorel, " The Loves of Ergasto."

If now English composers had been ready with English operas of value, here was a last chance. But it was not to materialize. Mrs. Tofts agitated for Italian opera, in which she was anxious to appear. Durfey wrote a comic opera in 1706, " Wonders in the Sun, or The Kingdom of the Birds," in which the species degenerated into pantomime, and even for that the music was written by Draghi. Saggione, an Italian double-bass player, produced another so-called opera in English, "The Temple of Love."   Nicola Haym, an Italo-German author, cellist and minor composer, adapted a libretto by Owen MacSwiney into an opera made up of adaptations from Bononcini.   Thomas Clayton, a musician in the queen's band, did the same kind of thing with songs and airs he had brought from Italy by fitting them to a piece by Motteux, "Arsinoë, Queen of Cyprus."   This set a new fashion for a sort of patchwork opera, the *pasticcio*, from which the English stage profited only by its later transformation into the ballad opera.

The final blow was dealt to English opera when a libretto written by no less a literary man than Addison, "Rosamond," proved a miserable failure because it had been composed by the incompetent Clayton.   Whereupon Addison himself turned savagely upon opera and opera-singers, English and Italian alike, in *The Spectator*, and completed the former's defeat.   The latter survived because it happened to be represented by stronger composers just then; and one who was a master in it, though not himself an Italian, came to England in 1710 to make the most of it and to sway English musical life in general for half a century and more.

CHAPTER VI

Handel and His Influence (1710–1760)

The German genius who did so much to influence English musical life in the eighteenth century reached London four years before the Hanoverian king, George I. He was even then in George's service at Hanover, but had obtained leave to go abroad for a year. He was graciously received by Queen Anne and must at once have felt, as he had done in Italy before, the freer air an artist could breathe away from a minor court. He was a self-willed, independent young man of twenty-five, more eager to join in the lively musical activities of the town and thus to make himself widely known than to dance attendance on the queen, whose interest in his art was superficial. The opportunities served him well, and the combative air and bickering criticism of the artistic world doubtless stimulated rather than dismayed him. There was an Italian opera at the Queen's Theatre in the Haymarket, frequented by polite society and well provided with good singers and orchestral players. When its manager, Aaron Hill, suggested that he should produce an opera there, he jumped at the chance with such alacrity that he threw the music for it together in a fortnight, mainly from his earlier works. This was "Rinaldo," the libretto of which, hastily sketched by Hill, was no less hurriedly versified by an Italian named Rossi.

With the possible exception of Wagner, Handel is music's greatest opportunist. He had already made much of his chances in Italy, where they were greater than he had found them either at his native Halle or in Hamburg, then the only German home of an opera that used the vernacular and was independent of a princely establishment; and he now made more of the many openings offered by London, which had by this time become cosmopolitan and was to remain so for the rest of the century. Handel was merely the greatest—immeasurably so, it is true—of many foreign musicians who sought their fortunes in Britain, and if he gave much to the country he made his own by naturalization in 1726, it must be remembered that he owed it at least as much. He made an excellent eighteenth-century Londoner, though by language and temperament never much of an Englishman, because he too was a true cosmopolitan, and it is absurd to suggest, as Chrysander and others have done, that he found himself lonely as an honest German amid a foreign quagmire of corruption, for what was corrupt in London much resembled what was so anywhere else in the early eighteenth century, including the German courts; and Handel made many friends in England who were among the noble characters of the age. As an artist he was far less German than he was Italianate and Anglicized. He set almost as few German texts to music as Gluck did later. Ready to absorb any influence that came his way, he wrote endless Italian operas that are indistinguishable in style from the genuine article, if nearly always superior in quality, and many of his melodies (e.g. some of the songs in "Acis and Galatea," several of the "Water Music" pieces, the chorus "Love and Hymen" in "Hercules," the "Hornpipe" in the B flat Concerto grosso, etc., etc.) strike one as having a distinctly English character, though it is easier to feel this than to say how the influence manifests itself technically.

The foreign influence that affected music so strongly after Purcell, who could have counteracted it single-handed, but who died when Handel, like Bach, was only ten years of age, did not come with Handel, nor principally from Germany. It was already there when he arrived and would indeed have swallowed him up too if he had not beaten it at its own games. Foreign musicians swarmed in Britain, as far off as Dublin, where a Hungarian, Cousser, was appointed organist at Christ Church Cathedral in 1710 and given the resounding title of Master of the Musick attending Her Majesty's State in Ireland. In London the Italians were uppermost. Old Draghi died about that time, but many of the operas produced in the Haymarket were by Italian composers who were actually on the spot, either as visitors or as holders of appointments, including the hapless Mancini, whose "L'Idaspe fedele," in which Nicolini appeared in combat with a lion, Addison ridiculed unmercifully. But Addison was prejudiced against opera by the failure of his preposterous "Rosamond" libretto.

Nicolini was the male soprano; Valentini the male alto. The Italian eunuch singers, if as melodious as nightingales, were also as vain as peacocks; but they strutted as successfully as they sang, for all the scorn that was openly poured upon them by satirists of the pen and the brush. (The singer in the fourth picture of Hogarth's "Marriage *à la mode*," which reappears in the levee in the first act of Strauss's "Rose Cavalier," is a caricature of Carestini.) English singers fared no better when some wit thought they had earned his abuse. It was Mrs. Tofts of whom Pope wrote:

"So bright is thy beauty, so charming thy song,
    As had drawn both the beasts and their Orpheus along;
  But such is thy avarice, and such is thy pride,
    That the beasts must have starved, and the poets have died."

Such spiteful treatment, however, was only a reaction, and singers got the worst of it because they had the greatest share of that excessive popularity which intelligence and balanced taste as well as envy are always sure to resent. For the singers were considered, because they arrogantly considered themselves, most important among the musicians of the day, more so than the instrumentalists, who in turn felt that they should have precedence of the composers. Handel was to change all that, but even he could not do so without the drastic expedients of overbearing rudeness and physical threats, nor did he assert the composer's supremacy until he had impressed the English musical world by a whole series of great achievements.

The native composers he found established on his arrival, it is true, made no impressive opposition. Aldrich, the venerable Oxford architect-musician, died that very year. Eccles, though barely fifty, was about to retire to Kingston-on-Thames, to take to fishing and content himself with the setting of annual odes for the queen's birthday and the new year. Daniel Purcell was but a feeble copy of his illustrious brother. William Babell and Henry Carey were only some twenty years of age, and the former was to take as much to harpsichord and violin playing as to composition, the latter to be as much a librettist and minor poet as a creative musician. Maurice Greene, one of Handel's more serious rivals, was still a boy of fifteen. Only Turner and Croft, both doctors of music and both Purcellians, counted for a good deal, and may have influenced Handel to some extent. They kept aloof from Italian opera, to which he devoted himself so largely at first, but their example may have done something to deter him from taking to it exclusively. Where else, indeed, could he have studied the English tradition, which certainly affected even such early works of his as the Chandos anthems (1716–18) and the masque of "Esther" (1729)? Who else could have so fitly shown him the style of Purcell, so little of whose work was published, but whose "Te Deum" and "Jubilate" of 1694 he imitated directly in the two similar works written to celebrate the peace of Utrecht in 1713?

The English Muse was thus not wholly disposed to accept Handel's rich gifts without forcing him to take some of her own, and so make him the richer. She also saw to it that in the very year of his arrival the two composers should be born in London who later on had something to give to English music that was in some ways unlike what he was giving it himself, though neither could escape his over-mastering influence altogether. They were Thomas Augustine Arne and William Boyce, both sons of small, respectable craftsmen, not of professional musicians. Arne's father was an upholsterer and Boyce's a cabinet-maker. A third musician of some distinction, whose exact age is uncertain, Charles Avison, a native of Newcastle-on-Tyne, may also have been born in 1710.

Meanwhile the dearth of home-bred composers of exceptional gifts, combined with the invasion by foreign executants, brought about a predominance of public interest in performance. Performers, native of or settled in the capital, were not slow to take advantage of the taste of the town. Public music-making became more and more frequent. What the nobility and gentry could afford to cultivate in their houses—no longer by their own activity, but by the hire of professionals—the middle classes were enabled to enjoy at such places as Lœillet's house, where weekly concerts for amateurs were held, or the Crown and Anchor tavern in the Strand, where Pepusch conducted the concerts of the Academy of Ancient Music, formed in the year of Handel's visit, during which he himself played the harpsichord at Thomas Britton's ramshackle warehouse in Clerkenwell. For the eccentric charcoal-vendor, who was now about sixty, not only continued his musical meetings, but attracted to them both the best musicians and the best society. In 1713 a dancing-master named Hickford opened a music-room between James Street and Panton Street, off the Haymarket, where the celebrities of the day appeared. Two of the outstanding Italian violinist-composers, Geminiani and Veracini, who both arrived in London in 1714 and the former of whom lived most of his life in England, also gave concerts in public as well as in private.

Handel's "visit" has just been mentioned. His coming to England amounted to no more at first, nor could it ever have done so had he been as docile as other court musicians or more firmly attached to the Elector of Hanover. He returned to his duties in 1711 but, having once tasted London's musical life, left Germany again the following year, with no intention of respecting the conditions of the formal leave that was all he had once more obtained from his patron. Having produced two more operas, "Il pastor fido" and "Teseo," at the Queen's Theatre in 1712 and written a birthday ode for the queen the next year to make the more certain that his music for the Utrecht celebration would be accepted at court from a foreigner, he only once, artistically speaking, looked back to his native country (when he set the Brockes Passion for Hamburg in 1716), though he visited it several times later on. Growing success, a royal annuity of £200 and an invitation from the Earl of Burlington to live at his palatial residence off Piccadilly were among the inducements that decided him to leave the elector in the lurch. Had he known that by 1714 Queen Anne would be dead and George of Hanover become George I of Great Britain, he might have thought twice about so dangerous a dereliction of duty; on the other hand he might not, for he lacked neither courage nor wilfulness. As for George, he was either capable of appreciating character or unable to resist Handel's music, for although he at first held him in disgrace, he forgave him in 1715 (charmed by the "Water Music," if the pretty story is true) and added another £200 a year to the late queen's bounty. Nothing, however, could turn Handel into a regular attendant upon the king. He never held any official post at court. Indeed he never held one anywhere: he was interested in the musical life at large, in which he took part when and where he pleased.

It was an interesting life, and though it was largely maintained by foreigners, there were two branches of musical activity which in the nature of things they could not touch, because the vernacular played an inevitable part in them: Anglican church music and the lighter stage entertainments in which music had some share. Composition for the church had languished since the death of Purcell, which was perhaps the reason why Lord Harley, afterwards Earl of Oxford, requested the Cambridge Professor of Music, Thomas Tudway, to make a great collection of English cathedral music, on which he at once embarked in 1714. Its six volumes began with the great works of the past, but in the end, in spite of the relative scarcity of good modern services and anthems, included a good many by contemporaries, with a liberal sprinkling of Tudway's own.

As for the theatre, it began to react against the vogue of Italian opera. Colley Cibber, writing of the early years of the century in *An Apology for his Life*, said that

"... as musick, by so profuse a dispensation of her beauties, could not always supply our dainty appetites with equal variety, nor for ever please us with the same objects; the opera, after one luxurious season, like the fine wife of a roving husband, began to lose its charms, and every day discovered to our satiety, imperfections which our former fondness had been blind to ..."

Cibber's allusion to "one season" is, of course, only part of his metaphor: it took opera of the Handelian type thirty years at least to fall wholly out of favour—in fact as long as Handel himself chose to produce such operas, which was until 1741, when his last, "Deidamia," appeared. But there had always been people to object to it, and to object more particularly, perhaps, to the dilettantish set that formed its chief patrons. Their strictures, both social and artistic, were quite understandable. The latter, so far as they were directed against the rigid form of the *da capo* aria, for instance, were by no means unjustifiable, for the Italian operas heard in London until the middle of the century were little more than strings of such arias, consisting of two contrasted sections the first of which was repeated after the second.

Now there is no reason to take exception to this musical form as such, any more than to the form of the Petrarchian sonnet, the two parts of which—the octave and the sestet —are at once different from and relevant to each other; and the *da capo* arias of Alessandro Scarlatti, Handel and other great masters give pleasure precisely by the beautiful relevance of their contrasted sections as well as by their symmetrical shapeliness, quite apart from the fact that their interest must often have been enhanced in their time by the new embellishments introduced into the voice-part by the singer at the return of the first section and, one is tempted to say —if one would only feel that the audiences paid attention to this—by the ingenuity of the continuo player at the harpsichord, who, if he was a good musician, doubtless varied his part in the repeat. On the other hand it must be admitted that this form of aria was in all normal circumstances of the stage hopelessly undramatic, unless its use was relieved by that of other musical structures, as it is in Purcell's "Dido," for instance, where the *da capo* device is the exception rather than the rule. Connoisseurs of the most artificially accomplished singing, snobs who liked only what they paid the highest prices for, sung in a language they did not understand, and some few cultivated persons who understood everything and had to make a point of being seen at the Opera continued for some decades to patronize Handel and the Italians more or less fitfully in the theatre; but there was a larger public of ordinary people who demanded something simpler, more natural, more alive and amusing, or if they did not actually demand it, gladly responded to it when it was offered to them in their own language. The opera snobs, it should be added, were just the same at the German and other continental courts, where Italian alone was sung.

It was John Rich, an enterprising man of the theatre, who in 1715 presented a new kind of light stage entertainment shrewdly devised to compete with outlandish opera that never deigned to stoop below the treatment of severely classical, legendary or historical subjects. He had opened a theatre in Lincoln's Inn Fields the previous year, with Pepusch as musical director, and was now ready to produce the masque of "Venus and Adonis" composed by that musician, who also wrote incidental music for various plays. Turner, who was quite old enough to remember the masques of Locke and Blow—we have seen that he was in the Chapel Royal with the latter as a child—helped with the revival of that typically seventeenth-century spectacle by supplying Rich with a specimen called "Presumptuous Love" in 1716, and another relic of Purcell's days, the bass singer Richard Leveridge, furnished him with the comic masque "Pyramus and Thisbe," based on the clowns' interlude in "A Midsummer Night's Dream." The fact that Handel, just then living at Canons near Edgware as composer and organist to the Duke of Chandos, had been temporarily drawn away from operatic composition happened to help Rich considerably. He was gradually securing for himself a following that was soon to enable him to deal Italian opera a stunning blow.

The foreign opposition, however, at first showed signs of growing more formidable than ever. The Opera in the Haymarket was formed, on the Parisian model, into a Royal Academy of Music, and Handel, entrusted with its direction, went abroad in 1719 in search of the best Italian singers, whom he sought, oddly enough, not in Italy, but in Germany, where they were attached to various courts. In 1720 Ariosti and Bononcini were engaged as composers in addition to himself, and there is a tradition that an opera,

"Muzio Scevola," produced in 1721, was the joint work of those three then friendly rivals, though it is possible that the act attributed to Ariosti was by the principal cellist in the orchestra, Filippo Mattei. However that may be, Handel and Bononcini were not allowed to remain on amicable terms for long. As in the case of Gluck and Piccinni or of Wagner and Brahms later on, critics and public, by disagreeing among themselves, saw to it that the two should be opposed to each other as deadly enemies, whether they agreed to such an attitude or not. Bononcini's "Cantate e duetti" were at once subscribed for by the Rutland, Queensberry, Sunderland and Marlborough families merely because they were hostile to George I and had to have a favourite composer to play off against Handel, who was patronized by the king. It was an artificially fomented squabble, and the two unwilling adversaries were sufficiently alike as composers for a satirist (John Byrom, not Pope) to express his astonishment that so much difference should be found between Tweedle-dum and Tweedle-dee.

Worse disruptions were to come. We have as yet reckoned without the singers. Several of great reputation now arrived in London and, true to their kind, they were not the people to suffer each other gladly. In 1720 came a famous male and a famous female soprano: Francesco Bernardi, surnamed Senesino, and Margherita Durastanti; in 1721 the tenor Benedetto Bernardi; in 1722 Francesca Cuzzoni, whom Handel is said to have held out of a window until she promised to withdraw her refusal to sing an aria, "Falsa immagine" in "Ottone," exactly as he had written it. (He was a strong enough man to justify such a story, and it may even be true.) Here was matter enough for trouble, for these artists, whose immense technical accomplishment was equalled only by their stupidity and bad manners, were unbelievably vain and jealous, and their own esteem of their profession cannot have been diminished when they found that an English colleague of theirs, Anastasia Robinson, married the Earl of Peterborough and Monmouth.

All sorts of dissensions must have been simmering, and occasionally boiling over, during these first years of the Royal Academy, which the patrons voted very successful. But a rare kettle of fish was put on the fire in 1726, when Faustina Bordoni arrived from Vienna to join the company, and it was Handel who stirred it. Thinking only of his opportunity in having two prima donnas at his disposal, he injudiciously or over-boldly decided to let them appear together in his very next opera, "Alessandro." They at once became implacable enemies. The fact that there was nothing to choose in difficulty or effectiveness between the two parts only made the situation worse, and unfortunately the two "first women" were not "ladies." The following year, at a performance of Bononcini's "Astyanax," they treated each other to a bout of fisticuffs on the open stage, unrestrained by the presence of the Princess of Wales. The season ended abruptly and the next opened with an insufficient list of subscribers. The Royal Academy, already weakened by the dismissal of Bononcini in 1724 and the departure of Ariosti the next year, began to totter.

Then, on January 29th 1728, came Rich's shrewd thrust. "The Beggar's Opera" harmed Italian opera not only because it made cruel fun of its conventions and aped the Cuzzoni-Bordoni quarrel in the brawls of Polly and Lucy, but also because John Gay's libretto was wittily satirical and the music to which his neatly polished verses were fitted had been cleverly chosen by him from the favourite airs of the day and of yesterday, with the aid of Pepusch, who arranged them with an accompaniment for a small orchestra including the inevitable harpsichord continuo. The piece not only had an immense success there and then: it began a fleeting vogue for a new kind of musical entertainment—the ballad-opera. If Gay had been assisted by a native musician he might have been more enterprising in his choice of tunes, though the study of folksong was not then an antiquarian pursuit. As it was, he took nearly all the airs from Durfey's "Wit and Mirth," as is proved by his naming them almost invariably according to the new words fitted to them by Durfey, not by those originally attached to the tunes, which were in most cases not particularly old. Some are theatre songs by Eccles, Barrett, Ramondon and others, some are known to be by such composers as Purcell, Leveridge, Jeremiah Clarke and —oh, irony!—Handel himself.

But great as its victory over Italian opera was for a season or two, it cost ballad-opera dear. The weapon that dealt the wound expended too much powder and shot all at once not to impoverish itself. "The Beggar's Opera" was not only the first ballad-opera, it was also much the best. Like Wagner's music-drama, it sowed the seeds of destruction in what it originated by immediately exhausting all its best possibilities. Gay's sequel, "Polly," might have succeeded in 1729 if the Lord Chamberlain had not interdicted its performance at the instigation of Walpole, who considered that he had been satirized in the part of Captain Macheath; but it was a much feebler production, marred by poisonous invective worthy of Swift and a plot that outdid Aphra Behn's "Oroonoko" in its extravagant exaltation of the "noble savage." Many ballad-operas poured forth, but few held the stage for more than a few performances. Their success did not depend on the tunes, which were all much the same in quality, but on the libretti, most of which were trash, and on the attraction of individual singers. In the very year "Polly" was suppressed appeared "Love in a Riddle" by Colley Cibber, "The Beggar's Wedding" by Charles Coffey and "Hurlothrumbo, or The Supernatural" by one Samuel Johnson, formerly a dancing-master. These names are, of course, those of the librettists, for the music of ballad-operas was never composed—it was collected and arranged.

Coffey was singularly successful, for his "The Devil to pay" (1731) and its sequel, "The Merry Cobbler" (1735), took on in Germany as a fascinating outlandish entertainment, much as the more sensational of the plays by the Elizabethan dramatists had once done, and they exercised a great influence on the earliest form of German comic opera, the *Singspiel*. "Hurlothrumbo" was an extravaganza that made sport of serious opera much as Fielding's "Tom Thumb" burlesqued bombastic drama. Fielding, by the way, himself wrote ballad-operas: "The Lottery" and "The Welsh Opera" were produced in 1731.

It has been said that the ballad-opera is in the first place a Scottish, not an English contribution to musical history, though nobody would attempt to deny (except possibly the Scotsman who said that his country would be larger than England if its mountains were flattened out) that its effect on that history dates from "The Beggar's Opera." It is quite true that something like it appeared early in Scotland: a pastoral play by Allan Ramsay, "The Gentle Shepherd"; but the whole truth is that in 1725 this came out as a spoken play and that not until after an Edinburgh production of Gay's piece in 1729 was a new version of Ramsay's given there with songs the tunes for which had been chosen from Scottish folksongs. This version was given in London, adapted by Theophilus Cibber as "Patie and Peggy," in 1730.

Scotland had by this time begun to show a keen interest in its native songs, more so than England, if we may judge by the fact that the songs in "The Beggar's Opera" were for the most part not folksongs, as we understand the term to-day. Ramsay, anticipating Burns and Moore in this kind of poetry of accommodation, had written words for tunes collected by the singer and teacher William Thomson under the title of "Orpheus Caledonius," which appeared in the same year as "The Gentle Shepherd." Other musical interests, too, showed themselves north of the Tweed. A New Royal Academy of Music was formed at Edinburgh in the autumn of 1728, with a mainly aristocratic membership.

Meanwhile a movement from which an ecclesiastical charity as well as music has profited to the present day was started in the English provinces in 1724. The Three Choirs Festival was inaugurated at Gloucester at the suggestion of Dr. Thomas Bisse, chancellor of Hereford. The cathedral choirs of Gloucester, Worcester and Hereford were united for the purpose of giving combined performances annually in aid of the orphans of the poorer clergy in the three dioceses, each town being the festival centre by turns. The model was the yearly festival held in London with a similar object by the Corporation of the Sons of the Clergy founded in 1655, which ever since that time has taken the form of a choral service accompanied by an appropriate sermon. The appointed place was St. Paul's Cathedral, but after the fire of London in 1666 these celebrations took place in other London churches until Wren's new building was ready in the reign of Queen Anne. The service and sermon remain a feature of the Three Choirs Festival, but are now held on the Sunday preceding the four days' music-making, which includes performances of standard oratorios and of new works specially commissioned from British composers who have won general recognition or aroused some form of local interest.

The operatic rivalries of the 1720's did not wholly absorb London's music-making: indeed the chaos they produced gave new chances to musicians whose main sphere was not the stage. Another convivial club was formed in 1726 by Greene, now organist at St. Paul's, Pepusch, Bernard Gates of the Chapel Royal and the organist Charles King, and began to hold its meetings at the Crown tavern in the Strand. Greene, though only just over thirty, was now one of the musical influences. His playing at St. Paul's attracted attention, as did that of Thomas Roseingrave at St. George's, Hanover Square, at whose examination he had been one of the judges, and it was he who was instrumental in obtaining the appointment as oboist at the Opera for Giuseppe Sammartini when he arrived in 1727; nor could Sammartini have published a dozen oboe sonatas so soon without having thus made himself known. In 1730 Greene became Professor of Music at Cambridge in succession to Tudway and he took the doctor's degree, his exercise being a setting of Pope's "Ode for St. Cecilia's Day." Handel too was busy outside the opera-house, especially in 1727, when he produced four anthems for the coronation of George II and turned out some minuets for a court ball held on the new king's birthday. He was granted another annuity of £200 that year as music-master to the princesses.

By 1732 Arne, aged twenty-two, was ready to meet the public. He had been giving singing-lessons to his young sister, Susanna Maria, with such success that at the age of eighteen she was able to appear in Carey's "Amelia," set to music by the German bassoon-player Lampe. In the hope of repaying her brother she suggested that he should make a new setting of Addison's opera, "Rosamond," which had failed so disastrously with Clayton's music. This was produced the next year and proved a more ambitious effort than any ballad-opera, a species with which Arne, even then quite capable of originating striking music and tunes as singable as any popular ditty of the day, desired to have nothing to do. "Rosamond" was a compromise between the easy manner of the English stage-pieces sponsored by Rich and the serious Italian style, and it is significant of the rapid decline of ballad-opera that other composers too endeavoured to approach the latter. Lampe in "Amelia" and John Christopher Smith, who was later to become Handel's amanuensis, did likewise, the latter in his setting of Carey's

"Teraminta." Only a few successful ballad-operas appeared, including Carey's "Betty, or The Country Bumpkin" and Fielding's "The Mock Doctor" (an adaptation of Molière's "Médecin malgré lui"), until in 1737 Carey and Lampe's "The Dragon of Wantley" had an enormous success almost rivalling that of "The Beggar's Opera," perhaps because of its almost impudently close imitation of Gay's manner rather than because it pointedly ridiculed Handel's latest stage work, "Giustino." It ran for sixty-seven nights and even then was taken off only because of Queen Caroline's death.

Handel went obstinately on producing opera after opera, undeterred by rival attractions, equally unwilling to follow new fashions and to consider reforms of stereotyped musico-dramatic procedures, and, if discouraged by adversities and disloyalties, doggedly determined not to admit defeat. Having rashly dismissed Senesino in 1733, he not only found the famous soprano contriving to raise subscriptions for the opening of a rival opera, but both Cuzzoni and the bass Montagnana following their colleague. Frederick, the young Prince of Wales, who was on the worst possible terms with his family, took the opportunity of supporting the truant artists for the sheer pleasure of helping to ruin his royal parents' favourite musician. Porpora, who was engaged as composer by the opposition, was not Handel's equal, but he was a sufficiently distinguished master to make a counter-attraction, at any rate so long as he was a newcomer fit to feed the curiosity of the town. Even the momentary sensation Handel was able to create by the appearance of a new leading man, Carestini, in 1734, was immediately counteracted by the arrival of the greatest of all male sopranos, Farinelli, at the rival house. Carestini left the following year, and Handel, broken in health, if not in spirit, had to go to Tunbridge Wells for a cure.

If in operatic composition he clung tenaciously to a tradition that had always served him well, he tried desperately

E

to offer the public some novelty of another sort in the theatre.
It was in 1732 that he made his first attempt with a choral
work on the stage, not an oratorio in this case, but a *serenata* or
pastoral cantata. It was the setting of Gay's charming "Acis
and Galatea," which was sung on the stage of the Haymarket theatre with Arne as conductor, his sister as Galatea
and Gustavus Waltz, a good bass who is said, on uncertain
evidence, to have been Handel's cook for a time, as Poly-
pheme. Part of an earlier Italian work on the same subject,
"Aci, Galatea e Polifemo," which Handel had written at
Naples in 1708, was also used, probably because some
Italian singers took part in the performance.

Choral works, commonly but loosely described as "oratorios," now became a regular feature at the Opera under
Handel's management, not only because he found that they
attracted the public—though "Deborah" failed in 1733
because of the high prices of admission, which gave the
impression of having been stimulated by Walpole's unpopular
new excise scheme—but also because they were the only
form of entertainment allowed there during Lent. He also
began to write organ concertos, which he himself played
between the parts—or acts, as they were called. This is
merely an outward indication of the fact that Handelian
oratorios or similar works hardly differed at all from Handelian
opera, except for the important share assigned to the chorus
in the former, which oddly enough made it the more
dramatic form of the two. Successions of arias connected
by recitative were characteristic of both. It is a critical
commonplace to call an early eighteenth-century opera "a
concert in costume"; one might just as reasonably say that
English oratorios as cultivated by Handel were operas
without action—and indeed they were not always given
without scenery and costumes. The "Acis" of 1732 indulged
in both.

Handel was not alone in producing oratorios. Young

William Boyce followed him in 1736 with "David's Lamentation over Saul and Jonathan," produced by the Apollo Society, another of those musical associations that flourished so well in an age which made even the coffee-house and the tavern homes of civilization away from home. Boyce was then but twenty-six, but he showed such great promise that he was appointed organist at St. Michael's Church in Cornhill and sworn a Gentleman of the Chapel Royal that year. Handel's choral concert-work just then was his setting of Dryden's "Alexander's Feast," which so impressed Pope, who doubtless considered himself the equal of Dryden, that he desired Handel to set a poem of his own. It is unfortunate that Handel refused the suggested subject of Orpheus and Eurydice: he was not so happy in his choice of poets, though their clerical qualifications may have seemed to fit them for the handling of biblical subjects, that he could afford to refuse the collaboration of Pope, who would have done better than the Rev. Thomas Morell, or whoever it was who perpetrated the following in "Solomon":

> "Can I see my infant gor'd
> With the fierce relentless sword?
>
> .   .   .   .
>
> And behold the purple tides
> Gushing down his tender sides?

Or than the Rev. James Miller, from whose "Joseph" a passage appropriate to this book must be quoted:

> "Ah jealousy, thou Pelican,
> That prey'st upon thy parent's bleeding heart!
> Though born of Love's greatest bane,
> Still cruel wounding her with her own dart."

However, one must remember that those words were especially designed for singing and also that many of them have changed their use and associations, so that now they sound ridiculous where formerly they may have been impressive.

Opera was going from bad to worse, although Montagnana returned to Handel in 1738 and two new singers arrested attention for a while: the male soprano Gaetano Majorano, known as Caffarelli, and Elisabeth Duparc, a Frenchwoman nicknamed La Francesina. Even the oratorios did not always do well. "Saul," one of the works that appealed to the Jewish section of society on account of their Old Testament subjects, was successful enough, but "Israel in Egypt" pleased nobody because it did not contain enough songs. The singers objected because there was no chance to display what Mozart used to call their "agile gullets"; the listeners because it was runs and trills and elaborate cadenzas for (and by) the soloists they were looking for; the publisher Walsh because he could not extract popular numbers from it for sale—for the fashion was not to publish whole vocal scores of operas and oratorios, but only the "favourite airs," arranged for voice and harpsichord, and sometimes for a violin or German flute.

Walsh, however, published the first set of the organ concertos in 1738, and although Handel was on the verge of bankruptcy and suffered from the after-effects of a paralytic stroke, he could not complain of any lack of popularity, however fickle he may have found the patrons of his theatre to be. So great, indeed, was his fame that a statue was made of him by Roubiliac that year, when he was fifty-three, and erected in Vauxhall Gardens—an honour that comes to very few artists in their lifetime.

Vauxhall was just about then coming into fashion, though it had been open as a pleasure-garden since the seventeenth century. In 1732 a *ridotto al fresco*—a kind of open-air carnival—was started and in 1737 an organ was installed on which the great musicians of the day were invited to play.

Famous singers appeared frequently, and bands of all kinds played for the delight of those who may in the first place have come to eat and drink, to converse or to flirt. Marylebone Gardens too had an orchestra, established for daily performances by their owner, Daniel Gough, and in 1742 Ranelagh Gardens were opened on the bank of the Thames at Chelsea. John Beard, the greatest English tenor of the day, sang at the ceremony. Breakfasts, suppers, balls and masquerades as well as music could be enjoyed at these most pleasant of London's places of entertainment, the like of which the modern metropolis has never known. The great exhibitions of the nineteenth and twentieth centuries may have taken their place in some ways, but it would be fantastic to pretend that they were ever intended for the cultivation of music.

There was plenty for musicians to do; yet the age did not differ from any other in that there was never quite enough for all of them. Some inevitably suffered neglect and want. Greene, with the violinist Michael Festing and the flautist Wiedemann, realizing this only too well, therefore decided in 1738 to form a Society of Musicians, to the first meeting of which they invited such distinguished people as Arne, Boyce, Carey, Handel and Pepusch, and a fund "for the support of decayed musicians and their families" was started which has done admirable work ever since. A charter granted by George III in 1789 turned the organization into the Royal Society of Musicians that still exists to-day. Another charity, the Foundling Hospital established by Captain Coram in 1739, interests us because Handel, like Hogarth, at once took a benevolent interest in it. He presented it with an organ later and gave annual performances of his "Messiah" there with the children forming part of the chorus.

We have seen that Handel went back to Dryden for a text worthy of his genius. In 1740 he went beyond Dryden to Milton, whose "L'Allegro" and "Il Penseroso" he set oratorio-fashion, unfortunately invalidating this evidence of good literary taste by adding to it a third part by Charles Jennens, a piece of work that bore a title beautifully indicative of its mediocrity—"Il Moderato." Arne too went to a dead author, as well as to a now almost obsolete form, when he set Congreve's masque "The Judgment of Paris." He had already made a setting of Milton's "Comus" in a remodelled version, doubtless considering Henry Lawes's score antiquated, and in 1740 he went to work on what is his best piece of the kind, for all that the words were by two less glorious if not mute Miltons: the Scot James Thomson, author of "The Seasons," and David Mallet, who was in the service of the Prince of Wales. It was at Frederick's residence at Cliveden in Buckinghamshire—above the Thames between Maidenhead and Cookham—that "Alfred" was produced. Its interest to-day lies in the one survival from its score, which is nothing less than the most familiar of all patriotic songs next to "God save the King," now always called by the opening words of its refrain: "Rule, Britannia." It may be a stilted piece and all too much starched by the mannerisms of its time, but it is unquestionably grand and stirring, not merely because of associations no English hearer can forget—for even if he is determined not to betray any patriotism they will haunt him as memories of childhood—but because the song shows an originating power and a strength of character worthy of Purcell, at any rate Purcell in his birthday-ode and welcome-song mood.

The masque, of course, could only be a sort of temporary resuscitation. It could not take the place of Italian opera any more than the ballad-opera had done, and there was little else that showed any new vigour. Music all round was going to seed in England towards the middle of the eighteenth century. The oratorio was only a kind of Lenten feast— and perhaps a penance to some people. Church music was flat and superficial compared with that of the seventeenth century, not to mention the wonders of the sixteenth. Handel himself, discouraged and financially ruined, decided to retire from opera after the "Deidamia" of 1741, which had added nothing to his glory.

His idea of retirement was to set to work immediately on the selection from the Bible which constitutes the book of "Messiah," made by Jennens (unless he took the credit for what was done by his secretary). Handel not only worked, he performed a miracle. The oratorio, begun on August 22nd 1741, was finished on September 12th—exactly three weeks later. True, the score was very sketchy, showing sometimes nothing more than the voice, first violin and bass parts, which had to be amplified in performance by continuo players at the harpsichord and the organ, according to the rules of thorough-bass which obtained roughly from 1600 to 1750 and consisted in playing more or less elaborate accompaniments according to the performer's skill—not from notes, but from figures which gave only an indication of the harmony required by the composer, but none of textures or chordal inversions.

The first performance of "Messiah" took place at the New Music Hall, Fishamble Street, Dublin, on April 13th 1742, for the benefit of several charitable objects including—how Handel must have sympathized!—the release of prisoners for debt. Tickets were sold in such numbers that the ladies were requested to leave their hoops at home in order to take up as little room as possible, and the sum of £400 was realized by a single performance—a fortune in those days.

There is no need to expatiate on the great qualities of "Messiah," which has always been favoured among Handel's works to an extent that is less than fair to its companions. But it must be pointed out that there are reasons for this preference beyond the obvious ones that the work deals with the greatest subject imaginable and uses the sublime language of the English Bible instead of the inanities of some reverend poetaster, chief among them being that "Messiah" is more dramatic than any other Handelian oratorio—or opera, for that matter—on account of the extraordinary new freedom and variety of its musical forms. The *da capo* aria, which never succeeded in becoming naturally absorbed into England's music, has almost wholly disappeared from "Messiah."

Arne's sister, now Mrs. Cibber, sang the contralto part in the new work. Handel had learnt to respect English singers, indeed to prefer them for his oratorios, the English words of which he did not always set with a native's feeling for prosody, but liked to hear intelligibly and idiomatically sung. There were by this time some excellent vocalists in London who bore homely names. Arne's wife, Cecilia Young, as well as his sister, won distinction, and Kitty Clive, though as much an actress as a singer, was a favourite in the lighter parts, as Lavinia Fenton, Gay's first Polly, had also been. Of the tenors John Beard and Thomas Lowe, and the bass Bernard Gates, two have already been mentioned.

Italian opera was all but dead. Even Galuppi (Browning's "brave Galuppi"), when he came to London in 1741 and produced his "Penelope," could hardly stir the flagging interest, and his "Sirbace" of 1744 aroused little more enthusiasm than two works by Veracini produced that year or two by Lampugnani, who replaced Galuppi later in the season. Gluck himself, who arrived in 1745, made little impression. It must be remembered, however, that he was then still a composer of ordinary fashionable operas cut to the conventional Italian pattern and that as a musical craftsman pure and simple he was considerably less gifted than the best of his Italian contemporaries. It is true that Handel's withering comment that Gluck knew no more of counterpoint than his cook loses its sting when we remember that the cook may have been Waltz, a good singer and presumably a very fair musician; but there is no denying that it contained a good deal of truth. Still, Gluck might have been more successful if his opera for London, "La caduta de' giganti," had not been a pasticcio perfunctorily thrown together from earlier works of his, with a few numbers hastily added for the occasion. Not that he alone indulged in concocting such pieces: the pasticcio was one of the artistic subterfuges of the day, of which most composers, Handel not excepted, were found guilty some time or other. Nobody, of course, regarded it as a crime. The proof of the opera was in the hearing, and if it sounded pleasing no awkward questions were asked about dramatic fitness, much less about the ethics of the matter. It was little worse for a composer to steal from others than from himself, and we know that Handel did both without compunction and without laying himself open to the charge of plagiarism.

Of the 1750's there is little to tell. Handel underwent an operation on his eyes in 1752. It was performed by one Taylor, often described as a famous surgeon, but apparently a charlatan who had exploited one foreign country after another until his successes were reversed by the discovery of his incompetence. He had already operated disastrously on Bach shortly before that master's death in 1750, and now he ruined Handel's sight, which perhaps nobody could have saved, however. Handel's tragedy was the greater, for he was blind for the last seven years of his life, whereas Bach had been sightless for hardly as many months. With the aid of the faithful Smith he nevertheless continued to compose, and he often appeared at the oratorios, playing the organ and enjoying the warm affection of his audience, which burst into tears with one accord when in the master's "Samson" the hero lamented his lost sight.

Handel died on April 14th 1759, but his influence persisted to the end of the century and beyond, even when the only other two foreign masters whose hold over English composers has remotely approached his own had begun to exercise theirs: Mendelssohn towards the middle of the nineteenth

century and Brahms at its end. All the same, there were
independent elements even in his lifetime. There was no
Handelian feeling and almost no Handelian manner, even,
in the songs in Shakespeare's plays set by Arne at various
times, with those in "The Tempest" coming as the crowning
achievement in 1746. They have a certain charmingly
simpering artificiality, like actresses masquerading prettily
as milkmaids dabbling in the dew. Other composers were
to follow Arne, and to improve on him in naturalness, by
producing songs destined to enrich the national treasury of
healthy, memorable and inimitable tunes. The best of them,
Charles Dibdin, was not born until 1745, but meanwhile
Boyce let in some fresh air upon instrumental music. He
also did a great service to the Anglican church by completing
a collection of "Cathedral Music" ranging from Henry
VIII (as a composer) to Clarke and Croft. This had been
begun in 1750 by Greene, who had inherited some money
which he devoted to this purpose; but Greene died in 1755,
entrusting his material to Boyce, who diligently added to it
until he was ready to publish the first of his three volumes in
1760. This, the year of George II's death, brings us to the
end of a period dominated by a great foreign musician,
whose greatness, however, might not have been what it
is had it not been stimulated both by the opportunities and
the adversities of musical life in his adopted country.

CHAPTER VII

The Later Eighteenth Century
(1760–1800)

Although Handel had died in 1759, the so-called foreign domination of musical England continued. Its characteristic manifestation, however, was not abject submission to the dictates of continental composers and executants: it was rather a high-handed annexation of many of them and an opportunist exploitation of the best they had to contribute to music. The capital and the sub-capitals of the British Isles, London, Edinburgh and Dublin, had many temptations to hold out which musicians from abroad willingly allowed to allure them, and even some of the provincial towns were not altogether without attractions. Bath, of course, was almost a little capital of its own—the capital of fashion. Thomas Linley taught and gave concerts there, and reared a musical family not unlike that of the Bachs and the Mozarts abroad. In the last quarter of the century Venanzio Rauzzini, one of the last male sopranos, lived there, retired from the stage but thriving as the most sought-after teacher of singing in the country.

In the earlier years covered by this chapter Mozart came to England as a child, to astonish everybody by his almost freakish accomplishments; during the last decade the aged Haydn came twice, to arouse wonder by the enduring vigour of his genius. London and other cities were visited by innumerable singers, fiddlers, keyboard players, composers and teachers, from Italy, from France, from Germany, from Bohemia. These had much to give, and English musicians, never inclined to entrench themselves behind their own traditions, profited where they could. But it is a superficial view, too often repeated and suggested only by the eighteenth-century decline in English composition, as distinct from English musical life as a whole, which holds that the profit was all on the English side. The foreigners benefited by no means only materially in a country musicians have always fantastically regarded as a gold-mine. Some of them learnt as much here as they imparted; a few—Clementi, for instance, as we shall see—owed so much to their adopted country that they can only be regarded, at any rate musically speaking, as Britishers. Even to Handel one refrains from assigning that status by only the smallest hesitation, by a scruple French people never feel in the very similar case of the Italian-born Lully. Elizabeth Weichsel, the daughter of a German oboist settled in London, and Maria Teresa Romanzini, an Italian Jewess, won fame as Mrs. Billington and Mrs. Bland, two thoroughly English singers, born and trained in London. The former's reputation was international.

The year 1760 was not uneventful for the resident musicians. Arne and Boyce, the two most distinguished composers now on the scene, both aged fifty, came forward with characteristic productions. Arne brought out his little opera, "Thomas and Sally," at Covent Garden, the one among his many stage pieces that has kept some hold on the public, though its ingenuously appealing plot may not be the best and its shapely and memorable tunes, all different in rhythm and melody, yet all beautifully matched in style, have their equals in many another work of his. Boyce published the first volume of his "Cathedral Music, being a Collection in Score of the Most Valuable and Useful Compositions for that Service by the several English Masters of the last Two Hundred Years." It contained the materials collected by Greene and left by him to Boyce, who however intended to continue the task, and did. And most valuable and useful his work has remained, for all that his editing needs the attention of later scholars, who have learnt more than he ever knew about the proper way of dealing with old music.

Musicology, too, received its due. Charles Burney and John Hawkins were working at their musical histories, both ready for publication in 1776 (Burney's first volume only: his work was completed in 1789), and both serviceable to this day, in spite of inaccuracies and prejudices (on the readers' as well as the authors' part). Hawkins, less reliable technically, took the more detached view of the true historian who endeavours to see things in the light of his own times; Burney, more readable, was interested—and is still interesting —only as a judge of all music preceding that of his own age as though it had been superseded by modern excellence and elegance. He is tolerant enough towards earlier schools, but no more. His contemporaries, however, he studied with a care and sympathy not understood by Hawkins in his professional detachment. Having begun his work in 1759, he found that he could not complete it without making two journeys, in 1770 and 1772, to France, Italy, Germany and the Netherlands in order to study musical conditions there and make the acquaintance of as many famous musicians as he was able to meet. His journals of these two tours are still entertaining and instructive to read: they present as virtues what the History shows as a glaring defect.

Burney's modern and international outlook was, of course, only that of his contemporaries in general. It would be absurd to suppose that eighteenth-century English musical life was a sort of stronghold too weakly defended by its garrison not to be taken by storm by foreign invaders. There was simply no question of any such national defence, in England or anywhere else. Paris was swarming at that time with successful German musicians; Italians held the best musical posts at the German secular courts; the ecclesiastical one at the Austrian Salzburg was thoroughly Italianized, as the Mozarts knew only too well; the early school of symphonists whose activities were fostered by the excellent orchestral conditions at Mannheim consisted of several Bohemians and at least one Italian. The state of musical affairs in London and elsewhere in Britain was thus nothing for English musicians to take exception to, as indeed they never thought of doing. It is nothing for historians to grow indignant about, as they have foolishly done for the last eighty years or so.

To the early development of the symphony as a form English composers did not feel called upon to add anything. They were quite content to leave this to foreigners, though Arne and Boyce made their contributions. This may be wounding to our pride, but it has at least saved us from joining in the futile squabbles of stalwart German critics anxious to prove that the Mannheimers were Sudeten-Germans, or that they were anticipated by C. P. E. Bach, and of touchy Italians who maintain hotly that the first symphonies came from G. B. Sammartini. Amusingly enough the species reached England through the great Bach's youngest son, Johann Christian, who had once been a pupil of his brother Carl Philipp Emanuel and came from Milan, where he must have been in touch with, if not actually influenced by, Sammartini. He came to London in 1762, went to live with his compatriot Carl Friedrich Abel, whom he had known at Leipzig, became music master to Queen Charlotte in 1764 and the next year began to give concerts with Abel at Carlisle House in Soho Square. This was a fashionable musical centre run by Teresa Cornelys, an Italian singer who had married a Dutchman. She induced the best musicians to perform there and the best society to listen to them. Unfortunately she took insufficient care to keep out less desirable attractions and less high-minded patrons, so that later she came into conflict with the law for keeping "nothing better than a common disorderly house." But Mrs. Cornelys at first deserved well of serious musical performers and composers for letting her assembly-rooms be used for good concerts, until their popularity was out-rivalled by that of the Pantheon in Oxford Street, a fine building in the classical style by James Wyatt, opened in 1772 as a sort of winter-garden Vauxhall for music, balls and masquerades, and by the opening of the Hanover Square Rooms in 1775 with one of the concerts given by Bach and Abel, who perhaps moved there from Soho Square because they were afraid of scandal.

If nothing, not even its early appearances in England, can give colour to a pretence that the symphony is anything but a purely continental growth, there is one musical species—a very much smaller and less important one—which became a wholly English musical phenomenon by its home cultivation during the latter half of the eighteenth century. The beginning of that cultivation is marked by the estab-lishment of the Noblemen's and Gentlemen's Catch Club in 1761. Catches, canons and rounds, of course, had become popular during the preceding century, where we find them as a sort of stunted (as to music) and debased (as to words) descendant of the madrigal. In fact such tavern songs appeared in Ravenscroft's "Pammelia," "Deuteromelia" and "Melismata" (1609–11) before the madrigal proper was extinct as a regular composers' practice. The most familiar of all songs in canon, "Three Blind Mice," comes from Ravenscroft.

In 1763, when Thomas Warren, the Catch Club's secretary, published a collection of such things, we find a new species added to them, for Warren's volume was entitled "Catches, Canons and Glees." It was the glee, which was not strictly in canon form, though it might contain canonic entries, that became the most characteristic eighteenth-century repre-sentative of this convivial kind of song. It was undoubtedly an offspring of the canzonets and balletts, the lightest pieces for combined voices written by the Elizabethan and Jacobean masters, and it even adopted their ringing, swinging "Fa-la" refrains. The glee continued to be cultivated all down the nineteenth century. The "merry madrigal" in "The Mikado" is not a madrigal at all, except by remote descent : it is a perfect glee, and so are other specimens in Sullivan's operettas, such as "Strange Adventure" in "The Yeomen of the Guard" and, most charming of all, "Where the buds are blossoming" in "Ruddigore." Among the first to come forward as glee composers was Samuel Webbe the elder.

More conspicuous, if less unique, were the English pieces for the stage in the latter half of the century. Although no longer ballad-operas, they were not always the work of one composer, for the pasticcio habit had by this time become a kind of amiable vice with theatre musicians. Arne's "Love in a Village" (1763), which has a libretto of some character by Isaac Bickerstaffe and finds its tunes wherever it can, is a good example of how well this sort of adaptation could be made by a musician of genius, though it should also have been a warning of how much better he would have done to let that genius become really creative, as he knew well how to do elsewhere and as Boyce had done in two pretty pastoral pieces, "The Chaplet" (1749) and "The Shepherd's Lottery" (1751). Arne, of course, contributed enough original work to the stage, including some scores that showed his ambition to rival the Italians as a composer of serious, large-scale opera. Libretti of literary pretensions by Apostolo Zeno and Metastasio had opened a new phase in Italian opera, and Arne, by setting his own translation of the latter's "Artaserse," hoped to produce a counterblast to the production of J. C. Bach's "Orione, ossia Diana vendicata," which kept up the purely Italian tradition. Arne produced his "Artaxerxes" in 1762, soon after "Orione." Not content, however, with having composed an English opera in the Italian manner, he made a setting of Metastasio's "Olimpiade" in the original in 1764, thus adding another to the many settings of one of the most frequently composed opera-books known to musical history (over forty settings are recorded). This must almost certainly have been heard by Mozart, aged eight, whose family had made the acquaintance in London of Manzuoli, the male soprano who sang in Arne's work, if not indeed of Arne himself. Mozart, like Handel a cosmopolitan artist open to any influence he came across on his travels, may thus have taken up a little of Arne into his creative consciousness, as well as much of J. C. Bach, whose music now sounds to us surprisingly Mozartian, whereas of course it is the other way about.

"L'Olimpiade" did not drive Italian opera from the London stage. Indeed it no longer needed driving at that time. The English pieces, feeble as their books often were and meagre as the music sometimes was, had already dealt the more opulent species a severe blow, so far as any sort of general public support was concerned. It was not a death-blow, though. Italian opera has never died out among us; but it was the late eighteenth century which finally put it in its place once and for all as an exotic entertainment for a very small minority of musical and a rather greater number of would-be musical people, an expensive luxury the greatest attraction of which has too often been the expense. The conspicuous exception, the finest musical figure among Italian opera composers, was to be Verdi, but so great is Verdi's vitality that he is just as enjoyable in a good performance in English as in one given by a cast of brilliant but wilful and undisciplined stars at Covent Garden, the international opera-house that has remained the great market for outlandish fruit down to the present day.

At least half a dozen young theatre composers came forward during the 1760–70's, none of them gifted with any great power as musical dramatists, but all possessing what was alone deemed desirable—melodic fertility. Little more was, in fact, required for the sort of success their inane libretti deserved, and we may be sure that it never occurred to them to think of their music as having any qualities of endurance. In providing music for the farcical or sentimental absurdities expected by their public they laid no stress on musical workmanship and were content if they could think of a number of catchy, varied and singable tunes. In this they succeeded admirably; indeed in so far as they achieved exactly what they intended they were considerable artists. True, they may have succeeded better than they knew or cared: it might have surprised them to be told by some musical fortune-teller that future generations would treasure many of their songs as part of the national heritage and that those who dip into their antiquated stage pieces would find many a forgotten ditty that has kept an astonishing freshness.

The best of these composers were, in order of age, Thomas Linley, whom we have already encountered, Jonathan Battishill, Arne's son Michael, Samuel Arnold, Charles Dibdin, James Hook and William Shield. They did not emerge as theatre composers in the same order. Linley was thirty-five when he first came forward with "The Royal Merchant" in 1768, and it was not until 1775 that he wrote and compiled music for his son-in-law Sheridan's "Duenna," aided by his son Thomas, then aged nineteen, who as a boy had struck up a great friendship at Florence with Mozart, his exact contemporary.

It was Dibdin, though one of the youngest, who came first. He was only sixteen when, in 1761, John Beard rescued him from Johnson's music warehouse and started him on the career of a singing actor at Covent Garden, bringing out his first piece, "The Shepherd's Artifice," for his benefit that year. At the age of nineteen Dibdin went to Birmingham, where he appeared with great success at the theatre and at Vauxhall, a provincial imitation of the London pleasure gardens; but in 1765 Beard recalled him to Covent Garden, where he appeared in Arnold's first opera, "The Maid of the Mill," partly an original work and partly a pasticcio, for it contained songs by J. C. Bach, Galuppi, Jommelli and others. But it established Arnold's reputation as a composer while it confirmed Dibdin's as a lively and attractive stage singer. Dibdin was altogether a man of the theatre, for he excelled also as a playwright. A good half of the libretti for his musical pieces are his own, and they are on the whole superior in content and structure to the average products of the period.

Meanwhile, in 1764, Battishill and Michael Arne had jointly produced an opera, "Almena," a respectable work for two young men of twenty-six and twenty-three to have written. But in this case the libretto was not acceptable even to the unexacting public of the day. The piece was withdrawn after five performances. The younger Arne had already produced "The Fairy Tale" the preceding year.

Hook came from Norwich, where he had been trained at the cathedral, to seek his fortune in the capital at the age of eighteen in 1764. His first dramatic piece was the "Love and Innocence" of 1769. Shield, a Northumbrian, the youngest, appeared last of all, with the comic piece "The Flitch of Bacon" in 1778, when he was thirty. After that there was no holding him: he brought forth an average of two pieces a year between this and the end of the century. A later collaborator of his, and of others, was William Reeve, his junior by nine years, who belongs to the same class of stage composers as the musicians just mentioned.

Their musical plays have not lasted, with a very few exceptions, such as "The Duenna," to which a great literary name is attached, and possibly one or two of Dibdin's vigorous pieces, which are quite capable of revival on the stage or the radio. But as song-writers these composers have survived and are well worth exploring afresh by those in search of good, undeservedly forgotten English tunes. Some of their melodies, such as Linley's "Here's to the maiden of bashful fifteen" in Sheridan's "The School for Scandal" (1777), Dibdin's "The Bells of Aberdovey" in "Liberty Hall" (1785) and Hook's "The Lass of Richmond Hill," are popular classics that will never die out, for they have assumed the status of folksongs. They must not, however, be mistaken for true folksongs, needless to say. They are compositions in exactly the same sense as, for example, "Fairest Isle" in Purcell's "King Arthur" is a composition, or the setting of Ben Jonson's "To Celia" ("Drink to me only with thine eyes"), which is not contemporary with the poet but belongs to the period now under discussion, being probably the work of Henry Harington, a physician and musical amateur at Bath. Other things of the sort, by some of the composers named above, are "No flower that blows" in Linley's "Selima and Azor," Battishill's "Kate of Aberdeen" and Shield's "The Ploughboy."

There was some excitement at Covent Garden on May 16th 1767, at a revival of "The Beggar's Opera"; for the playbill announced that after the first act "Miss Brickler will sing a favourite song from 'Judith,' accompanied by Mr. Dibdin on a new instrument call'd Piano Forte." And the same year J. C. Bach played a new concerto of his own composed especially for the *fortepiano*. The instrument, so called because it could be played loudly and softly at will on a single keyboard, which had not been possible on the harpsichord and could be done only to a very limited extent on the clavichord, had already begun to make its way on the Continent, although J. S. Bach, for one, had shown a certain distrust of it, and the two older types of instrument continued to linger on in musical households, if only because everybody could not afford to replace them by the new-fangled invention. In England the harpsichord did not finally disappear from the concert-platform until 1795, when it was used for the rehearsal of a birthday ode for the king, but was replaced by a pianoforte at the performance; and abroad even Beethoven's first sonatas were described by their publisher in 1796 as being playable on either the new or the old instrument, though doubtless for purely commercial reasons not countenanced by the composer.

The invention of the pianoforte has been another subject for disputes between Italy and Germany. The victory in this case is Italy's, one must decide, for although a larger number of German instruments of the kind dating from the early eighteenth century have been preserved, Bartolommeo Cristofori of Florence is known to have made four of them with a hammer action—as distinct from the plectra of the harpsichord and the tangents of the clavichord—in 1709, whereas the first instruments by Gottfried Silbermann date from about 1725. But another German, Christoph Gottlieb Schröter, appears to have devised some sort of a hammer action between 1717 and 1721, and a Frenchman named Marius about 1716.

To complicate the matter still further, the first pianoforte seen in England was made in Rome by Father Wood, an English monk, according to Burney; and the introduction of the hammer action which enabled J. C. Bach to write concertos in a new style is, again, said to have been due to a German craftsman, Johannes Zumpe, who had long been employed by Burkat Shudi (really Burkhardt Tschudi), a Swiss harpsichord maker settled in London, whose daughter Barbara married another of her father's workmen, John Broadwood, in 1769. It was Broadwood who towards the last quarter of the century invented an adaptation of the wing shape of the harpsichord to the pianoforte, which had previously retained the square shape of the spinet. Broadwood thus originated the modern grand piano while another English maker, Robert Stodart, with the help of two ingenious assistants, introduced the iron frame whereby the weight and tension of the strings could be enormously increased and the tone consequently made much fuller and more sustained.

The new instrument, capable of producing not only harmony but a range of dynamics undreamt of by harpsichord players, was eagerly studied not by virtuosi alone but by would-be composers, in whom improvisation could not fail to stimulate novel departures. Thus arose the new race of pianist-composers which so conspicuously helps to people the musical history of this period, and to which even Mozart and Beethoven in a sense belong, though in them the creative impulse immensely outranged the reproductive. It was a curious tribe. Many of its members who over-ran the Continent and often paid lucrative visits to England succeeded by effrontery rather than by genuine gifts. The brilliance of their technique enabled them to disguise the shallowness of their extemporizations, which were a fleeting type of composition not written down on paper and forgotten as soon as the performance was over, but leaving a spurious impression of dazzling cleverness. The easiest way of making this impression was to take a familiar tune, either a popular song or an air from a favourite opera, and embroider it with variations which gave neither structural solidity nor additional character to the original, but merely broke up its surface into flashy figuration. The great bulk of these temporary effusions were mercifully disposed of almost as soon as their players had risen from the instrument; but frequently things of this sort were written down and published, and even serious composers were sometimes tempted by the easy success of such ornamented presentations of favoured tunes to adopt a style that was well enough suited to improvisation, but perpetuated work rarely worth preserving in print.

In spite of Beethoven's surpassingly great example in making the variation form a vehicle for composition on the grandest scale, this sort of thing continued to be perfunctorily done well into the nineteenth century: as late as 1841 Mendelssohn was moved to protest against it by writing a cautionary set he deliberately entitled "Variations sérieuses," which was as good as calling the work of Herz, Thalberg and their like *variations frivoles*.

Not all pianist-composers were charlatans, however. Three who worked in England stood out as fine artists. The eldest concentrated his activities on London all his adult life, with some interruptions. He was the Italian Muzio Clementi, who was brought to England in 1766 as a boy of fourteen by a Mr. (or Sir) Peter Beckford, a member of Parliament and wealthy country gentleman who may have been an uncle of William Beckford, the author of "Vathek." Beckford settled the gifted boy at Fonthill Abbey, his estate in Wiltshire, where he gave him the free run of his library and looked after his education. Clementi studied any music he could lay hands on, including works by J. S. Bach, and became a highly accomplished performer and a composer of decided originality, as his sonatas show, many of which are transcriptions of works at first performed in an orchestral form as symphonies. The second was Jan Ladislav Dussek, a Bohemian who came to London in 1790 at the age of twenty-nine, driven there from Paris by the Revolution, and stayed for ten years as a very successful pianist, teacher and composer until he was forced to leave surreptitiously in 1800 because, less successful as a publisher, he was threatened with bankruptcy. Dussek's sonatas are even more remarkable than Clementi's for the richness and variety of their keyboard-writing and for the astonishing number of anticipations of stylistic features found in later composers—as late as Schumann and Brahms—which they contain.

The youngest of these three exceptional performer-composers was the Irishman John Field, who very early astonished Dublin by his precocious gifts, even before Hummel, aged twelve, did the same on a visit to Edinburgh in 1790. Field's grandfather and father kept a kind of musical academy at Dublin, but they moved to Bath in 1793, where John, then eleven, amazed the smart set, and soon afterwards to London, where he became an apprentice in Clementi's music warehouse. The Anglo-Italian master undertook to teach him in return for his services, plus a hundred guineas. Clementi did well out of the talented boy, whom he employed to display the pianofortes in his showrooms; but at least Field in this way learnt all there was to know about improvisation, and Clementi saw to it that his taste should not be spoilt thereby, as may be judged from Field's compositions, which at their best lack neither character nor refinement. Settled in Russia later in life, he wrote a good deal of fashionable keyboard music, but also anticipated Chopin in being the first to invent lyrical pieces to which he gave the title of Nocturnes, less beautiful but more varied than the Polish master's, whom he influenced considerably.

Field was by no means the only musical child-prodigy. Wonder-children were all the rage. Little Mozart and his sister had shown how to captivate the great world, from the royal family downwards, by feats of performance or composition expected only from grown-up and highly trained artists. English parents too were anxious to show that their offspring could do as well as Irish and foreign infant phenomena. Indeed a babe at Norwich named William Crotch outdid even Mozart at the age of three, when he began to play the organ in 1778, an instrument made especially for him by his father, a music-loving carpenter. He was brought to London the following year and fashionable people could hear him play daily at the establishment of Mrs. Hart, a milliner in Piccadilly. His aural faculty for detecting faulty intonation was found to be as miraculous as his keyboard technique and his gift of improvisation. Both Burney and the Hon. Daines Barrington, the latter of whom had already done the same in Mozart's case, published accounts of the child's accomplishments, Burney's being read before the Royal Society and published in the "Philosophical Transactions." At the age of eleven Crotch was assistant organist at Trinity and King's Colleges at Cambridge, at fourteen he wrote an oratorio, "The Captivity of Judah," and at twenty-two he succeeded Philip Hayes as Professor of Music in the University of Oxford, which appears to have been somewhat reckless in these matters at that time. His chants are still used in the Anglican church, and one of them contains a characteristic example of his technical skill: the notes of all four parts in the first section go backwards in the second and make perfect progressions in each. All the same, though some of his anthems too have remained serviceable, Crotch does not prove that even the most marvellous early development necessarily guarantees future greatness, as it happened to do in Mozart's case. We cannot speak of "The Captivity," as we do of "Don Giovanni," with the certainty of instantly conveying the composer's name without mentioning it. In fact we do not speak of it at all.

Thomas Busby, later an organist, composer and scholar, had already followed the new fashion by appearing as a singer and harpsichord player of fourteen at Vauxhall in 1768, at a salary of ten guineas.

The Wesleys, though a family of a different kind of fame, were also a highly musical one. They too produced a prodigy: Samuel, the son of the Rev. Charles Wesley and nephew of the founder of Methodism. He too played the organ at three, and his first oratorio, "Ruth," dates from his eighth year. At thirteen, in 1779, he and his elder brother Charles began to give concerts at their father's London house in Marylebone.

Girls as well as boys shone by precocious gifts. We have already met the singers who later became Mrs. Bland and Mrs. Billington. Both established their fame in their early teens about 1780–83. Nancy Storace (really Anna Selina Sorace, for although London-born, she was the daughter of an Italian double-bass player) sang at the oratorio concerts at Covent Garden and at the Hereford Festival in 1777, aged eleven. It was she who only nine years later was to be Mozart's first Susanna in the Vienna production of "Le nozze di Figaro." Linley's daughter Elizabeth was another singer who appeared at a tender age. Having already sung at her father's concerts at Bath before she was sixteen, she came out in London at that age in 1770, three years before her romantic marriage to Sheridan, who was supposed to take her to a nunnery in France as a protection from the advances of several undesirable suitors. She must have attracted the public as much by her beauty as by her voice, if we are to believe Reynolds's exquisite portrait of her. She sang immediately at all the Three Choirs Festivals: at Worcester in 1770, at Hereford in 1771 and at Gloucester in 1772.

These festivals flourished greatly, so that other cities followed their example. Birmingham established a triennial one in aid of the General Hospital in 1768, Norwich held a single one tentatively in 1770 (there was no regular event there until 1824), Chester began in 1772, York in 1791.

Large-scale works were required at the festivals and for the admirable choral societies England possessed up and down the country, who liked to collaborate with brilliant solo singers. It was due to them, above all, that the oratorio continued to be cultivated after the death of Handel. The form was clearly not particularly congenial to English musicians, who were content—one may almost say up to the appearance of Elgar's "Dream of Gerontius"—to treat it conventionally in the Handelian manner. We may in fact

doubt whether it would have held its own in England at all
but for the special conditions attaching to the festivals, and it
seems to be a mistake to regard it as a specifically English
musical phenomenon, except in so far as those conditions are
peculiar to England.

Not so with church music. That too, it is true, was
determined by special demands made on composers—the
peculiar requirements of the Anglican service, with its
generous provision for musical settings both in Matins and
Evensong, particularly the "Magnificat" and "Nunc dimittis"
of the latter, apart from the place it reserves for the voluntary
anthem. But there have always been groups of composers
to whom it seems to have appealed, as the oratorio has never
done, as especially suited to the native temperament. In the
later eighteenth century it languished somewhat, one must
admit; still, other musicians than Boyce gave it their attention. James Nares, then Master of the Children at the Chapel
Royal, published a collection of anthems in 1778. William
Jackson, organist at Exeter Cathedral from 1777 to his death
in 1803, did much honest if insipid work for the church; a
"Te Deum" of his is still sung, though perhaps for sentimental rather than artistic reasons. Other church musicians
of the time are Edmund Ayrton, who succeeded Nares in
1780; John Alcock, who worked successively at churches at
Plymouth and Reading and at Lichfield Cathedral; Theodore
Aylward, who began at London city churches, became
Professor of Music at Gresham College and finally went to
St. George's Chapel, Windsor; Battishill, also a city organist,
who contributed anthems and chants. Crotch, a little later,
did much work for the church; Arnold too began to devote
himself to its music when he joined Ayrton as organist at
the Chapel Royal in 1783.

These composers were, of course, entirely home-grown.
Others now began to go abroad for study, a thing older
English musicians had very rarely done, though they had

often carried their matured talents into the service of foreign employers. Studying abroad grew from a habit into a fashion in the nineteenth century, not always to the advantage of English music as such. In 1782 a young musician of seventeen, Thomas Attwood, appeared at a concert at Buckingham House, where the Prince of Wales (afterwards George IV) took a keen interest in him. The prince was himself something of a musician, a pupil of John Crosdill the violoncellist, who was that year appointed chamber musician to Queen Charlotte. When George came of age the following year and took up separate residence at Carlton House, he sent Attwood to Italy for further study. But the young man desired to become a pupil of Mozart in Vienna, where he found a little group of musical compatriots: Nancy Storace, her brother Stephen, a promising young man who learnt much about stage music from the composer of "Figaro," the work in which not only his sister appeared, but also the third of the group, the Irishman Michael Kelly (sometimes called O'Kelly and described in the playbill of "Figaro," in which he was the first Basilio, as "Signor Ochelly"). Kelly, who left delightful memoirs including an admirable prose-sketch of Mozart, also tried his hand at composition. Later on he wrote music for many light English stage pieces of the kind already discussed—many more than Storace, who attempted something more substantial in opera ("The Haunted Tower," "The Siege of Belgrade," etc.), but died at the age of thirty-three.

To study under foreign musicians it was, of course, not necessary to go abroad. There were plenty of them in Britain. Mozart himself, who was dissatisfied with his poor chances in Vienna, was nearly induced to follow his four friends to England when they returned in 1787. Clementi, who at the age of thirty-two came back from abroad, where he had greatly enhanced his reputation, took part in the foundation of the Grand Professional Concerts held at the

Hanover Square Rooms and soon had many pupils for the now fashionable pianoforte. He produced his first symphony at the new concerts two years later, in 1786, and followed it up by four more the same year. Cherubini came to London as opera composer for two years in 1784. The German-Jewish violinist Johann Peter Salomon began to do much for serious music in the eighties, giving subscription concerts of his own at which he played and conducted. It was he who first introduced symphonies by Haydn and Mozart to the English public. The French violinist Barthélemon became a Londoner by his marriage to the singer Mary Young, a niece of Mrs. Arne's, and was active in the Irish as well as in the English capital. The brothers Giordani, a musician and a dancer, enlivened the stage at Dublin. Gertrud Elisabeth Mara, a German singer who had begun her career as a violinist, astonished London at the Pantheon. French as well as German and Italian music caught on. The pretty, sentimental and melodious comic operas of Monsigny and Philidor had some vogue, though the latter was better known as a great chess player, in which capacity he was almost more at home in London than in Paris. Burney had already adapted Jean-Jacques Rousseau's amateurish, simpering but charmingly tuneful little opera, "Le Devin du village," in 1766 as "The Cunning Man." Twenty years later Linley and Shield contributed some music to what was mainly an adaptation of Grétry's "Richard, Cœur de Lion" by General John Burgoyne.

Among the Italian music-teachers in London was Gabriele Piozzi, who married Mrs. Thrale in 1784, much to the annoyance of her friends, who thought her infatuation with a man much younger than herself ridiculous. These friends were, of course, the circle that included Dr. Johnson as despotic arbiter, Burney and his gifted daughter Fanny, Burke, Garrick (before his death in 1779), Reynolds and Mrs. Delany, who had been a great friend of Handel's. There were many gatherings at Burney's house in St. Martin's Street. Not all the friends were musical; Johnson was notoriously ignorant of the art, though he seems to have made rather a pose of his lack of ear and not to have disliked music as much as he pretended. He felt at home, at any rate, at the house of a musician for whom and whose daughter he had a great affection, a house, too, at which literature, the stage, painting, politics, society and the prosperous middle-class were represented as well as music.

Among painters Reynolds was by no means the only one who showed marked fondness for music or kept in touch with musicians. Gainsborough painted portraits of both Abel and J. C. Bach, with whom he was on terms of friendship. Fanny Burney left a delightful account in her diary of how she overheard an overture by Piccinni played by the family at an inn at Devizes which was the childhood home of Lawrence. Both Clementi and Dussek dedicated sonatas to the wife of George Chinnery, the painter and engraver, and Viotti also became friendly with the Chinnerys after his settlement in London as another of the many musicians exiled from France by the Revolution. A more famous engraver, Francesco Bartolozzi, and his wife also made friends in the same circle.

The royal family itself showed a benevolent interest in musicians, if not a passionate one in music. Soon after his accession George III had made much of the greatest of wonder-children, Mozart. In 1785 he made Cherubini "Composer to the King." The Prince of Wales, whose interest was more active, also admired that gifted young Italian, who was two years older than himself and who seems very nearly to have settled for good in London, as he did later in Paris. The Concerts of Ancient Music were regularly attended by royalty and therefore began to be called "The King's Concerts" in 1785. The following year, when Arnold projected a complete edition of Handel's works, the king subscribed for twenty-five copies.   The Prince of Wales had a chamber band of his own at Carlton House.   His younger brother, the Duke of Clarence (afterwards William IV) became a member of the Catch Club in 1789, at the age of twenty-four—perhaps for the sake of conviviality rather than for a keen love of music.

The Catch Club continued more flourishing than ever under such patronage.   It encouraged some new composers to cultivate its specialities.   In 1785 a youth of nineteen, John Callcott, won its prizes with a glee, a canon and a catch, and, perhaps to show that he was not prepared to devote himself to musical frivolities alone, took the Mus. B. at Oxford at the same time.   A more admonitory demonstration of seriousness was the foundation of the Caecilian Society that year by amateur musicians who had the strange notion of gathering at each other's houses to sing hymns and anthems, performances that may well have been as awful in the literal sense of the word as the Victorian drawing-room musical evenings were colloquially speaking.   But again, these domestic solemnities were offset by Linley and Webbe when they established the Glee Club in 1787.   That the Catch Club was not thereby put out of countenance is proved by the fact that Callcott alone submitted nearly a hundred pieces to it that year.

Something of the sociable spirit of these clubs was brought to a larger public by Dibdin, who in 1787 began to tour through England with miscellaneous performances which later developed into his famous Table Entertainments.   The next year Dibdin set sail for India, but his vessel being driven into Torbay by a violent storm, he decided to abandon this plan and return to London.   Which did not prevent him from becoming the sea-dog of British music and writing sturdy tunes for many a stout mariners' song.   He started his new venture at Hutchins's Auction Rooms in King Street, Covent Garden, where he sang the songs composed by himself to his own words. The first entertainment, called "The Whim of the Moment," was very poorly attended; but he did not lose heart and brought out "The Oddities" at the Lyceum, where he had a resounding success with a number of songs that included "Tom Bowling," a bluff but moving elegy on the death of his brother, Captain Thomas Dibdin. In 1790 the entertainment called "The Wags"—it would in the present century have been called "The Dibdin Follies," perhaps, for in some ways these diversions were the fore-runners of those of Pélissier and his followers—was repeated more than a hundred times, and the sale of a song, "Poor Jack," made £500 for the publisher, which decided Dibdin to publish for himself in the future. In 1796 he opened a small theatre specially built for his Table Entertainments in Leicester Place.

The great events of the 1790's, of course, were Haydn's two visits to England. It was Salomon who invited him to come and conduct his own symphonies and, more than that, to write new works of the kind especially for London. In the course of his two visits in 1791–2 and 1794–5, stimulated by the fine orchestral playing he found at the Grand Professional Concerts, he responded with a set of twelve works which are his last and greatest in a series of more than a hundred. Earlier works of his were also played, needless to say, including the Symphony in G major of 1788, performed at Oxford when that University conferred its musical doctor's degree on him, *honoris causa*. Though not composed in England, it has been known as the "Oxford" Symphony ever since.

Haydn did not conduct his symphonies; he sat at the harpsichord while Salomon led at the first violin desk. Although Haydn's later symphonies are fully scored to sound complete without a keyboard part, the custom still prevailed in performance of retaining the *continuo*, the player of which often spared a hand or two to beat time.

The term *continuo*, having been used before (Chapters III and VI), had better be briefly explained here. It describes a part for a subsidiary keyboard instrument (harpsichord or organ, or even, in later instances, pianoforte) used to fill up the harmony in chamber, orchestral and choral works, the parts of which were often harmonically incomplete in themselves. The *continuo* part was not fully written out by the composer, but showed as a rule nothing but the line of the bass identical with that played by the lowest bass instruments, so far as actual notes were concerned. In addition to these notes there was a kind of shorthand system of numerals indicating, according to an accepted convention, the harmony required, but not the exact vertical position of each chord, which the player was at liberty to space and invert as he pleased, so long as the constituent notes were correct. He was also, not only at liberty, but actually expected to enrich his part with such figuration and passages of imitation as he was skilful enough to invent on the spur of the moment. Such "figured bass" parts, which demanded a highly specialized art of playing, were called the *continuo* because with very few exceptions they went on uninterruptedly all through a composition. The practice belongs to the seventeenth and eighteenth centuries, but, already superseded in the second half of the latter and wholly superfluous in Haydn's last symphonies, it fell into complete disuse by 1800, though it must still be resorted to in some way or other for the performance of old music.

Haydn made many friends in England and renewed old friendships, such as that with his former pupil Pleyel, in spite of the fact that the younger man was introduced as a rival. He also got into touch with George Thomson, an enthusiastic Scottish amateur collector of Scots, Irish and Welsh folksongs, who hit upon the curious idea of having the tunes set to more or less lavish accompaniments by various foreign composers of note—a request to which these composers naturally responded more or less unsuitably. Beethoven's work for Thomson's collection belongs to the period covered by the next chapter, but although Thomson had at first approached Pleyel, he met Haydn in 1791, and eventually the result of the acquaintance was a contribution of no less than 187 settings from Haydn's pen.

Thomson's were not the earliest publications of the sort. In 1784 a Scots fiddler, Nathaniel Gow, published the first "Collection of Strathspey Reels" at Dunkeld, assisted by his son Neil. Four years later Malcolm M'Donald, a cellist and minor composer attached to Gow's band at Edinburgh, issued his own first book of "Strathspeys and Reels." A similar service was rendered to Wales in 1784 by the Welsh harper Edward Jones, a young man of thirty-two who bore the proud title of "Bard to the Prince of Wales" (which indicates some sort of notion of the prince's due to his own title) and published a work called "Musical and Poetical Relicks of the Welsh Bards, with a General History of the Bards and Druids, and a Dissertation on the Musical Instruments of the Aboriginal Britons."

By the end of the century concerts had really become public institutions in London and in the provinces. Opera, on the other hand, always confined to the capital, did badly even there, both materially and artistically. Vanbrugh's splendid King's Theatre in the Haymarket was burnt to the ground in 1789, and the conversion of the Pantheon into a theatre was only a makeshift. Besides, it too was destroyed by fire in 1792, and when it was reopened it was once more a place of non-theatrical entertainment. Perhaps the conflagration was regarded as a punishment for having taken to a kind of musical performance always regarded with some suspicion in England. Be that as it may, opera was certainly not given its chance at that time. Covent Garden continued to be given over largely to the production of sentimental comedies and silly farces larded with songs and embellished with sometimes very flimsy musical pieces. Worse than that, in 1792 it carried the iniquities of the pasticcio to the length of allowing Reeve to "adapt" Gluck's "Orfeo" and to write some new music for it himself. "Orfeo" was the first of Gluck's works showing him fully aware that an opera should be all of a piece as a work of art and a musical composition. To tamper with the least detail of its score was to show an utter lack of understanding of all that opera means, or should mean. But London did not heed this in those days, or indeed later, when it butchered Mozart's "Figaro" and "Don Giovanni" in much the same way and enjoyed the ghastly disfigurements.

The musical stage productions of the year 1800 may thus not have represented England's operatic nadir; but they are worth glancing at for a specimen of the kind of thing that went on. The titles of many of the pieces alone are significant of complete insignificance: i.e. Arnold's "Obi, or Three-fingered Jack," Attwood's "Harlequin's Tour," Kelly's "Of Age To-morrow," and Reeve's "Jamie and Anna." Doubtless "Zenobia" was not the least successful opera of the season, for was it not the composition of Richard, Earl of Mount-Edgcumbe? (This nobleman, a musical dilettante of very modest creative gifts, became better known later in life as a writer of excellent gossip about operatic life of the past.) Busby contributed incidental music to an English version of "Joanna" by Kotzebue, whose well-made but shallow and slightly risky comedies were all the rage. "Paul and Virginia," by Reeve and Joseph Mazzinghi, had at least the merit of a libretto based on Bernardin de Saint-Pierre's languidly romantic novel. Its music has no more claim to remembrance than that of its rival "operas" of the end of the eighteenth century. If it was no worse than they, it still shows how low the operatic standard had sunk.

CHAPTER VIII

The Early Nineteenth Century
(1801–1837)

The last eleven years of George III's active reign, the nine of the Regency, the ten under George IV and the seven under William IV saw the birth of no British composer of more than moderate distinction, while abroad the years 1803–13 alone produced Berlioz, Mendelssohn, Chopin, Schumann, Liszt, Verdi and Wagner. What is more, the first third of the nineteenth century, or more exactly the first thirty-six and a half years up to the accession of Queen Victoria, produced scarcely a British musical work one may designate as bearing the marks of genius, though its composers did contrive to turn out some things that achieved immortality of a kind—the immortality conferred by sentimental affection rather than artistic discernment. Bishop's song, "Home, sweet home," may at once be singled out as a typical product of the kind.

An English opera appeared which is honoured by musicians though almost wholly unperformed anywhere: "Oberon"; but its music was by a German master. Two great overtures found their inspirational sources in Britain, one being for "A Midsummer Night's Dream," the other depicting seascapes in the Hebrides; but they were by a composer who must still, in spite of Nazi decrees and in spite of his temperamental acclimatization to England, be called a German. The new British literary romantics, especially Scott and Byron, gave fresh matter to composers for operas and symphonic works; but the important results of this association were destined to appear mainly abroad (e.g. Rossini's, Donizetti's,

Marschner's and Bizet's operas on Scott subjects, Berlioz's Byronic "Harold en Italie," etc., etc.).

All the same, the period, though not strikingly productive, was eventful in several ways. It made Beethoven known to an English public enthusiastically ready to lend him an ear. It includes Mendelssohn's first visits, which proved as stimulating to him as to English musical life—indeed more so, since in some respects he became a drag upon its activities. It saw the rise of fine orchestral playing, at any rate in London, and confirmed the habit of concert-going. It turned choral singing into a sort of artistic national sport by making attendance at the great festivals something like a national duty. It produced English singers who could compete successfully, sometimes triumphantly, with their foreign rivals. It gave English pianoforte makers precedence over all others.

Two of these singers returned from Italy in 1801: Mrs. Billington with fresh laurels to her crown, and the Jewish tenor, John Braham, who was not yet thirty and had appeared with Nancy Storace at the Pergola in Florence and the Scala in Milan, among other places, and encountered Mrs. Billington too upon the Italian stage. He went to Covent Garden and became so great a favourite in English "opera" that the public tolerated the feeblest pieces in which he appeared and insisted on his singing songs composed by himself, the rest of the score being entrusted to a hack like Reeve.

Concerts were more serious and showed some enterprise. That same year not only a comparatively modern work, Mozart's Requiem, was given together with Handel's "L'Allegro," but a novelty was played, more adventurously than suitably, between the two: John Field, now aged nineteen, played a piano concerto of his own. It was the following year that Clementi took Field on a foreign tour which included France and Germany and ended in Russia, where the young Irish genius settled down, at St. Petersburg, as teacher of his instrument. The chief reason may have been the warm reception given him by Russian music-lovers, but it may not be too fantastic to suppose that he was tired of doing business on behalf of Clementi, even though his duties at the music warehouse called for a musician's skill.

Not that musicians were at that time disinclined to do business. Kelly not only opened a music shop in Pall Mall early in the century, while he went on busily turning out imitative musical stage pieces; he also, like Viotti, traded as a wine merchant. ("Composer of wines and importer of music," Sheridan called him.) Taking no great interest in his shop, he made John Addison, another stage composer and a double-bass player at the Italian Opera and the Ancient Vocal Concerts, manager of it. We have seen that Clementi was a publisher as well as a pianoforte maker and that Dussek came to grief over a publishing venture. This, however, was carried on with more success by his father-in-law, Domenico Corri, who was also a composer and produced an opera, "The Travellers," in 1806. Dibdin, too, though over sixty, had to set up a music shop in the Strand when a government pension of £200 granted him about 1804 was lost to him on the death of Pitt and the change to Grenville's Ministry of all the Talents formed in 1806. Dibdin's special talents, doubtless, were not those esteemed by the statesmen of the hour. He thought of appealing to the king, but refrained because George III was then well on the way towards the blindness and insanity which obscured the last years of his reign.

In 1811 Vincent Novello, the English-born son of an Italian father, who had already won some distinction as organist and composer, founded the publishing house which still exists, beginning as editor of "A Collection of Sacred Music." The following year the firm of Chappell & Co. was established by Samuel Chappell, Francis Tatton Latour and Johann Baptist Cramer, the last of whom at least was a musician by profession, German-born but London-bred. As a pianist and composer for his instrument Cramer fell little short of Clementi; indeed his Studies are finer music than Clementi's "Gradus ad Parnassum," written for similar instructive purposes.

The Scottish and Irish capitals had their own musician-publishers. Pietro Urbani, an Italian singer and composer, brought out a collection of Scottish songs, rivalling Thomson's, in six volumes, the last of which appeared at Edinburgh in 1804; and the young Irish violinist Thomas Simpson Cooke (Tom Cooke) kept a music shop at Dublin from 1806 to 1812, giving it up only to devote himself to playing and composing. He later joined the motley company of successful but frivolous stage composers. The Gows at Edinburgh also went on publishing, thus becoming involved in the financial difficulties which seemed to be the rule rather than the exception for musicians who ventured into business.

If not always profitable, publishing could be quite serious. John Stafford Smith, son of a former Gloucester Cathedral organist and once a pupil of Boyce, composer of glees, catches and songs (one of which, "Anacreon in Heaven," is the tune now known as "The Star-spangled Banner"), issued in 1812 a collection in two volumes, "Musica Antiqua," containing specimens of music selected from the twelfth to the eighteenth century. Smith was then Master of the Children in the Chapel Royal. Such antiquarian interest in the past, however, was rare in a period that was still, like the eighteenth century, interested almost exclusively in contemporary music. Even the great Johann Sebastian Bach seemed to belong to a dead past. Still, in 1813, Samuel Wesley, together with Karl Friedrich Horn, a German settled in London, father of Charles Edward Horn, the composer of "Cherry Ripe" and another of the purveyors of the quasi-operatic stage, issued an English edition of "The Well-tempered Clavier," following a similar edition of the German master's organ Trios published in 1810.

Wesley had already in 1808 begun a correspondence on Bach with the organist Benjamin Jacob, who had invited him and Crotch to join him in giving recitals at the Surrey Chapel, where Wesley played much of the music he was the first to introduce to England in a systematic way. But if Bach became known here more than half a century too late, it must be remembered that his own country knew him hardly any better until Mendelssohn began an enthusiastic revival with his Berlin performance of the St. Matthew Passion in 1829. In his own lifetime Bach had been widely known only by repute in Germany as an exceptionally gifted organist; his compositions, almost all of which remained unpublished until long after his death, were thought of, with few exceptions, as having only the local importance of music turned out in the ordinary course of his duties as cantor at St. Thomas's Church and as of no interest beyond Leipzig. Such works as the B minor Mass, written for the Dresden court, or the "Musical Offering" dedicated to Frederick the Great had an unusually wide aim, and even they did not become generally known.

A newly-awakened interest in German music, a subject on which Callcott gave special lectures at the Royal Institution, and which only now began to compete seriously with Italian and French music, was by no means concentrated on Bach alone. Indeed it centred on him only through the exceptional efforts of a man who happened to have a rare interest in the past. The musical public in general still preferred to pay attention to modern music, or at any rate, if that suggests an interest too far above mere curiosity, to living composers. And the great modern composer now coming into view was Beethoven. England, devoid of outstanding native musicians of creative genius, was quick to seize upon a new master who hurled surprise after surprise into a musical world that may have been complacent enough in its acceptance of Italianate conventions, but had learnt to face new

departures from Haydn, whose work taught it to understand Beethoven's earlier symphonies and concertos.

It was the foundation of the Philharmonic Society in 1813
which established Beethoven in London, and thence quickly
throughout the country, though his work had been by no
means unknown before. The new organization was established for the purpose of performing great orchestral music
adequately. Chamber music was done as well, a custom
that prevailed for many years. The founders were the
veteran violinist William Dance, J. B. Cramer and Philip
Anthony Corri, Domenico's son. Attwood, Henry Smart,
leader of the orchestra at Drury Lane, his elder brother, Sir
George Smart, organist and conductor, and Henry Bishop,
who had lately come forward as theatre composer, were
among the first members. Crotch and a young man of the
odd name of Cipriani Potter were elected associates, the
latter becoming a full member on reaching his majority later
in the year. Clementi was appointed conductor, though his
advanced years made it necessary for Bishop or George
Smart to take his place sometimes. They still conducted at the
keyboard, while Salomon led at the first violin desk. Clementi
took to the composition of symphonies again, writing now
in friendly rivalry, no longer to Haydn but to Beethoven.
Viotti too, at the age of sixty, again took a share in musical
life after his retirement: keenly interested in the Philharmonic,
he willingly played as a subordinate violinist for the sheer
pleasure of forming part of the splendid new orchestra.

The opening concert took place at the old Argyll Rooms
on March 8th 1813. From 1820 onwards the Society's
headquarters showed its modern and ambitious outlook as
clearly as did its inclusion of Beethoven in the programmes,
which contained three of his symphonies and his Septet
during the first season. The new Argyll Rooms were situated
in John Nash's magnificent, mile-long Regent Street, the
finest piece of town-planning London has ever known, or

at least has ever carried out since it rejected Wren's plan for the lay-out of St. Paul's Cathedral. For it was all one design in Nash's stately, yet delightfully domesticated stucco, stretching from Carlton House, the Prince Regent's town residence, to Regent's Park, where a splendid country house was to be built for him. The new Argyll Rooms were as opulent as the rest of the street, and the patrons, who paid heavy subscriptions, were among the most affluent people in town. For years afterwards, until the Argyll Rooms were burnt down in 1829, patrons were requested as a matter of course in the programmes to be set down at the doors "with their horses' heads towards Piccadilly."

Those programmes were incredibly substantial. As a rule they contained more than twice the amount of music a normal twentieth-century audience would expect to endure and almost double the quantity even the most insatiable Queen's Hall "Promenader" could have faced. The custom was to give not one symphony, but two, not one overture, but three, with at least one concerto in addition, together with some vocal items and a quartet or other chamber work thrown in for make-weight. The past century had already accustomed English audiences to monstrous musical feasts by Handel's oratorios with organ concertos between the "acts"; but it was now that concert-goers were deliberately induced to display a Gargantuan appetite for music if they loved it or to endure prolonged agonies of boredom with stoical politeness if they attended only for social reasons or for the sake of some other snobbish gratification.

But if not all those who went to the concerts loved music, the Philharmonic promoters themselves certainly lived up to their chosen name. They continued to cultivate Beethoven's work and caught up with its new manifestations more and more quickly. They first performed the "Eroica" Symphony eleven and the fifth nine years after their composition, the seventh only five years later, and the ninth had but two years to wait for a hearing in London. When Beethoven lay dying in 1827, and it became known in England that he was financially embarrassed, the Philharmonic Society sent him a gift of £100 with a tactful letter that made acceptance easy. It was not the first present he had received from England. In 1818, the year in which Potter went to Vienna and was received by him with much kindness, Broadwood's sent him one of their best pianofortes—which meant one of the finest keyboard instruments then to be had in Europe. He expressed admiration for the English character and thought the British constitution exemplary, and he was nearly induced by the Philharmonic and by his pupil Ferdinand Ries, who had married an Englishwoman and lived in London for several years, to follow Mozart's and Haydn's example by paying a visit to the island that has never ceased to allure foreign musicians, though they have sometimes—like Wagner—allowed themselves to be tempted for the wrong reasons.

It must be said that by the time of Wagner's visit (which does not come within the present chapter) the Philharmonic's early spirit of enthusiasm seems to have yielded to a certain humdrum complacency, a fault that often mars the activities of well-established organizations which have existed long enough to pride themselves upon their traditions. From that reproach the Society was, of course, free in its early days, as it has indeed again been in its latest phases. The institution at which such an accusation could have been levelled with some justice in the years round about the Regency was the Church of England. It had, indeed, great traditions to live upon, and so far it did its work of musical cultivation well enough; but it had no new creative musicians to show who could enrich it with an ecclesiastical art of a strong and distinctive style reflecting the period—as indeed it could not do in architecture either. All Souls' Church in Langham

Place, freakishly designed by Nash to close the vista of Regent Street, is a quaint, amusing and characteristic period-piece not remotely comparable with the exquisite Wren churches, much less with the three English Gothic styles; and the few active church composers of the time—Attwood, Callcott, Crotch, J. S. Smith—have nothing to show that one would dream of calling the equal of Byrd or Purcell. Attwood was the only living composer who had something to contribute to a memorial service for Nelson held in 1806, and his coronation anthems for George IV ("I was glad") and for William IV ("O Lord, grant the King long Life"— William, like Attwood, was then sixty-five!) are characterless compared with Purcell's similar work for James II. The best church musician, considered as a creative artist, was Samuel Wesley: his motets, including the splendid "In exitu Israel," and some of his anthems and parochial Psalm-tunes more particularly designed for the Anglican service, have qualities of originality unapproached by any of his contemporaries. Some of the older church composers died early in the century: Aylward and Battishill in 1801, Arnold in 1802 and Ayrton in 1808.

If, however, the church lived smugly upon fine traditions, the stage had no standards at all. It continued to give a public that was easily pleased knockabout fun and insipid sentimentality mated to music which was thought good enough if it included a few catchy tunes, as indeed these pieces, to do them justice, did more often than not. Bishop, at eighteen, joined the older generation of theatrical purveyors in 1804 with a tentative production of his first piece, "Angelina," at Margate, of all places. He came to town with several dramatic pieces the next year, and steadily went on turning out similar things with more industry than care, producing for instance no fewer than six of them in 1808. He was unlucky, however. On February 24th 1809 Drury Lane Theatre, suffering the same fate as Covent Garden had

done on September 19th 1808, was burnt to the ground, and
the score of "The Circassian Bride," which he had produced
only the night before the fire, perished in the flames.   For all
we know it may have been his masterpiece.   As it is, apart
from a few prettily stilted songs, including the charmingly
mock-Handelian "Should he upbraid," his fame rests mainly
on "Home, sweet home."   Its history in the careers of great
prima donnas is well-known; its origin is more curious, for
it appeared in a piece entitled "Clari, or The Maid of Milan"
in 1823 as a distinct anticipation of that indispensable attribute
of modern musical comedy—the theme-song.   It is not
merely sung once by a single voice, but is used both in the
overture and as a final chorus, as well as in various transformations of key and time, and scraps of it even turn up
in the manner of the Wagnerian *Leitmotiv*.

In 1806 Bishop came to the fore as the first English composer to write music for ballets designed as complete stage
entertainments, as distinct from the dances forming part of
masques, as in the seventeenth century, or interpolated into
operas, as in the eighteenth.   The ballet as a separate form
of art had gradually detached itself from the masque in France
at the time of Lully, and it remained almost wholly French
during the eighteenth century.   It is significant that the titles
of Bishop's new contributions of the kind were still French:
"Tamerlan et Bajazet," "Armide et Renaud," "Narcisse et
les Grâces."   In this they followed the example of two
foreign musicians who came to London in the first place as
pianoforte virtuosi and composers for their instrument, but
who both succeeded in producing ballets at the King's Theatre,
where that species was now cultivated side by side with
Italian opera.   They were the German Daniel Steibelt, who
came out in 1804 with "Le Jugement du berger Pâris" and
in 1805 with "La Belle Laitière," and the Austrian Joseph
Woelfl, whose "La Surprise de Diane" was given in the
latter year.   The predominance of subjects from classical

mythology and from history was as much a convention of French ballet as it was of the Italian opera libretti by Zeno and Metastasio. With the appearance in London during the 1820's of Marie Sophie Taglioni, whom Thackeray called "the most beautiful and gracious of all dancers," an Italian element, always present abroad, came into the London ballets; but the species remained obstinately French. Not until a century later did English composers begin to take it seriously, and then their inspiration came not from France, where during the nineteenth century the ballet became effete from an excess of conventionality, but from Russia.

The musical stage might have been re-invigorated by the influence of literary romanticism, if only a great composer had been present to respond to it adequately. As it was, the pieces adapted for that stage from the novels of Walter Scott amounted to nothing more than dramatized versions with incidental music or so-called operas which differed little from those versions except that they contained rather more music, though the scores were hardly more highly organized. Thus Bishop produced "Guy Mannering" in 1816 and "The Heart of Midlothian" in 1819, the Welshman John Parry wrote incidental music to a play based on *Ivanhoe* in 1820, and later, in 1832, Bishop came forward again with a *Waverley* "opera" and music for a *Kenilworth* play. Scott, by the way, was one of the organizers of a musical festival held at Edinburgh in 1815, an event repeated later though not permanently established. That same year Byron also came into touch with musical life: a Jewish singer and minor composer, Isaac Nathan, began to publish settings for voice and pianoforte of his "Hebrew Melodies." A similar service had already been rendered by an Irishman, John Stevenson, to Thomas Moore, whose "Irish Melodies with Symphonies and Accompaniments" were set by that musician and began to be published by William Power of Dublin in 1808. It was there, in 1818, that C. E. Horn produced an opera on Moore's

Lalla Rookh, with little success for himself, while the same year Kelly brought out a piece based on Byron's "Bride of Abydos" in London.

For the outstanding romantic English opera of the time the composer had to be sought abroad. Covent Garden, rebuilt in a handsomely porticoed classical style and reopened on September 18th 1809, a day less than a year after the fire, had hankerings after an opera that could seriously rival the works of Rossini, fifteen of which had been produced in London by the time "Oberon" was commissioned by the new theatre. The project was ambitious. The choice of a composer fell on Weber, whose "Freischütz" had become the talk of the town when Covent Garden (1824), Drury Lane (1824) and the Lyceum (1825) all produced English versions of it. The subject was to be one of literary pretensions, for the libretto of "Oberon" by the young critic James Robinson Planché was founded on Wieland's epic poem of the same name, which was itself derived partly from Shakespeare and partly from the old French romance of *Huon of Bordeaux*, which had been treated in English as early as 1534 by Lord Berners. Unfortunately Planché excelled neither in dramatic structure nor in poetry. Bearing in mind the admirable mechanical devices of the new Covent Garden stage and the spectacular displays which they led the public to expect, he turned his opera into a pantomime with as many changes of scene, transformations and scenic effects as possible. As for his verse, it must have been beneath even his own criticism. Sir Huon, virtuously resisting the charms of a bevy of oriental houris, is not above declaring that

> "There is no charm that can yield delight
> In the wanton's hand, be it never so white.
> Sooner its fingers should o'er me stray
> When the worm hath eaten the flesh away!"

Happily Weber knew very little English. What he did know he had in fact learnt especially in order to do justice to this commission. He was therefore quite unaware that Planché's words were sheer fustian, and so managed to write music to it that is glamorous and enchanting, if rarely as truly dramatic as it becomes in Rezia's great scene, "Ocean, thou mighty monster." What even he could not do with a libretto that suffered constant scenic interruptions and was cut up by spoken dialogue was to make a really organic and convincing whole of a work that remains fascinating by fits and starts. The overture is an admirable musical structure, devised according to his new way of building up symphonically a number of themes from the opera itself; but once the curtain has risen "Oberon" goes sadly to pieces, though most of the pieces are in themselves most engaging.

The first performance took place on April 12th 1826, after some vexatious rehearsing and preparing, which had included the re-writing of some of Huon's music to suit the convenience of Braham, who was now over fifty and could not sing the exacting part as Weber had intended it. One of the new arias interpolated for him is, not unnaturally, almost as poor as if, according to his old custom, he had written it himself. Still, Braham was in his way an artist. So were three at least of the women singers, Mary Anne Paton, then aged twenty-four, with whose Rezia Weber was delighted, Lucia Elizabeth Vestris, who sang Fatima, and a girl of twenty-one, Mary Anne Goward, who sang the Mermaid's song delightfully. Some of the artists were already experienced in Weber's style: Paton had sung Agathe in the "Freischütz" performances; Braham had been the Max at Covent Garden and Goward the Aennchen at the Lyceum. Another English singer who greatly pleased Weber was Catherine Stephens, who sang at a concert of his own a setting he made for her of "From Chindara's warbling fount" from *Lalla Rookh*.

Weber's visit stimulated some curious and questionable activities. Drury Lane, which had also been splendidly rebuilt and opened on October 10th 1812 with an address by Byron, was anxious to vie with Covent Garden in the production of a grand spectacular opera; but it succeeded in staging nothing better than Bishop's "Aladdin," which, although he had taken exceptional care over it, has no claim to remembrance, except perhaps as an interesting study for those who wish to trace the genesis of the many Christmas pantomimes of the same name. For it is a fact that the English pantomime contains in a debased form many features of opera, notably the hero played by a woman, who is quite plainly in the tradition of the long-extinct male soprano and has many forerunners and followers in later opera (e.g. Cherubino in Mozart's "Figaro," the pages in Meyerbeer, Verdi and Wagner, Octavian in Strauss's "Rose Cavalier," etc.). The traditional Dandini in the Cinderella pantomimes comes straight from Rossini's "Cenerentola."

Tom Cooke impudently adapted Weber's "Abu Hassan" and even "Oberon" itself, and added music of his own to them. That Weber remained unaware of these things may soften the tragedy of his London visit a little. He had arrived very unwell on March 5th, and the conducting of twelve performances as well as the rehearsals of "Oberon" and taking part in half a dozen concerts given by the opera artists and others so exhausted him that hasty preparations were made for his return home early in June. But it was too late. He retired to bed at the house of his host, Sir George Smart, in the evening of June 4th. The following morning he was found dead.

Some of the singers then in London were good musicians. Braham, after all, knew something about composition. Paton had appeared as an infant prodigy at Edinburgh in 1810, when she was eight years of age, not only as a singer, but as a pianist, violinist and harpist, and she had also published

some compositions. The age of wonder-children was by
no means past. An Irish boy of seven, Michael Balfe at
Wexford, who had already made great progress on the violin,
composed a "Polacca" and scored it without assistance. In
1824, when he was deputy leader at Drury Lane, he wished
to become an opera singer and went to Norwich to appear
in a garbled version of "Freischütz." Later he sang on the
stage in Italy. He turned naturally to composition and wrote
three Italian operas before his first English work, "The
Siege of Rochelle," appeared at Drury Lane in 1835. Other
musicians who showed gifts in early youth were John
Barnett, who began to compose at the age of nine and sang
on the Lyceum stage when he was eleven, producing a musical
farce, "Before Breakfast," there in 1825, when he was twenty-
three; and William Sterndale Bennett, who entered the
Royal Academy of Music, of which he was one day to become
principal, before he was ten.

Barnett became a more serious composer than his first
work had indicated. But he did not, any more than other
English composers of the time, do what even "Oberon"
was unable to do—improve English opera. It continued
gaily in its trivial round. The theatre of Sadler's Wells at
Islington, then a country resort, though within walking
distance of the City of London, famous for its dairies and its
mineral waters, now produced the real thing in pantomimes,
with the great clown Joseph Grimaldi as the chief attraction.
In 1819, for instance, an organist and composer named John
Whitaker wrote music for one of those heterogeneous entertainments, including "Hot Codlins," a song for Grimaldi
that took the town by storm and may be regarded as a kind
of link between the old London street-cries and the later
music-hall songs. A similar song appeared in Scotland in
1824, in the fifth volume of *The Scottish Minstrel*, a large
collection of Scots songs begun in 1820, published by Robert
Archibald Smith of Paisley under the auspices of Lady Nairne

and other noblewomen. Smith contributed many songs of his own, but the most familiar one, "Caller Herrin'," was a tune by Gow, previously known as an instrumental piece, but supplied with the well-known words by Lady Nairne.

Sadler's Wells was hardly more frivolous than the theatres in town. When they did not produce new pieces of the accepted light sort, which might be derived from the farces of Kotzebue or from the French *comédie larmoyante*, they continued to adapt works by foreign composers. Even Rossini's "Barber of Seville" was not light enough as it stood: it had to be adapted by Bishop for production in English at Covent Garden in 1818, though already heard in the original in the Haymarket. Trying to get grander and grander in competition with Italian opera, Bishop's adaptations went at last to the length of including Auber's "Masaniello" in 1824 and Rossini's "Guillaume Tell" in 1830. It is entirely characteristic of the unscrupulous procedures of the time that the latter work was given as "Hofer the Tell of the Tyrol." One suspects that the change to Andreas Hofer must have been made solely because the theatre happened to possess a stock of Tyrolese costumes, but no Swiss wardrobe. It may be added, if it matters, that the librettist was the egregious Planché. Rossini even suffered in the company of Scott: in 1829 the violinist and actor Michael Lacy made a libretto out of *Ivanhoe* (evidently the Rebecca episode), called it "The Maid of Judah," and fitted to it music from, of all incredible things, "Semiramide." The new romanticism affected even the lightest musical stage after "Oberon." An even greater curiosity than "The Maid of Judah," perhaps, was an operetta by the manager and musical director of the Adelphi Theatre, George Herbert Bonaparte Rodwell, the title of which was no other than "The Flying Dutchman." As late as 1833 the influence of "Oberon" showed itself in a ballet, "Sir Huon," written by Costa for the King's Theatre.

No one but a great native composer could save English opera from the encroachments the Italian variety was now beginning to make upon the London stage once more—the kind of composer who regards opera not as a living or a diversion, but as a mission. No such man existed. Revivals of stock pieces like "The Beggar's Opera" or "Artaxerxes" could do nothing, nor did Bishop succeed when for once he showed unusual taste by setting a libretto based on Thomas Love Peacock's "Maid Marian" in 1822, when the novel was as yet unpublished. Barnett had aspirations beyond his fellows, it is true, for in 1833 he went to Susanna Centlivre, the celebrated literary wife of Queen Anne's cook, for a libretto, taking her most famous comedy, "A Bold Stroke for a Wife," as his subject. But he was not a strong enough composer to impose such a new departure, and although his music pleased, the book was not to the taste of the time, a taste that could tolerate only the mildest unspiced fare. Barnett was unlucky, too, because that very year Italian opera received a fresh stimulant in London by the visit of Bellini, whose "Sonnambula" had already been produced in the Haymarket on May 1st and whose "Norma" was then given its first performance in England on June 20th.

The first great nineteenth-century Italian singer to reach England had been Giuditta Pasta, who appeared in 1817 in Cimarosa's "Penelope." She was only nineteen and had no great success, but she returned in 1824, when she made a sensation in Rossini's "Otello." Maria Felicita Garcia, the daughter of a great Spanish singer and teacher, came out at the Italian Opera in 1826. She was then eighteen, and her father gave her in marriage to an elderly French merchant named Malibran, whom she left the following year, never to return to him, though she sang under her married name for the rest of her short life. Rossini came to England with his wife, Isabella Colbran, another famous singer, in 1823 and was taken by the Russian ambassador to Brighton to be

presented to George IV, who greatly delighted in his music
and his winning personality.   About the same time Rossini,
who was greatly favoured by the patrons of the Italian Opera,
wrote two cantatas on the death of Byron, news of which
had come from Greece.   In 1834 a dazzling Italian girl-singer
of eighteen, Giulia Grisi, appeared in Rossini's "Gazza
ladra."

Not all singers of Italian opera were Italians.   Colbran as
well as Malibran was Spanish.   Paton and Maria Caradori
(later Caradori-Allen, an Alsatian) appeared at King's in
"Figaro," as Susanna and Cherubino, in 1822.   Henriette
Sontag, who made her first London appearance as Rosina in
"Il barbiere di Siviglia" in 1828, was a German.   On the
other hand, not all the new Italians were singers.   Michele
Costa started in that capacity by a mere accident when he
was sent by Zingarelli to conduct one of that master's works
at the Birmingham Festival of 1829 and found that he was
expected instead to sing the tenor part.   He made the best
of the situation and thereafter decided, no doubt, that it
would be safe to remain in England in any musical capacity.
At any rate, he became a composer and was appointed
conductor at the Italian Opera later on.

Again, all foreign opera was no longer Italian, or even
French.   In 1832 and 1833 a German company including the
great dramatic soprano Wilhelmine Schröder-Devrient and
the Austrian tenor Anton Haitzinger came to London with
Hummel and the French-born Hippolyte Chelard as conductors.   They produced Beethoven's "Fidelio" and Chelard's "Macbeth" among other works, besides starting the
horribly provincial habit of doing Mozart's "Don Giovanni"
in a German translation, which is tolerable nowhere but in
countries where that language is the vernacular.

Foreign concert artists continued to pay their visits to
London and the provinces.   Spohr was invited by the Philharmonic Society in 1820 to come and play one of his violin

concertos and conduct a new Symphony composed for the purpose. He was the first to conduct with a stick from a rostrum, and thus did away at last with the old *maestro al cembalo* habit, which however persisted much later at the Opera. Moscheles played for the same Society in 1821 and later made London his home. In 1824 Liszt arrived as a boy of thirteen to play at many private concerts in town and amaze everybody by his virtuosity and his improvisations. Paganini turned up at the Dublin Festival of 1831, where Vincent Wallace, the future composer of "Maritana," also played the violin as a youth of nineteen. The following year, Field, now aged fifty and almost a foreigner, returned from Russia as another visitor to the Philharmonic. He stayed long enough to be the chief mourner at Clementi's funeral in Westminster Abbey and to take part with Cramer and Moscheles in a Haydn centenary concert. Meyerbeer came to England for the first time later that year. In 1834 the Austrian pianist and composer Sigismund Neukomm settled in England and produced an oratorio, "David," at the Birmingham Festival. For oratorio, though moribund, was not dead: the festivals, who needed just that kind of work for their large choral societies and brilliant solo singers, saw to it that it was kept precariously alive by commissioning new specimens from composers to whom it was more or less congenial. In 1836 Julius Benedict, formerly a pupil of Weber's, also settled in London, at first as musical director of the Opera Buffa at the Lyceum Theatre.

The most important visitor, of course, was Mendelssohn; but since he belongs essentially to the Victorian age, little need be said about him in this chapter, which covers only a few noteworthy events of his earlier career. He first came across the Channel in 1829, at the age of twenty. A friendship with Attwood, who was forty-four years older, must have made him feel that he had come a little closer to Mozart. Between these two musicians was re-enacted, on a smaller

scale, John Stuart Mill's and Carlyle's tragedy of the manuscript of the latter's "French Revolution": Attwood left
the MS. score of the "Midsummer Night's Dream" Overture
in a hackney carriage and lost it.   It is said that Mendelssohn
re-wrote the work from memory without a single mistake.
He might, of course, have reconstructed it from the parts,
but that would have robbed him of the credit for a staggering
feat.   On May 25th he first conducted the Philharmonic,
of which he was made an honorary member later in the year.
He gave his C minor Symphony, characteristically replacing
the original minuet by the scherzo from the string Octet,
scored for full orchestra for the purpose.   A scherzo in 2–4
time may have been new to London, though it was anticipated by Beethoven; what was certainly new was the fresh
individuality of Mendelssohn's fairy music in this movement
and in the Shakespearean overture.

He played much at fashionable houses and became a
favourite in society.   It was largely due to his own social
standing and to his ease of manner that it began to be possible
for musicians to be asked to the homes of the great on terms
of something like equality, though as late as the Victorian
days it was no unheard-of thing for them to be admitted only
at the servants' entrance and roped off from the guests.   But
no doubt they did not always know that any other demeanour
except that of servility might be tolerated by their patrons.
Mendelssohn showed that a gentleman could be a musician
without loss of dignity and so started a tradition to which
an exaggerated importance has perhaps since been attached
in English musical circles.   A gentleman has as much right
to be a musician, if he chooses, as anybody else; what matters
more is that the musician should be, broadly speaking, a
gentleman, and very much more that, whatever else he is,
he should be a genius.

Mendelssohn went to York, Durham and Edinburgh
during his first visit, and then made a long tour of Scotland.

At Holyrood Palace he sketched the opening bars of the later "Scottish" Symphony and in the Hebrides he jotted down the opening of the "Fingal's Cave" overture, as it is actually called. This was produced at the Philharmonic during his second visit in 1832, first in a primitive and later in the present revised version. At that time Novello published Mendelssohn's "Original Melodies for the Pianoforte," the first book of what were afterwards the "Songs Without Words." The "Italian" Symphony was first heard during his fourth visit in 1833.

A few outstanding events of the early nineteenth century remain to be enumerated to tidy up this chapter. In 1816 Richard, Viscount Fitzwilliam, died at the age of seventy-one and left his valuable collection of music, books, paintings, engravings and other treasures to the University of Cambridge, with an annual income to be devoted to the erection and maintenance of a museum to house it. It included manuscripts of Elizabethan virginal music, later to be published as *The Fitzwilliam Virginal Book* (1899).

In 1822 the Royal Academy of Music was founded by a committee presided over by John Fane, Lord Burghersh (later Earl of Westmorland). A house in Tenterden Street, Hanover Square, was taken for the purpose, and there the R.A.M. remained until 1911, when it moved to its present building at York Gate. Crotch, then aged forty-seven, was appointed its first principal. He was succeeded by Potter in 1832.

Dublin established a Philharmonic Society in 1826, and in London the Sacred Harmonic Society was founded in 1832. That year Samuel Sebastian Wesley, Samuel's son, was appointed organist of Hereford Cathedral, though he was only twenty-two. Younger still was Clara Novello, Vincent's daughter, when she first sang at a public concert at Windsor in 1833, aged fifteen, and was immediately engaged by the Ancient and Philharmonic concerts and for the Worcester Festival. About the same time the tenor John

Templeton was chosen by Malibran to appear with her in Bellini's "Sonnambula," with the composer's full approval. In 1834 Edward James Loder came of age and reached the public with the production of his first opera, "Nourjahad," given at the opening of a New English Opera House. He had been a pupil of Ries at Frankfort. That year George Alexander Macfarren, who was born the same year as Loder, finished his studies at the R.A.M. and was immediately appointed professor. He produced a Symphony in F minor at a concert of the Society of British Musicians and brought out a picturesque overture of the kind suggested by Mendelssohn, "Chevy Chase," in 1836. Other young composers made their mark, though none with works that could be called great. Balfe's first English opera, given at Drury Lane in 1835, was "The Siege of Rochelle." It had an enormous success and was played continuously for three months. Although negligible musically compared with "Fidelio" or the "Freischütz," it showed at least an effort to improve on the common run of English opera of the time, and Malibran herself did not disdain a part specially written for her by Balfe in his next Drury Lane opera, "The Maid of Artois" of 1836. Another young Academy student, William Sterndale Bennett, produced a piano concerto there in 1835, at the age of nineteen, as well as one of those concert overtures, "The Naiads," a romantic piece that has remained valuable in spite of its mildness and is superior to Mendelssohn's weaker overtures. There was in fact no reason to doubt that Bennett could turn into an English Mendelssohn, which indeed he did to a certain extent, and he was therefore sent to Leipzig to continue his studies. The pianoforte firm of Broadwood offered to pay the expense of a year's study. Bennett not only made friends with Mendelssohn and Schumann there, but had some success with his compositions, even at the austere and exclusive Gewandhaus concerts.

Towards the end of William IV's reign, in 1836, Dickens came into touch with musicians. He married the daughter of George Hogarth, music critic of *The Morning Chronicle*, then engaged on the writing of his *Memoirs of the Musical Drama*, and he met John Hullah, a young man of twenty-four who studied singing at the R.A.M., but was an amateur as a composer, as Dickens may be said to have been at verse. Nevertheless, the upshot of the acquaintance was an opera, "The Village Coquettes," with a libretto by Dickens and music by Hullah. It was even produced, though without success, at the St. James's Theatre.

The last great Italian singer to come to England before the death of William was the bass Luigi Lablache, who appeared at the King's Theatre—so soon to be the Queen's. What is more, he became singing-master to a young girl of seventeen who is now to come very prominently into our picture, out of the seclusion of Kensington Palace. She was no other than the king's niece, Princess Victoria, who succeeded him with dramatic suddenness on June 20th 1837.

CHAPTER IX

The Victorian Era (1837–1880)

The age of Queen Victoria, of which the earlier and most characteristic years only fall within this chapter, is as a rule held up to scorn by the modern world, when it does not happen to be the fad of the moment in Chelsea or Bloomsbury. It is regarded as all that is prim, priggish, tasteless and middle-class. True, the rise of industrialism and the power of mere wealth resulting from it gave the more fortunate, the cleverest and also sometimes the least scrupulous members of the middle classes their chance to dictate to many people, artists included; and money alone being incapable of raising either taste or sentiment above mediocrity, this new influence undoubtedly encouraged a great deal of valueless production of all kinds. The arts took their share, and more than their legitimate share, in commercial enterprise.

All the same, the period was very far from being one of mere shallow material indulgence. It was after all the period of Palmerston, Disraeli and Gladstone; the period of the penny postage, the steam engine and compulsory education; of Faraday and Darwin, Livingstone and Florence Nightingale, Spencer and Huxley; of a literary galaxy not easily rivalled anywhere or at any time, including Carlyle, Ruskin, Macaulay, Browning, Tennyson, Dickens, Thackeray, the Brontës, George Eliot, Meredith.

Music, however, represented the earlier Victorianism at its worst. It must be said that the period at which we have now arrived is the nadir in British music, so far as actual artistic production, as distinct from an active musical life, is concerned. That it was merely the darkest hour before dawn does not concern us for the moment, though it will become significant before long. There were many accomplished composers, some of them well fitted to please the taste of the day, and there were a few with positive if mild tastes of their own: there was no outstanding genius comparable with the best composers who were now active or beginning to be active on the Continent, among whom were, in order of age, Berlioz, Mendelssohn, Chopin, Schumann, Liszt, Wagner and Verdi. There was not even an established master of the second rank like Cherubini or Spohr, much less a champion of musical nationalism like Glinka. That there was no operatic composer comparable with Spontini, Auber, Meyerbeer, Rossini or Donizetti is, of course, not to be wondered at in view of the state of the English musical stage. What seems much more surprising is that one British operatic musician, Balfe, came nearer to their status, even in continental opinion, than the present estimation of him would lead one to suppose.

Other evidences of appreciation of English musicians abroad were not wanting. Sterndale Bennett's Leipzig friendships bore fruit in the year of Victoria's accession in Schumann's "Études symphoniques," which were not only dedicated to Bennett but contained a tribute to his country: the finale contains allusions to Marschner's romantic "Ivanhoe" opera, "The Templar and the Jewess," where the original words are a tribute to England.

All sorts of musical cross-currents between the British Isles and the Continent showed themselves. The festivities attendant on the young queen's coronation included the visit of the elder Johann Strauss, who thus established the Viennese waltz in England as soon as the sovereign came to the throne whose name we somehow associate with the vogue of that dance in its most glamorous and musicianly ballroom cultivation. In 1838 Mozart's "Magic Flute" was given for the first time in English, the Papageno being no other than Balfe, who that same year produced a "Falstaff" opera at what was now *Her* Majesty's Theatre in the Haymarket. Julius Benedict, now firmly settled in London, brought out his first English opera, "The Gypsy's Warning," about the same time; and Loder, back from his studies in Germany, had an opera, "Francis I," done at Drury Lane. But this was mainly a publisher's advertisement, for it was hastily and loosely put together from a number of Loder's songs, which he was bound by agreement to turn out at the rate of one a week—a horrifying practice which, though in a modified form, has been known to cramp the inspiration of more than one composer still in our midst. If Loder had written fewer songs, it is possible that more of them would now be remembered. With one exception they are forgotten, perhaps undeservedly, for that exception, "The Brooklet," set to a translation of the second song in Schubert's "Fair Maid of the Mill," is so good that it could take its place in the Austrian master's cycle without loss of quality or incongruity of style.

Spontini at the age of sixty-four had the enterprise to come to England to study history and local colour for a second opera on the subject of Milton. It is a little difficult to imagine where he could have found the latter in Victorian England, which, though in some ways reverting at least outwardly to a Puritan England, was certainly not Miltonic. Musically it was so largely foreign that the Italian composer might just as well have relied on his imagination in any other surroundings. Still, in a modest way British folk music, or at least popular music, continued to be looked after. In 1838 William Chappell began to publish a collection of "National English Airs," edited by himself, and Paterson & Roy of Edinburgh brought out a third volume of their "Vocal Melodies of Scotland," to which another of those artistic-patriotic noblewomen, Lady Montague Douglas-Scott, contributed what has remained one of the most favoured of Scots pseudo-folksongs, "Annie Laurie."

In the coronation year, 1838, during which Strauss visited a large number of provincial towns and thus introduced a new type of light concert to many places, London began a new departure of the kind that was much later to grow into the most important means of popular musical cultivation. The English Opera House, as the Lyceum Theatre then called itself, established a series of Promenade Concerts on the model of those run very successfully in Paris by Philippe Musard, a conductor of dance music who took his profession as seriously as did Strauss. He came to London himself in 1840 to conduct a rival venture started at Drury Lane, but went over to the Lyceum the next year, Drury Lane finding a new attraction in Louis Antoine Jullien, an eccentric French musician nearly twenty years younger than Musard, who created a sensation at the "Concerts d'hiver" by displaying a judicious blend of the attributes of charlatan and genius. He had the discernment to include Beethoven in his otherwise rather frivolous programmes, but advertised it by using a jewelled baton for such occasions and by putting on a clean pair of kid gloves handed to him on a salver. The "Concerts d'hiver" were the answer to the "Concerts d'été," as Musard called his series at the Lyceum, which was more soberly conducted. It was pointed out by Thomas Hood as a curiosity that there was "no bit of a *Fop*" about the older of the two rivals.

Light entertainments more or less in the manner of those invented by Dibdin continued to be given. John Orlando Parry, a harpist, pianist and singer, took to this kind of production in 1840, when he also began a series of highly successful comic songs with one entitled "Wanted, a Governess." Three years later the stage baritone Henry Phillips gave table entertainments not only in England, but also in the U.S.A., and in 1844 Samuel Lover, an author, miniature painter and singer, who was obliged to give up writing and painting owing to bad eyesight, began a series of "Irish

Entertainments." Another venture of the kind came in 1855, described—very characteristically for the age—as intended for people who objected to or disliked the theatre. It was managed by Thomas German Reed, a pianist, conductor and impresario, and his wife Priscilla, a singer and actress, and held at St. Martin's Hall in Long Acre. It lasted long enough to give his first real chance to a young composer who did not object to the stage and was to write much for people who did anything but dislike the theatre: in 1867 they produced "Cox and Box," the libretto of which had been made for Arthur Sullivan by F. C. Burnand from a farce by Madison Morton.

But we return to the early years of the Victorian reign and its foreign musical traffic, to which perhaps in a sense the queen's marriage to Prince Albert of Saxe-Coburg-Gotha in 1840 may be said to belong. For the consort, who like his wife was then just of age, was musical in an intelligently dilettantish way. He was particularly attached to Mendelssohn, who produced the "Hymn of Praise" at the Birmingham Festival that year, and in 1842 was not only permitted to visit the royal couple, but to dedicate his "Scottish" Symphony, produced by the Philharmonic Society, to the queen. We may be sure that it was the gentlemanly Mendelssohn—and no doubt the wealthy Mendelssohn too—who showed Victoria that musicians could be regarded as members of society not beneath the notice of the highest in the land, provided that they knew how to mind their manners—and were not too poor to keep up appearances. And it was Victoria who came to admit that musicians might even be worthy of a knighthood occasionally, all things besides talent being suitable. Her first musical knight was Bishop, which perhaps went some way towards consoling him for the loss of his second wife who, twenty-eight years younger than he, had eloped with Bochsa, the harp virtuoso, in 1839. Whether her French lover compensated her for the loss of the rare distinction of being Lady Bishop may be questioned, for he was only three years younger than her husband and had a dubious reputation. (Bishop's marriage to Ann Rivière, who was a promising singer fresh from the Academy, had taken place in 1831, the year in which he had produced a piece with the ominous title of "The Romance of a Day.")

The queen, though not especially musical, was aware that a certain amount of interest in music would become her, if only for her adored husband's sake, and she was not unmindful of what was due to native composers. It was not her fault that she could not posthumously create a Sir William Byrd or Sir Henry Purcell, great masters who had remained plain "misters," and that even the eminent musician who, oddly enough, lent his name to the emblematic representative of the "unmusical" British nation was never Sir John Bull. Less illustrious though her musical contemporaries were, she did her best for them, according to her lights and according to the reports she had from her advisers; and however much favour foreigners of distinction found at court, state occasions were duly left for natives to celebrate. For the coronation it was Macfarren, then aged twenty-seven, who produced "An Emblematic Tribute on the Queen's Marriage" at Drury Lane and Bishop who brought out a topical stage piece—his last—entitled "The Fortunate Isles."

The home-bred musicians themselves could take their profession very seriously on occasion. When the young musical historian, lecturer and writer Edward Rimbault was instrumental in founding the Musical Antiquarian Society in 1840, Macfarren undertook an edition of Purcell's "Dido and Aeneas" on its behalf. The following year, when serious concerts began to be given in connection with the Reid professorship at Edinburgh University, the professor, John Thomson, not only conducted them but wrote analytical notes on the music, thus starting in a scholarly way a useful feature that has distinguished British concert programmes

ever since and found its most learned and witty exponent
in a much later Edinburgh professor, Donald Francis Tovey.
In 1843 Bishop became conductor of the Antient Concerts,
whose avocation is indicated by its title and emphasized by
the spelling of the adjective; and Sterndale Bennett instituted
a series of chamber concerts. The Handel Society also
flourished at that time, Macfarren editing several of Handel's
works for it. The cultivation of chamber music was further
upheld by the establishment of the Music Union in 1845, by
the violinist and critic John Ella, whose aim it was to have
classical chamber works performed by the best artists that
could be found. Ella also wrote his own programme notes.
Another series described as Classical Concerts was given at
the magnificent fifteenth-century Crosby Hall in Bishops-
gate, by Ann Sheppard Mounsey, one of the few women
organists of distinction recorded by musical history.

London was not alone in these praiseworthy endeavours.
A small body of amateurs at Cambridge founded what at
first they called the Peterhouse Musical Society in 1843 and
began to give concerts at the Red Lion in Petty Cury. It
was from this organization that the Cambridge University
Musical Society was to spring later.

Meanwhile the Philharmonic Society, settling down to
comfortable middle age, was becoming smugly conservative.
The orchestra, consisting of musicians of standing and in too
many cases of advancing years, felt that it had nothing to
learn and showed a polite but stubborn hostility towards
new ideas. Even Mendelssohn, whose conducting does not
seem to have been in the least revolutionary, and whose
conduct was always beyond reproach, asked too much in
1844, when he introduced a symphony by the young Danish
composer Niels Gade, to whose work one could now object
only on account of its excessive tameness, and the orchestra
became unpleasantly refractory at the rehearsal of Schubert's
C major Symphony, which Schumann had not long before

G

come across in Vienna and Mendelssohn had enthusiastically taken up. No doubt the many dignified string players objected to being kept hard at it in the finale playing pages and pages of mere accompaniment. However, the Philharmonic remained enterprising in bringing forward promising new artists at an early stage of their careers. That same year it not only engaged the Italian cellist Alfredo Piatti, who was then twenty-two, but also a boy violinist of Hungarian extraction, aged thirteen, who gave the highest promise—Joseph Joachim. These two artists were often to combine later in giving London and other cities some of their finest experiences in chamber music. Joachim was actually brought to England by Benedict, who invited him to his own series of concerts, for which he also engaged Offenbach, who first came over, not as a composer of operettas, but as a cellist. Among the great instrumentalists of the time who visited England, Scotland and Ireland was Liszt; he played in many towns in 1840, gave three concerts in London and appeared before the queen at Windsor.

Foreign operatic artists continued to come out. 1839 saw the first London appearance, at Her Majesty's, of the great tenor Mario and a remarkable mezzo-soprano of eighteen, Pauline Garcia (later Viardot-Garcia). For Italian opera persisted in its fashionable course at the Haymarket, until it transferred itself in 1847 to Covent Garden, the interior of which was reconstructed for the purpose. The works of Rossini, Bellini and Donizetti formed the backbone of the repertory, the chief *chevaux de bataille* for new sopranos being the heroines in "La Sonnambula" and "Lucia di Lammermoor." There was a sprinkling of early Verdi in the forties, but Verdi was disliked by the two chief critics, Chorley and Davison, who chose to take offence at the crudity of such works as "I Lombardi" and "Ernani" rather than recognize their vitality and directness. The public took to him the more slowly because he happened to be unfortunate with a work written especially for London in 1847, "I Masnadieri," a lurid melodramatic piece based on Schiller's callow schoolboy drama, "Die Räuber." Even the fact that the work contained a part for Jenny Lind, who had shortly before made her London début in Meyerbeer's "Robert le Diable," did not save it, and Verdi left England disappointed as an artist, though fascinated by the life of London.

No sooner had Covent Garden begun its career as an Italian opera house, with Costa transferred to it as conductor from Her Majesty's, than Drury Lane opened as an "English Opera" under French management (Jullien's) with a translation of an Italian work, "Lucia," the Scott subject of which, however, was perhaps considered as making it British. What is significant is that it was done in English and that a new tenor, Sims Reeves, just back from a course of study in Italy, made his first London stage appearance in it, after an earlier tentative venture as a baritone at Newcastle-on-Tyne. He also sang in Balfe's latest work, "The Maid of Honour," produced at Drury Lane in December 1847, soon after the opening of Jullien's enterprise. Balfe's best and only enduring opera, relatively speaking, "The Bohemian Girl," had already come out at Drury Lane on November 27th 1843, followed on November 15th 1845 by its close rival, Wallace's "Maritana." The two Irish composers were now settled in London again, after Balfe's successful visit to Paris and Wallace's ten years' travels in many parts of the world. A third Anglo-Irish opera of the same kind, though the composer was German by birth, was Benedict's "The Lily of Killarney," based on Dion Boucicault's "Colleen Bawn." It was produced in 1862.

"The Maid of Honour," it is amusing to recall, was conducted by another Frenchman, who had been engaged by Jullien, and a very eminent one—Berlioz. He came to know

London and its musical life well from now on—too well, as he had sometimes reason to think. However, it was Jullien who failed him, mainly, for the "English Opera" collapsed in 1848 and his engagement was abruptly cut short. Of his reception as a composer he had no reason to complain. A concert of his own works given at Drury Lane earlier that year was so successful that the same programme had to be repeated at the Hanover Square Rooms, a huge and exacting one containing the "Carnaval romain" and "Benvenuto Cellini" overtures, "Harold en Italie" and fragments of the Requiem, "Faust" and the "Symphonie funèbre." Interminably long performances, however, were the order of the day, and it was largely owing to the feats of endurance imposed on their audiences by the provincial festivals—once in three years, after which they could go to sleep for all the charitable committees cared—that the British public acquired the habit of listening to music for hours on end, or to make a show of well-bred attention when listening was no longer possible. Mendelssohn's "Elijah" is in itself a long enough work to satisfy any hearer for a day, but its production at the 1846 Birmingham Festival started the tradition of giving it as a rule at such demonstrations of musical gluttony, where it is preceded or followed by at least one other full-length concert.

The performance that set on its endless career a festival work which comes second only to Handel's "Messiah" in the affection of an unwaveringly loyal public was conducted by Mendelssohn himself. The principal soloists were Maria Caradori-Allen ("so pleasing, so pretty, so elegant—so slovenly, so devoid both of soul and head," wrote Mendelssohn in comic exasperation), Maria Hawes, Charley Lockey, a promising young vicar-choral at St. Paul's Cathedral, and the Austrian bass Joseph Staudigl. The following year Mendelssohn came again—for the tenth and last time before his early death—and not only went to court, but played at the Prussian Embassy, where Gladstone was in the audience.

Other famous visitors from abroad at that time were Spohr, whose luscious oratorios had by then become fashionable, and a second genius destined for a premature death very soon afterwards—Chopin. He had already paid a visit to London earlier, but had then seen hardly anybody apart from the Broadwoods, in whose pianofortes he was much interested, and had not appeared in public. In 1848, however, he came at the suggestion of his Scottish pupil Jane Stirling and, though already gravely ill, played at many private houses and gave recitals at Manchester, Glasgow and Edinburgh before he went to stay for a rest-cure at the country estate of Jane's brother-in-law, Lord Torphichen, in Scotland. On his return to London he made what proved to be his last public appearance at a Polish ball and concert at the Guildhall on November 16th.

Berlioz next came to London in 1851, sent by the French Government to report on the musical instruments at the Great Exhibition. It was the age of exhibitions, one of the less disagreeable manifestations of an era of commercialism. If not disagreeable, the craze was monstrous. Everything was done on a vast scale, like some of Berlioz's compositions, one of which he would doubtless have dearly loved to perform with a chorus of 3,000, an orchestra of 500, several brass bands and an accompaniment of cannons and mortars in the vast edifice of iron girders and glass (that it was crystal was only a pretence) which had been erected in Hyde Park. But the Crystal Palace was not then available for music, and the only French choral work done in London that year was the "Messe solennelle" by Gounod, who at the age of thirty-three had been invited by John Hullah, the work being given by Hullah's recently established school of choral singing for schoolmasters, which had begun in 1847 with four concerts illustrating the evolution of English vocal music.

That music was now in rather a bad way. Just as English opera had been able to produce nothing more impressive than "The Bohemian Girl" and "Maritana," so English oratorio, content to be outshone by "Elijah," yet mildly stirred to emulation by it, could muster nothing more lasting than such works as the Norwich Festival produced in 1852: "Israel Restored" by William Bexfield and "Jerusalem" by Henry Hugo Pearson (who later went to live in Germany and called himself Pierson). There was much controversy as to the relative merits of these two works, and Macfarren wrote an article on "Jerusalem" in *The Musical Times*. For all that, they are long forgotten. But if no choral works of great value came from British composers, choral singing flourished as much as ever, thanks not only to the festivals, but to the foundation of various choirs that went on ceaselessly up and down the country. Even those who could not read music were encouraged to sing together by the invention of the Tonic Solfa system, based on the old solmization, by John Curwen, a Nonconformist minister and educationist, who in 1853 founded the Tonic Solfa Association to promote its dissemination.

In the Exhibition year the New Philharmonic Society was formed as a more progressive rival to the organization which had by then reached its thirty-eighth season. It did not outdo the old Philharmonic in audacity by asking Spohr to conduct in 1853, when he was nearly seventy; but perhaps the opportunity was merely taken because he happened to be in London for the production of his "Jessonda" at Covent Garden—in Italian, of course, as all operas were done for a long time to come, even Wagner's "Lohengrin" and "Mastersingers." More adventurous was the engagement of Berlioz two years later, for although he was then fifty-two, he had remained as modern in his outlook as anyone, not excepting Wagner, though the latter was ten years younger. Wagner came that same season (1855) at the invitation of the old Philharmonic Society. He and Berlioz met and liked each other personally, though they had little use for each other's work. Much nonsense has been written about their mutual commiseration for being at the mercy of the London orchestras. Those orchestras were highly competent, and if the old Philharmonic players were inclined to ride the high horse and tried to keep foreign musicians whom they knew to be very well paid for their engagements in their place, Wagner was the last man to stand any nonsense of that kind and quite capable of looking after himself, especially as he had no wish to ingratiate himself with anyone in England. One gathers, in fact, that he went out of his way to ask for trouble by making himself as disagreeable as possible. Adulatory biographers have wasted their pity on him for being constrained to spend his valuable time on the rehearsing of music in which he had no interest; but he knew from the beginning that he was not accepting the engagement for his enjoyment, but simply because he was in need of money, and it is absurd to look upon him as a saintly martyr because he was expected to keep to the terms of a contract of which he was perfectly well aware from the first. Besides, he could disguise his feelings quite amiably when he chose. He took any amount of trouble over a symphony by old Cipriani Potter, whom he happened to like, perhaps because he found in him a man who had known Beethoven or perhaps only because Potter was appreciative and deferential. As for Wagner's criticism of the humdrum orchestral playing, it may have proceeded from his dislike of ways he recognized as due to the influence of Mendelssohn, whom he had had good reason to distrust; and one cannot help suspecting, on weighing the evidence in a matter so difficult to judge as the conducting of the past, that his handling of the classics, though admirably justified by his own notions and literary discussions, must have been not only unorthodox enough to upset a conservative orchestra, but wildly wrong-headed according to modern ideas. There is no doubt that he played fast and loose with tempos and dynamics, which may have been excitingly venturesome as a reaction against Spohr and Mendelssohn, but no less reprehensible than what one fancies must have been the latter's lifelessly correct readings. What makes one doubtful is that Wagner thought even Berlioz disappointing as a conductor. It is difficult to imagine Berlioz as erring on the side of conventionality.

On the other hand it must be borne in mind that Chorley and Davison were probably unjust to Wagner, as they had been to Verdi, in their criticism. Whether that was due to his perfectly well-justified refusal to call on them may be doubted. It makes a good, dramatic biographer's tale of virtue and villainy, and one perfectly credible in countries where so iniquitous a custom prevails. There is no evidence that it had any existence in the London of Wagner's time except possibly in his own and his satellites' imagination. If it did, it has happily not survived. No critic can prevent artists from calling on him if they are misguided enough to do so, but they will merely find that they have made it more difficult for him to give them unqualified praise.

Of his reception by the public Wagner had no reason to complain, nor could he have thought the queen and the prince consort wanting in breadth of mind when they came to one of his Philharmonic concerts, seeing that he was living in exile in Switzerland after his revolutionary participation in the continental turmoils of 1848. Even the wickedly sensual and starkly modern welter in the "Tannhäuser" overture seems to have pleased rather than shocked them, for they demanded to hear the piece a second time.

The old Philharmonic continued to engage eminent foreign artists as soloists. In 1856 Clara Schumann, compelled to earn her own living by the tragic mental collapse of her husband, appeared twice, and in 1857 came Anton Rubinstein. At the Italian Opera, too, great singers continued to come forward: Therese Tietjens in 1859, Adelina Patti in 1861 and Zelia Trebelli in 1862. The stage was still the place where women could become musically active with the greatest ease and at the earliest age. Patti was eighteen when she came to Covent Garden; Clara Schumann was thirty-seven before the Philharmonic engaged her. As for composition, it was almost freakish for a woman to take to it, although about the seventies Alice Mary Smith (Mrs. Meadows White) did so, writing chamber music and other works, including a clarinet concerto. While Louisa Vinning, a young soprano, sprang instantly to fame on taking the place of an indisposed singer at a performance of "Messiah" in 1856, Elizabeth Stirling, who was of the same age as Clara Schumann and well known as a pianist and as organist at St. Andrew Undershaft, found that a Psalm setting for five voices and orchestra submitted for the Mus. B. at Oxford, though highly approved of by the examiners, was powerless to remove the rule that women should be ineligible for the degree. However, less than two years later a colonel's wife was delivered of a daughter who was to secure not only a Mus. B. but a Mus. D., to compose *con furore* and to see to it that her works, approved or not, were performed. Her name was Ethel Smyth.

The monstrous structure for the 1851 Exhibition had been a miraculous engineering feat in Hyde Park. What was even more marvellous about the Crystal Palace was that it proved to be collapsible and transportable; for it arose again on a commanding site at the top of a slope at Sydenham for the purpose of housing a number of more permanent exhibits and of making a new popular resort rather on the lines of the eighteenth-century pleasure gardens, but with acres of indoor space in which people could walk themselves tired by merely going round once. There were buildings within the buildings which almost disappeared, including a theatre and a concert hall; there was an ornamental garden and there were incredibly lavish fireworks out of doors; all the rest took place inside that gigantic conservatory, which in due time became a sort of monumental epitome of all that Victorianism stood for, gradually grew more and more shabby and deserted, and finally, in November 1936, ended in a fire which put even its grandest pyrotechnic displays of the past in the shade. There had, of course, to be music. In 1855 a German bandmaster who had been engaged to take the problem in hand, no doubt originally with the idea that he should give performances with a military band, started the orchestral Crystal Palace Saturday Concerts, which turned out to be classical affairs of good standing. For August Manns, an enterprising young man of thirty, was an excellent musician anxious to cultivate the best orchestral music, which he did not only by performing masterpieces of the past, but also by adding to them first performances of new works by promising British composers. In 1862, for instance, incidental music written for Shakespeare's "Tempest" by Sullivan, who was then twenty, was given by Manns with such success that it was afterwards taken up by the Hallé Orchestra at Manchester, established by the pianist and conductor Charles Hallé for use at an exhibition held there in 1857 and afterwards retained. Sullivan had written the music, not for a performance of the play, but as an exercise during his student days at Leipzig, where he had gone after an excellent training in the Chapel Royal and at the R.A.M.

But some time before that the Crystal Palace had become a centre of a live musical culture. In 1856 its secretary, George Grove, a man of extraordinary versatility in science, literature and music, had begun to write analytical notes of great value for Manns's concerts, the first being a commentary on a Mozart centenary performance. The following year a kind of Victorian musical monster exhibit was tried out: a Handel Festival on a scale that would have satisfied even Berlioz, especially if one of his instead of one of Handel's works had been given. Although only the transept of the palace was set aside for it, even that alone made incomparably the largest concert-hall any sane musical person could possibly wish to conceive. The experiment was deemed successful, as indeed it must have been according to the notions of those days. It was repeated in 1859 as a commemoration of the centenary of Handel's death and thereafter became a triennial event, like the provincial festivals, to which one at Leeds had been added provisionally in 1858. There was, needless to say, no chance to achieve balance between the massed choirs, the orchestra and the soloists, and the performers were so widely scattered and so far from the audience that even unanimity was difficult to obtain and delicacy of effect impossible; but at their moments of climax these functions were impressive.

The Crystal Palace, of course, needed an enormous organ, and got it. Organ recitals became one of its features. Elsewhere too they were popular, and good organ playing had become widespread in England, the Wesleys having done a great deal to spread the cultivation of Bach. Among the exponents of the instrument the Liverpool organist William Thomas Best easily justified his surname. He had published a "Modern Organ School" in 1853, come to London to play regularly—and characteristically for the period—at the Panopticon of Science and Art (in another word, waxworks) in Leicester Square and to become organist at the neighbouring church of St. Martin-in-the-Fields, only to return to Liverpool as organist of St. George's Hall. What was "modern" about Best's performances was his daring method of registration and his talent for arranging elaborately scored orchestral works. John Stainer was another musician who early distinguished himself as an organist. He was only sixteen when the Rev. Sir Frederick Gore Ouseley founded St. Michael's College at Tenbury as a school for the training of church choristers in music and giving them a classical education, yet it was he who was appointed the first organist there.

An even more important series of concerts in some ways than those at the Crystal Palace was that of the Popular Monday Concerts, affectionately called the "Monday Pops" and so referred to even in such a classic as "The Mikado." They were founded in 1858 and held at the new St. James's Hall, opposite the church of that name, on the site now occupied by the Piccadilly Hotel. There was a great and a minor hall, the former not too "great" to make it an ideal place for chamber music—or so it would have been had not the occupants of the minor hall, the Christy Minstrels, sometimes threatened to make themselves heard where they were not wanted. Between the opening of St. James's Hall and its destruction in 1905, few of the greatest and most serious musical performers in Europe failed to appear there at some time or other, or would have refused to do so if they had been asked. A similar series of concerts was offered on Saturday afternoons.

In 1862 an International Exhibition brought three distinguished foreign composers to London as representatives of other nations. France chose the veteran Auber, who was eighty; Germany, oddly enough, sent Meyerbeer, with his Italianized name of Giacomo and those out-and-out French grand operas to his credit; Italy made the obviously right choice of Verdi. England itself was represented by Sterndale Bennett, who was now Professor of Music at Cambridge and set an Ode especially written by Tennyson to music for the occasion. Meyerbeer wrote an overture containing the tune of "Rule, Britannia" and Verdi composed an "Inno delle nazioni" in which national anthems appeared in contrapuntal combinations.

Several boys showing exceptional musical promise appeared in various parts of the country. At Edinburgh Alexander

Mackenzie was so promising on the violin that he was sent to Germany at the age of ten and before long played and conducted there; Frederick Cowen also was taken there to study when he was thirteen, though he had already won a scholarship in London; at Worcester Edward Elgar picked up astonishingly wide and varied knowledge in his father's music shop; at Bradford Frederick Delius, the son of a wealthy manufacturer of German provenance, improvised at the piano and was able to hear the best artists of the day in his own cultivated home. At Eton Hubert Parry, the son of a Gloucestershire country squire, showed uncommon talent for composition. An organ fugue on three subjects, written by him at the age of seventeen, was performed by George Elvey, the organist of St. George's Chapel in Windsor Castle, in 1865. Three years later Parry went to Oxford, where in 1872 he, with Charles Lloyd, another undergraduate with a musical career before him, founded the Oxford University Musical Club. Meanwhile Charles Villiers Stanford, the gifted son of a Dublin lawyer, went to Cambridge as organ scholar in 1870 and three years later became organist at Trinity College. Thus, although the mid-Victorian period still went on without showing any striking events in musical creation, it stored up rich promise for the not far distant future.

For the moment, in the sixties and seventies, the composer who attracted the greatest attention, Arthur Sullivan, was a remarkable personality enough, though not a great one. Greatness was later to be thrust on him in a way that he certainly neither expected nor desired in his early days. The ballet he produced at Covent Garden in 1864, at the age of twenty-two, "L'Ile enchantée" (ballets still had French titles), doubtless interested him far less than the "Kenilworth" cantata sung at the Birmingham Festival that year or the Irish Symphony he wrote for a visit to Ireland; and he did not feel a sufficiently strong bent for the stage to finish his first attempt at opera, "The Sapphire Necklace." In 1866, when he was appointed professor of composition at the R.A.M., his new cello Concerto was played by Piatti at the Crystal Palace and he wrote a concert overture, "In Memoriam," on the death of his father. Only then came his stage success with "Cox and Box," and the German Reeds also produced another piece of his, "The Contrabandista." But it was in 1871 that he first associated with the librettist whose name is inseparably connected with his own—indeed sometimes absurdly so, for people will talk even of a selection played by a seaside band as being "by Gilbert and Sullivan."

The new firm's first effort, "Thespis, or The Gods grown old," produced at the Gaiety Theatre, was not a success; in fact it was not until Richard D'Oyly Carte, who in 1875 managed a season of Offenbach operettas at the Royalty Theatre, invited the two to collaborate again in a one-act comic opera, that they really began their sometimes contentious but incredibly successful joint career. The little work was "Trial by Jury," and the first full-length operetta (for the species is not well described by the popular name of "Gilbert and Sullivan operas") was "The Sorcerer," which ran for a hundred and seventy-five nights at the Opéra-Comique in 1877, to be eclipsed only by "H.M.S. Pinafore" the next year, against which even Planquette's "Les Cloches de Corneville" at the Folly Theatre could not stand up.

It was in the operettas that Sullivan found himself, though he would never quite admit it and his friends persisted in misguidedly trying to persuade him that he was destined to achieve greatness in symphonies and oratorios—which he never did. He was, of course, a serious musician for all that. It was he whom Grove chose as a companion for an expedition to Vienna in search of Schubert manuscripts, which was as excitingly rewarded as Schumann had been when he found the C major Symphony. Indeed it was

Sullivan's admirable musicianship, combined with a nimble wit and an inexhaustible gift of invention, which enabled him to make his light stage pieces so durable. They are more finely wrought and orchestrated than anything done in the same line by Offenbach or the younger Johann Strauss, in whom it would also be vain to look for anything so technically accomplished as the fugal passages associated with the Lord Chancellor in "Iolanthe" or the many fine examples of contrapuntal combination of two distinct melodies. But Sullivan lacks something of the former's amusing impertinence and the latter's peppery verve, though he excels both in the enchanting delineation of gracefully high-spirited young girls. He can be tiresomely sentimental and occasionally rather stale; but it is very clearly evident that his lapses always coincide with Gilbert's own: with the librettist's unpleasant gibes at unfortunate characters, the weak dénouements of his last-act finales and the mawkish moods in which he sometimes indulged. What Gilbert did offer Sullivan was an endless and stimulating variety of metrical devices, which the composer not only matched but sometimes improved on in rhythmic resourcefulness, and a pleasing, not too harsh vein of satire that brought out Sullivan's delightful gift of musical parody, an aspect of his genius that cannot be fully appreciated by the public at large—and his public has always been very large indeed. It is by such things as the universally admired "Mikado" (marred only by Gilbert's sadistic treatment of Katisha), the rich musical solidity of "The Yeomen of the Guard" (almost miniature "Mastersingers" at times) and the musically most ample and as good as impeccable "Gondoliers" that Sullivan lives on, not by such an ambitious effort as the Worcester Festival oratorio of 1869, "The Prodigal Son," though it was sung by such grandees as Tietjens, Trebelli, Sims Reeves and Santley— the last now well on the way to becoming the greatest English bass-baritone—or even by the rather likeable "Golden

Legend." As for his hymn-tunes, they show him at his very worst.

Church music, indeed, which began to come under the deplorable influence of the American hymn-book compilers Sankey and Moody, was in even lower waters than any other during a period the discussion of which must now be wound up with a mere summary of a few more events that deserve attention. John Francis Barnett, a nephew of the John Barnett whom we have already encountered, tried to improve the festival cantata by his choice of good literary subjects, such as Coleridge's "The Ancient Mariner" in 1867 or Moore's "Paradise and the Peri," which had already been treated by Schumann, in 1870. Foreign visitors continued to come, including the Swedish soprano Christine Nilssen, who first sang at Covent Garden and the Crystal Palace in 1867; the Canadian Emma Albani, who appeared in 1872 in the stock part of Amina in "La Sonnambula"; Gounod, who like Napoleon III was a refugee in London during the Franco-Prussian war and stayed on for some time afterwards to make some contributions to the grandiose choral performances encouraged by the Crystal Palace and by another monster building, the new Royal Albert Hall, erected on part of the ground occupied by the 1851 Exhibition, at the suggestion of Prince Albert, part of whose memorial it formed after his death; and Anton Bruckner, then known even in Austria only as a remarkable organist, who played with Best and others at the inauguration of the Albert Hall organ in 1871 and was tempted to stay on in England. (One wonders, incidentally, what would have become of him as a symphonist if he had done so.)

The Royal Choral Society was twin-born with the Albert Hall, which has remained its home, and about the same time Joseph Barnby, the organist at St. Anne's, Soho, gave Bach's St. Matthew Passion—then almost unknown to London—at Westminster Abbey and instituted the long-lived annual performances of the St. John Passion at his own church, on a much more modest scale but in a manner that must have closely resembled the composer's own at St. Thomas's in Leipzig. In 1875 the Bach Choir was founded by Otto Goldschmidt, Jenny Lind's husband. In the country too choral singing was further encouraged by the establishment of the Bristol Festival in 1873 and the turning of the casual Leeds Festival into a triennial event.

Instrumental music and scholarship also advanced in 1874, when Mackenzie began a series of Classical Chamber Concerts at Edinburgh, and Ouseley and Stainer founded the Musical Association "for the discussion of the science and art of music," an organization that still functions, giving a series of scholarly lectures each year and publishing them in the "Proceedings" which by now make a valuable library of learned essays on a great variety of subjects. An important new teaching institution, the National Training School for Music, the immediate forerunner of the Royal College, was opened in 1876 with Sullivan as principal and Stainer, Ebenezer Prout and others as professors.

In 1877 Joachim was given the musical doctor's degree at Cambridge, and it was also offered to Brahms, who declined it, in spite of Joachim's urgent appeal to join him, for the sole reason that it had to be received in person and he could not face the idea of having to visit this country, though it had already begun to cultivate his work. Wagner, on the other hand, though equally disdainful, did not hesitate to come again when he was offered the chance that year of performing excerpts from his works at the Albert Hall. He cannot have greatly objected to meeting Browning, Burne-Jones, George Eliot, George Henry Lewes, Grove and others, to being presented to Edward, Prince of Wales, and Princess Alexandra at his third concert, or to being received by Queen Victoria at Windsor. He also condescended to sit to Herkomer for a portrait. Two other visitors of 1877, one of

whom, like Joachim, was always glad to come again, while
the other stayed eventually and became naturalized, were
Hans Richter, who acted as assistant conductor to Wagner,
and the baritone Georg Henschel.

The last two years of the period just discussed contain
two events that augured well for the future.   1878 saw the
foundation of the People's Concert Society for the purpose
of giving good music a hearing in the poorer parts of London.
This was taken over in 1887 by the South Place Ethical
Society, which has given admirable Sunday chamber concerts ever since, for long at South Place in the City of London
and later farther west, at the Conway Hall in Red Lion
Square.   It admits its audience free and contents itself with
a modest silver or even copper collection; yet innumerable
artists of repute have been happy to appear there.   In 1879
Grove published the first volume of his *Dictionary of Music
and Musicians*, the earliest English work of reference with
which no musical library in Britain or abroad can afford to
dispense. But altogether the future looked promising.
Not the whole of Victoria's reign was to be the darkest age
for British musicians.

CHAPTER X

The Renascence (1880–1900)

The beginning of the vast improvements in British composition which have led to its present rehabilitation is usually
dated from the production of a choral work by Parry, the
scenes from Shelley's "Prometheus Unbound," at the
Gloucester Three Choirs Festival of 1880. The landmark is
convenient, but must not be taken as a rigid demarcation
between a period of utter obscurity and another of sudden
enlightenment. There can be no definite borderline between
bad and good in art fixed by a date in its history any more
than there is a clean division between good and evil in
human affairs. Parry's festival work was not revolutionary.
It was remarkable for its excellent literary choice, though in
this matter it had been anticipated by J. F. Barnett and others,
and it showed a striking nobility of musical thinking, a constant regard for quality of texture and above all a very keen
understanding of English prosody, of how to handle it in
composition without damage either to the verbal declamation
or to the musical phrase.

All this was not by any means new to English music.
Older English composers had known all about texture as
well as word-setting: Purcell was past-master in both and
even a composer of the second rank like Henry Lawes had
been praised by Milton in a sonnet for having "first taught
our English music how to span words with just note and
accent," which, of course, was only partially true, for the
lutenists, for example, had been quite capable of impeccable
"spanning." But Parry revived these virtues and applied
them in a new way.

In other respects Parry was, after all, still Victorian, and he remained so to the end. His invention was tame, he had little creative passion and his orchestration was neutral and lifeless. He was often visited by magnificent notions, to begin with, but carried them on only by an infallible skill in knowing how to proceed technically, producing a steady glow without being able to keep the flame alive. A work or movement of his often begins by holding out the greatest possible promise—the thrilling opening of the Miltonic "Blest Pair of Sirens" is a familiar instance—but before long one listens only with interest and sympathy, unable to find oneself continually enthralled. He could always go on writing fluently and flawlessly, but he carried on a composition as an electric train continues to move for some time after the current has been shut off. One feels that he could sit down to composition at any time, whenever his busy administrative life left him an hour to spare; he enjoyed it like a physical recreation, and it has been said that his pleasure in handling fine English words would have led him to set the whole Bible to music, if he had only had leisure enough. None but his most devoted friends and grateful protégés, however—and there were many for whom his benevolent and helpful patronage remained a precious memory—could have wished that he had written more than he did, for if anything he wrote too much; and too much has been claimed for him, for his reputation rests in the last resort more on influence than on genius. In many ways his case is, *mutatis mutandis*, curiously similar to that of Mendelssohn. His amiability, his social standing and his scholastic authority secured him a large and enthusiastic if somewhat mixed following, and it was natural that many people sincerely thought that they were impressed by his work when in reality they had been won by his personality. All the same, to be comparable to Mendelssohn is no mean thing, and what Parry has done in helping to further England's musical regeneration amounts to a monument to his memory that will stand for ever. And several of his works will, after all, go on decorating that monument very aptly.

"Prometheus Unbound" did not stand alone, even in that one year 1880. Parry himself produced a piano Concerto and finished a string Quartet at that time, while Stanford wrote an Evening Service for chorus, orchestra and organ for the Festival of the Sons of the Clergy in St. Paul's Cathedral. Stanford, beginning to be as active as his immediate contemporaries, was then twenty-eight, and so was Cowen, whose "Scandinavian Symphony," his third, was heard at St. James's Hall. Mackenzie and Parry were thirty-three and thirty-two respectively. With them may be counted a musician who made an enviable place for himself in church and choral music: Charles Harford Lloyd, who was then thirty-one.

If we draw up a composers' calendar for 1880, we shall be astonished to find how much young blood there was in the British school, how much promise for the future and how little elderly respectability of the kind we associate with the period. A glance at the creative musicians surrounding these newcomers on either side will show that there was only one old stager left—Macfarren, then in his sixty-seventh year—that the only two middle-aged composers who counted had but just reached the riper years, Stainer being forty and Sullivan thirty-eight, and that on the other hand a whole bevy of youngsters and children were growing up who among them were in charge of a future of the most varied and in several instances incalculably rich promise. The following list of names, with the ages reached in 1880 shown in brackets, will need no comment to be revealing:

Ethel Smyth (22), Frederick Delius (18), Edward German (18), Arthur Somervell (17), Granville Bantock (12), Hamish MacCunn (12), John McEwen (12), Walford Davies (11), Ralph Vaughan Williams (8), Gustav Holst

(6), Samuel Coleridge-Taylor (5), Cyril Rootham (5), Donald Francis Tovey (5), Thomas Dunhill (3), Roger Quilter (3), Rutland Boughton (2), Josef Holbrooke (2), Frank Bridge (1), John Ireland (1), Cyril Scott (1).

One name, the most important of all, has been omitted. Edward Elgar was twenty-three, but although the eldest, not the most promising, so far as anyone then knew. Ethel Smyth had already studied at Leipzig and performed her first works among fellow-students and friends there; Edward German had already organized a band at his native Whitchurch in Shropshire; but Elgar, though he had attracted some local attention at Worcester, was rather left behind for his age. He was still constrained to find such instruction as he could by picking up technical books and scores at his father's shop. Luckily his was the kind of mind that thrives without outside stimulation, and he had the good sense to seek practical experience wherever he could, in whatever odd or humble surroundings. His organ playing at the Roman Catholic church, his visits to London when he could afford a few violin lessons—the only teaching he ever had— his playing the bassoon in an amateur wind quintet and conducting the band at the County Lunatic Asylum, with the attendants for players and the inmates for audience, all helped to make him an uncommonly versatile and resourceful musician. Fortunately both the quintet and the asylum band were so queerly constituted that he was forced to rearrange the music they wished to perform, with the result that he developed an extraordinary knowledge of instrumental technique and effect. He acquired such a practised hand at scoring that no orchestral problem ever presented him with any difficulty later in his career. Elgar's artistic opportunism is one of the great curiosities in musical history, and it is characteristically English. Indeed it is singularly significant that the only musician who became a composer of the front rank without any academic or other professional teaching belonged to a country which has so often succeeded better with improvisation than with organization.

There was nothing wrong with this period of the Victorian era, compared with the earlier phase of stagnation, so far as the enterprise of young composers was concerned. Why, then, do we persist in feeling that nevertheless there was something dreadfully wrong with it? The answer is that although it is a fact that composers were doing astonishingly well in paving the way for a great new evolution of creative musical art, musical life was still in a deplorably bad way. Musical life as a whole, that is, not the concert world, which was well enough provided for by artists many of whom fully deserved their great reputations, if not yet by a great permanent orchestra. The trouble was that the standard of taste among the public at large was lamentably low and that there was no central influence outside the circle of professional musicians and scholars to improve it. The church encouraged a liking for the most flaccid hymns, and the contemporary settings of the services were at best insipid, in the manner of—to name the most favoured religious work of the time—Stainer's "Crucifixion." The day schools did next to nothing and bestowed not even the sometimes doubtful blessing of "musical appreciation" on the children, nor had more than one or two of the public schools made so much as a beginning with the splendid modern cultivation of music which makes it incumbent nowadays, not only on Eton and Harrow, but on Rugby, Wellington, Oundle, Shrewsbury, Clifton, Uppingham and the rest to have their scholarly music master, their choir and their orchestra.

There was no adequate musical life in people's homes either, though there were numerous exceptions, of course. Here and there chamber music was lovingly fostered by families of musical leanings. As a rule, however, music was still deemed nothing more than a genteel accomplishment young ladies had better be induced to acquire in moderation. So maidens tinkled their prayers on the pianoforte and played, at best, Mendelssohn's "Songs Without Words" or, perhaps not at worst, Sydney Smith and "The Battle of Prague." Even that was preferable to their singing, an attainment thought to be within the reach of all who could open their mouths (not too wide!) and produce a few timid, piping notes which family affection was capable of finding attractive. A few young people learnt to sing, some from reputable and some from fraudulent teachers; the rest satisfied their parents' ambitions without ever having had a lesson. Great songs were seldom taught and even more rarely discovered by the untaught. What was generally sung was the vocal equivalent of Sydney Smith. For this was the period of the drawing-room ballad.

It is difficult to say where exactly lay the origin of the Victorian ballad, which later became Edwardian and even neo-Georgian, as those of us know who are unfortunately old enough to remember how our hearts used to sink when Jessie was encouraged to take her turn or Mabel was asked if she had brought her music. The ballads were partly the debased descendants of the more sentimental songs in the English operas or so-called operas of the preceding generation, partly watered-down Mendelssohn and partly of Italian provenance. For in 1880 two Italian writers of light songs were both settled in London: Paolo Tosti and Luigi Denza; and a third, Luigi Arditi, returned to England that year. Tosti's tearful ditties in particular pleased the young ladies, but were also quite unblushingly performed by the great celebrities of the day, who technically could have sung most of the present vocalists' heads off, but were often sadly deficient in any sort of musical discernment. Tosti was even appointed professor of singing to the royal family.

Arditi's "Il bacio" was a favourite and Denza's successes were also of the sentimental kind in many instances, though the greatest of them was that spicy Neapolitan canzonet, "Funiculì, funiculà," one of the most popular comic songs ever written. (Richard Strauss actually incorporated it in the finale of his "Aus Italien" symphony under the impression that it was a folksong; but then Germans have always had a surprisingly vague notion of what is and what is not a genuine folksong, even where their own national music is concerned.)

"Funiculì" was, of course, less often sung by young ladies than by gentlemen of various ages who had some vocal pretensions. For indeed gentlemen were sometimes allowed to sing too, and they usually had the two species of song reserved for them which were felt to be just a little too, too "forward" for a young woman to attempt: the comic and the religious. The fair sex sang almost exclusively about two things. One of them was LOVE (pronounced "Lohve" in obedience to Italianized teachers), the other was A GARDEN (sung "gardén"), though the moon and some roses were usually thrown in for make-weight.

It was in the music-hall, however, that the comic song spread itself most luxuriantly, and it was refreshing, if sometimes rather too breezy, to turn into one of these theatres, which bore so oddly unsuitable a name; for the "halls" were the last places where anybody would have thought of going for the sake of music. Here vulgarity in word and tune was rampant, and the "orchestral" accompaniment was brazen in the extreme. Still, the reaction of honest if sometimes unclean fun was not unhealthy, if it can be admitted that one bad thing will sometimes blot out another; in any case it was natural that the eternal simpering of the drawing-room song, and the archness of some of the songs in the lighter musical stage pieces too, should drive a large section of the public to a periodical orgy of indulgence in sheer blatant crudity, more particularly because it was often associated with capital fooling and always presented with a professional virtuosity that was in its own way as amazingly finished as the home performances were incompetent. One does not take such things as "Champagne Charlie" or "A Bicycle made for two" seriously as music, but there is no doubt that even in artistic vitality they surpass any amatory and horticultural ballad ever written.

In spite of all this, great English song-writing began to be cultivated once again quite early in the period of renascence. In 1881 Parry wrote the first two sets of his large collection of "English Lyrics," settings of an anthology of verse chosen with singular discernment from the great poets of the past and often turned into songs of much refinement, grace or exquisiteness; and the following year Stanford made a notable contribution by his profoundly musicianly arrangements of "Songs of Old Ireland." There were also, during those twenty years now under discussion, several minor writers who bridged the gulf between the ballad and the "art-song" with some charming work of an unpretentious kind. They included two talented women composers: Maude Valérie White and Liza Lehmann. Much more important were Arthur Somervell's settings of poems from Tennyson's "Maud," which have remained among the world's few great song-cycles. They are apt to the words, constructed as a symphonic whole and have eloquence, feeling and flavour.

Stanford's Irish birth and English upbringing blend attractively in his work. He is a natural singer with a much readier gift for a memorable tune than we ever find in Parry, for even in the latter's noble and justly popular setting of Blake's "Jerusalem," there is something laboured. This spontaneous songfulness in Stanford is admirably disciplined by fine schooling. In his best songs, such as the perfect "The Fairy Lough" and the unforgettable "A Soft Day," haunting melody is blended with the most beautifully finished accompaniments in such a way that the singer and player cannot resist doing a little more than their best. Stanford wrote much music of all kinds, including symphonies and operas, but it is with his songs, one or two choral works such as the fine "The Revenge," perhaps, and with some of his chamber music that he is most likely to survive, though the orchestral "Irish Rhapsodies" are far better and more musical things of their kind than Liszt's "Hungarian Rhapsodies," and the clarinet Concerto would be well worth a revival. The influence of Brahms, whom he revered, is sometimes too plainly evident in the chamber music to make it quite convincing as an individual enlargement of the repertory, and sometimes Stanford can be stolid or too obviously picturesque; but, himself a great teacher who handled mere experimentation severely without ever attempting to curb true creative originality, he is seldom academic in his own work. What he lacks is fantasy, sometimes even poetry, but even so he was the greatest composer who ever came out of Ireland. He narrowly missed, one cannot quite tell why, becoming an Irish Dvořák, as Mackenzie missed, rather less narrowly, being a Scottish national representative of that stature.

Like Parry, Stanford came forward in good earnest in the early eighties. Both had symphonies produced in 1882, Parry his first at the Birmingham Festival and Stanford his second, the "Elegiac Symphony," in London. The following year Mackenzie had his symphonic poem on Keats's "La Belle Dame sans Merci" accepted for a Philharmonic concert, and Elgar, who had joined Stockley's orchestra at Birmingham, at last appeared outside his native county with one of his own works, the "Sérénade mauresque." He toyed at that time with the idea of going to Leipzig to supplement his studies, but found that he could not afford to do so. It may have been just as well: Leipzig might have cost him more than money he could ill spare—his independence.

The habit of studying in Germany was on the decrease altogether, though Ethel Smyth was still at Leipzig and Somervell went to Berlin that year. Neither Parry nor Stanford had done more than pay brief visits to German teachers, and it was becoming quite possible to learn at home all a composer could need. Not only was the Royal Academy of Music an excellent teaching institution: in 1880 the Corporation of the City of London founded its own, the Guildhall School of Music, and two years later the Prince of Wales, at a meeting held in St. James's Palace, became president of the new Royal College of Music, which opened in 1883, with Grove, newly knighted, as director, in the building next to the Albert Hall now occupied by the Royal College of Organists. The R.C.M. moved to its own extensive building in Prince Consort Road in 1894.

If British composers no longer went to Germany merely to profit by its great musical organization, they now had to give it something of their own. In 1881 Stanford had his first opera, "The Veiled Prophet," produced at Hanover. The libretto was by the young musicologist William Barclay Squire, who in 1885, at the age of thirty, was appointed music librarian at the British Museum. Another of Stanford's operas, "Savonarola," was first heard at Hamburg in 1884 before it was conducted by Richter at Covent Garden. The same year the Carl Rosa Opera Company gave his third stage work, "The Canterbury Pilgrims," at Drury Lane. Several of Mackenzie's early works were also done in various German cities.

In the international musical exchange, however, England still had more to take than to give, as indeed a single country always will if it deals with a number of others. The outstanding composer who contributed several choral works to the musical festivals during the eighties was Dvořák, who came at least half a dozen times and wrote "The Spectre's

Bride" for Birmingham and "St. Ludmilla" for Leeds in 1885–6. During one of his visits to Birmingham, when he stayed at the Oratory, Cardinal Newman showed him "The Dream of Gerontius," which in a moment of rash enthusiasm he declared he would set to music. It is interesting to speculate what the Czech master, among whose surpassingly great gifts there certainly was no turn for mysticism, would have made of Newman's poem; it is almost terrifying for many people to reflect that he very nearly deprived them of a masterpiece of rejuvenated English oratorio.

English opera continued to languish, in spite of Stanford's good work, which failed to reach the public for lack of the kind of organization indigenous opera needs to remain alive. Given such an organization, together with a dramatic composer of Mozart's stature, the musical stage could have occasionally turned the elements of even its lowest entertainments to good account. The Christmas pantomime, for instance, could easily have given back to opera as much as it had taken: it might have engendered an English "Magic Flute" by as lucky a chance as its Viennese counterpart, the "fairy farce," had thrown up Mozart's German masterpiece. The operettas might have stimulated things as great as his Italian comic operas. Here it was only the lack of a composer disposed to take the writing of comic opera seriously, and perhaps the lack of a librettist as gifted as but less flippant than Gilbert, which withheld from us an English "Figaro."

Meanwhile the operettas were often very good. Sullivan's were supremely so in the eighties, but his was not the only deserved success. In 1886 Alfred Cellier made a great hit with the pretty "Dorothy," which had an enormously long run, and Frederick Clay had already produced many attractive though slight things of the kind, "Princess Toto" of 1876 being perhaps the best. It was in 1886, too, that Edward German, at the age of twenty-four, brought out a first operetta, "The Rival Poets." He came nearest to Sullivan in refinement and solidity of craftsmanship—and he in fact completed "The Emerald Isle," left unfinished at Sullivan's death in 1900—but he had no genuine comic vein and was deficient in Sullivan's spark of mischief. Neither could he parody a style; he could only imitate it without penetrating to its essence, with the result that his "Merrie England" of 1902 is a piece of sham Tudor. The names of one or two operettas later than the eighties having slipped out, two other purveyors of the species who deserve grateful recollection may be mentioned here: Sydney Jones, whose very well-made "Geisha" (1896) captivated even Germany, reaching its thousandth performance in Berlin alone by 1904, and Leslie Stuart, whose most successful piece was the tuneful "Florodora" (1899). Ballet found a gifted exponent of a more serious kind in Dora Bright.

Returning to the earlier years of our period, we find a good effort at more serious opera in Goring Thomas's "Nadeshda," produced by the Carl Rosa Company in 1885. Its Russian setting was engaging and it contains some excellent but not particularly dramatic music in a vein that rather improves and modernizes Balfe and Wallace. The Scottish composer Hamish MacCunn made some mark with two operas, "Jeanie Deans" and "Diarmid," in the nineties, but he is now remembered only for his fine concert overture, "The Land of the Mountain and the Flood," written at the age of nineteen and produced at the Crystal Palace in 1887, a work which admirably paints the Highland landscape and leaves the memory of its tunes behind long after a performance.

In the year 1887 came Queen Victoria's Jubilee. She was sixty-eight and had reigned for fifty years. Musicians took their part in the celebrations as a matter of course. Mackenzie produced a "Jubilee Ode," Stanford, now Professor of Music at Cambridge, set a "Carmen Saeculare" written especially by the Poet Laureate, Tennyson, and Covent

Garden, managed by Augustus Harris, arranged an exceptionally brilliant season, with Mancinelli as chief conductor.

Covent Garden was about to bring forward a new British
star of the first lustre, the Australian soprano Nellie Melba,
who had already sung Gilda in "Rigoletto" at the Brussels
Théâtre de la Monnaie in 1887 and came out in London the
following year, still in the traditional first-appearance part
of Lucia. Not musical or interested in anything but opera,
Melba was gifted with a phenomenal technique and a voice
as luscious as the sweet that was subsequently named after
her. Much the same criticism applies to the astonishing
contralto Clara Butt, who first appeared in 1892, except that
for "opera" in the preceding sentence must be read "oratorio"
and "drawing-room ballads." A few other outstanding
British singers of what was on the whole a great period for
them must be mentioned, such as the Irish baritone Harry
Plunkett Greene, who never had a great voice, but became
a surpassingly fine interpreter of songs, and the Welsh baritone
David Ffrangcon-Davies, a more dramatic singer, who came
out the same year as Greene (1890), while the tenor Ben
Davies, an exponent of impeccable *bel canto*, was then mainly
on the stage. In 1893 the striking and temperamental mezzo-
soprano Louisa Kirkby Lunn first made her mark in a Royal
College students' performance of Schumann's "Genoveva,"
as Clara Butt had done in a similar one of Gluck's "Orfeo";
in 1896 another mezzo with a most beautiful voice and
plenty of intelligence, Muriel Foster, first sang in Parry's
new "King Saul" at Bradford while still a College student.
This enumeration of singers may now be concluded with a
great quartet: the soprano Agnes Nicholls, the contralto
Ada Crossley, the tenor Edward Lloyd and the bass Robert
Radford. All these could have served as ideal models for
later vocalists, at any rate so far as technical perfection goes,
for their accomplishment is very rarely matched nowadays.
(For that reason, and also because of the impossibility of

discriminating fairly, it will be advisable to mention no later singers, or indeed other executive musicians from now on, except in cases where the latter may be intimately connected with some musical organization or enterprise that calls for notice.)

A few instrumental performers of the end of the nineteenth century, however, yet remain to be remembered. The profoundly musical pianist Fanny Davies, for instance, who at the age of twenty-four finished her studies with Clara Schumann in Germany, reappearing at the Crystal Palace in 1885 and for the first time playing at the St. James's Hall Monday Popular Concerts—the "Monday Pops"—musically alluded to by Sullivan in "The Mikado" with a quotation from Bach's "great" G minor organ fugue. Another fine Clara Schumann pupil was Leonard Borwick, who not only appeared in the Schumann Concerto at a Philharmonic concert in 1890, but played Beethoven at Frankfort and Brahms (under Richter) in Vienna. A young Scottish pianist, Frederick Lamond, had already played in Berlin at the age of seventeen and laid the foundations of a great international reputation when he appeared at Glasgow in 1886 and then gave several recitals in London. It may here be mentioned, perhaps, that Eugen (formerly Eugène) d'Albert too was born in Scotland, of French parents, and that he began his studies at the R.C.M., though during the war of 1914–18 he declared his own hostility to Britain.

Lamond was heard and highly approved of by Liszt, who came to London again in 1886, after many years, for a performance of his "Legend of St. Elizabeth." Among other foreign visitors of distinction about that time were Grieg and his wife, the former being engaged as pianist, conductor and composer by the Philharmonic, while Nina sang his songs at several private musical evenings. They had met Frederick Delius, aged twenty-five and just back from Florida, whither he had escaped from business at Bradford intending to cultivate oranges but unable to resist cultivating music instead. It was Grieg who urged Delius's father to allow the young man to take seriously to composition, with the result that he was sent to Paris to study as he felt inclined. At Covent Garden the de Reszkes, first Edouard and then Jean, began to appear, and in 1894 Puccini visited England and that theatre for the first time, when his "Manon Lescaut" was produced.

Four factors of importance to the renascence must not be overlooked: the revival of folksong (to be dealt with separately in the next chapter), the growth of competition festivals, a renewed concern with musical scholarship and notable developments in orchestral performance. The competition festivals are not held for charity or for the display of choral societies—another one was founded for the latter purpose at Sheffield in 1896 by the remarkable choral conductor Henry Coward—but for the purpose of giving amateur performers, including children, an opportunity of engaging in friendly contests and a chance of gaining a modest prize for an outstanding performance. The competitors were at first intended to be mainly choral bodies, but the movement inevitably extended to solo performers, both vocal and instrumental. The first festivals of the kind were those at Stratford (East London) and at Kendal in Westmorland founded by John Spencer Curwen and by Mary Wakefield in 1882 and 1886 respectively. The Kendal Festival quickly developed by the sheer enthusiasm of those who ran it and of those who attended, and in 1891 Somervell, himself a native of Westmorland, wrote "A Song of Praise" for performance there by the massed choruses and an orchestra which by this time formed part of the function. Many competitive festivals have since established themselves up and down the country, as at Blackpool or Leamington, for instance, and for days on end many hundreds of performers appear before adjudicators chosen from among the most distinguished pedagogic and administrative musicians, such as the late Geoffrey Shaw, H.M.'s Staff Inspector of Music.

The idea of such musical mass competitions was not altogether new, though Mary Wakefield's scheme carried it out in a new way. It had a very ancient forerunner, going back to the seventh century or beyond, in the Welsh Eisteddfod, originally a meeting of bards as exclusively professional as an ecclesiastical commission, but nowadays a competitive gathering on a vast scale, held each year at a different Welsh town. The Cornish Gorsedd is a similar institution with a pronounced Celtic bias, and so is the more important Irish Feis Ceoil, founded in 1897 and first held at Dublin that year.

As for scholarship, it was well upheld at the two senior universities. We have seen that Stanford was given the professorship at Cambridge; Parry succeeded Stainer in the chair of music at Oxford in 1900. Both these Oxford professors had by then done valuable literary work. Stainer's book on *Dufay and his Contemporaries* is a far more enduring monument to his memory than "The Crucifixion" or any of his tame church music, and Parry, who had already written *The Art of Music* in 1896, contributed a third volume to *The Oxford History of Music*, published under the general editorship of William Henry Hadow, a brilliantly versatile scholar whose interests ranged far beyond music, but who had been appointed lecturer in that subject at Worcester College, Oxford, at the early age of twenty-six in 1885. The *Oxford History*, which is now to be replaced by a *New Oxford History of Music*, was somewhat haphazard in plan; but it was a handsome testimony to the English scholarship that was taking on new vigour towards the end of the century, as indeed English music was doing altogether, even in the eyes of the world at large, for in 1891 it was possible for a German scholar, Willibald Nagel, to publish a *Geschichte der Musik in England*. Editing as well as authorship took its share: in 1889 the young musicologist Godfrey Arkwright began his

Old English Edition, a valuable collection of works by old masters which had been previously more or less inaccessible.

Criticism also improved. One of the contributors to the *Oxford History*, John Alexander Fuller Maitland, was appointed chief music critic to *The Times*, which has never since ceased to treat music generously and seriously. But the best critic of the time, or at any rate the best writer on music, was no other than George Bernard Shaw, who wrote for *The Star* in 1888–9 and for *The World* in 1890–4. Needless to say Shaw annoyed many people and, as in a different sphere since, meant to do so. His strictures on Parry and Stanford, for instance, who drew things much too mild for his Wagnerian taste, were taken as personal insults. But they cease to look suspicious if one remembers that Shaw wrote just as disparagingly about Brahms or Dvořák and realizes that he has always said precisely what he felt, rightly or wrongly, about anything whatsoever, with a detachment the like of which those who came under Parry's or Stanford's influence could not be expected to appreciate. Shaw was severe, outspoken and, if one likes, perverse; he was certainly not spiteful, much less capable of any sort of dishonesty. The future author of *The Perfect Wagnerite* was that already, seen from the egotistic Wagnerian point of view, when he wrote his musical criticism, and his major fault was that, like Wagner, he would see no good in any contemporaries, either because they really were the Bayreuth master's inferiors or, on the other hand, because they were his serious rivals. For the classics Shaw had a genuine feeling and understanding, his knowledge of Italian opera, acquired from his mother, was minute down to chapter and verse, his English was then as lucid as it has remained ever since and his wit at least as keen.

Orchestral conditions improved, particularly in London, Manchester and Scotland. Richter was appointed permanent conductor of the Hallé Orchestra in 1897, to the great benefit of the two largest Lancashire towns, for Liverpool as well as Manchester had the benefit of the organization; and in 1891 the Scottish Orchestra was founded for the purpose of providing Glasgow and Edinburgh, and in a smaller measure other towns in Scotland, with orchestral music. Henschel was appointed conductor in 1893, when the concerts actually started.

It was during that year that London opened its new concert hall, Queen's Hall in Langham Place, which remained the centre of orchestral music and the happy hunting-ground for innumerable new experiences until the fatal day it was destroyed in one of the air-raids of 1941. The place was ugly and uncomfortable, until the recent removal of most of the uncomeliness and the installation of beautiful lighting and luxurious seating; but it was acoustically perfect and had an atmosphere of studious seriousness that conduced to good listening. Its real beginning came in 1895, when Robert Newman was appointed manager and engaged an almost startlingly promising young conductor, Henry J. Wood, to direct a series of nightly Promenade Concerts in the summer and early autumn. Their programmes at first resembled those of the old "Concerts d'été," including light overtures and selections from popular stage works, introducing bassoon and euphonium soloists among others and encouraging singers to sing ballads and double them with more ballads by way of encores. But Wood soon saw to it that the public taste should be improved, as it was during all those years of an activity that did not cease with his death. The Queen's Hall Orchestra, from which in due course the London Symphony Orchestra stemmed while the earlier body was re-formed, gradually began to play classical programmes and, more than that, to introduce new music, among which that of Tchaikovsky was the earliest, quite soon after the Russian composer had paid two not very successful visits to the Philharmonic Society. Wood not only looked round for new continental works, but did his best to encourage British composers by bringing forward promising novelties, a policy he steadily pursued ever after. In 1897 things had advanced sufficiently to make it possible to add Saturday afternoon symphony concerts to the Queen's Hall enterprise.

Wood was not alone in defending the British composer's cause, which others too felt to be worth an effort. That Granville Bantock should do so was perhaps not surprising, since he was himself one of the composers who had something new to say. However, Bantock did a great deal for others. After a performance of some of his work at a students' concert at the Royal Academy he succeeded in having an opera, "Caedmar," staged at the theatre in the Crystal Palace and afterwards repeated at the Olympic Theatre in town. He was only twenty-four then. Four years later he gave an orchestral concert with a programme entirely devoted to young British composers. In 1897 he held a similar concert of chamber music, and when he was appointed conductor of the Tower band at New Brighton he did not rest until he had converted it into an orchestra capable of doing justice to the new works he was anxious to bring out, including his own, of course, but also those of other promising young people, such as Josef Holbrooke, an Academy student of ambitious talent and eccentric personality who had been sent packing when at a students' recital he played a piece of his own instead of that set down for him and afterwards spent much time wandering in search of any musical job he could manage to pick up.

Such orchestras were deplorable enough in those days, with the exception of that at New Brighton and another at Bournemouth, where the young bandmaster Dan Godfrey had been appointed in 1892. He too insisted on an orchestra and in course of time persuaded the town council that good concerts would attract more visitors to the flourishing seaside resort. For many years Godfrey gave weekly symphony concerts and championed new work, sometimes merely because it was new, but often with profit to music in general as well as to young composers. Harrogate, Torquay, Scarborough, Hastings, Eastbourne and other resorts also made efforts at various times to provide good performances.

The outstanding new works not yet mentioned that appeared in the last decade of the nineteenth century had better be briefly enumerated, since they decidedly belong to the renascence, whereafter that aspect of our story too will have to be left to the records of living memory. Ethel Smyth had a Serenade and an overture to "Anthony and Cleopatra" done at the Crystal Palace in 1890. German's first Symphony was also done there by Manns. The next year saw the production of Stanford's "Eden," a large choral work notable for being set to words by Robert Bridges. Stanford had as good a literary taste as Parry, one of whose large biblical oratorios, "Job," came out at the Gloucester Festival of 1892. That year Cowen produced an opera, "Signa," in Milan and German wrote incidental music for Irving's Lyceum production of Shakespeare's "Henry VIII," containing the dances which have remained so popular but exhibit his "olde Englishe tea-shoppe" manner at its most spurious. His second Symphony, a much finer work often curiously suggesting Elgar, was done at the Norwich Festival that year.

Another musical Shropshire lad, Walford Davies, when still at the R.C.M. in 1893, wrote an overture, set an ode by Milton and composed two piano quartets and two violin sonatas. Ethel Smyth's Mass was done by Barnby at the Albert Hall—not the first work of the kind by an English-woman, for portions of one by Maude Valérie White had already been heard. Donald Tovey went to Oxford that year and astonished everyone by his amazing musical memory and his profound interpretations of the pianoforte classics, and he attracted Joachim's attention as a composer of very

serious classicist leanings. Joachim also liked a clarinet
Quintet by the coloured College student Samuel Coleridge-
Taylor, so much that he did it at Berlin in 1897, a year after
the composer of twenty-one had already had a Symphony
performed at St. James's Hall. But he cannot be said to
have fulfilled such promise. His "Hiawatha's Wedding
Feast" of 1898 and the other Longfellow settings and similar
choral works that came later were no more than attractively
picturesque. They had a great popular vogue, but have
not lasted. The year 1896 brought forward two good
works by Stanford, however: the opera "Shamus O'Brien,"
based on Sheridan Le Fanu's ballad, which was conducted
first by Wood in London and then by Bantock in the
provinces, and the splendid choral ballad on the same poet's
"Phaudrig Crohoore," which came out at Norwich.

In the year 1897 the queen's Diamond Jubilee again produced, as a matter of course, a number of official works,
including Cowen's ode, "All hail the glorious reign," German's orchestral fantasy, "In Commemoration," and Elgar's
"Imperial March" and a cantata, "The Banner of St. George."
Bantock that year finished a set of six cycles entitled "Songs
of the East" which began that oriental phase of his that found
its culmination in the colossal setting for soloists, chorus and
orchestra of Fitzgerald's whole "Omar Khayyám" "translation." Bantock's eastern works were all, so to speak,
made in Birmingham—most of them literally, indeed, for
he became principal of the Midland Institute School of
Music there later; but if they are no more genuine than
Fitzgerald's quatrains, which are nevertheless splendid English
poetry, they are English music that made its mark in its time
by a rich and glowing if somewhat over-sumptuous invention
and not least by the composer's magnificent handling of the
orchestra, a virtue not cultivated by the earliest composers
of the renascence, but looked upon by them rather as though
they suspected it to be an insidious vice.

In 1899 Delius gave a concert of works of his own at the St. James's Hall. They were understood neither by the public nor by the critics, who nevertheless showed a sincere desire to come to terms with them. It was to be a long time, however, before Delius came into his own; he was appreciated to some extent in Germany before his music conquered England, where he belongs decidedly to the twentieth century. So does Elgar, in so far as almost all his really important work came after 1900. Nevertheless he is the crowning figure of the renascence this chapter has attempted to outline, so that a brief discussion of his work may aptly conclude it.

Edward Elgar was longer in coming before the musical world than any master of his standing had ever been before him. We have seen that this was due to his provincial obscurity and his lack of contact with teachers and fellow-learners; but there is also the fact to be reckoned with that, owing to these very circumstances, he matured more slowly than any other great composer, with the possible exception of Wagner. Not until he was thirty-two, in 1889, did he settle in London, after his marriage, in the hope of at last gaining a footing in the musical world and having his works adequately performed and published. But the "Froissart" overture of 1890 was still done only at Worcester, and so was the cantata, "The Black Knight," in 1893, not at the Festival, but only by the Festival Choral Society. The Festival of 1896 at last did the oratorio, "Lux Christi," and the North Staffordshire Festival at Hanley of the same year the cantata, "King Olaf." Still London was not conquered, and it must have been a galling coincidence, if perhaps also a characteristic one in view of his later devotion to the court, that his first works to attract attention in the capital should have been the two written for the Diamond Jubilee. Elgar thus became an official composer before he was recognized as a great master.

That real master, it is true, did not become apparent until 1899, ten years after he had hopefully come to London. Now, however, success came like a torrent, together with mature inspiration. "Caractacus" was produced at the Leeds Festival, the "Sea Pictures" for contralto and orchestra were done at that of Norwich and, best of all, Richter took enthusiastically to the "Enigma Variations," which he performed at St. James's Hall and elsewhere. The work is now a classic of the orchestral repertory, and of the English repertory alone only because an English musical classic is still, by tradition and prejudice, a contradiction in terms for foreign conductors and audiences. Moreover Elgar planned that year a symphony of which Gordon was to be the hero—later to become simply Symphony No. 1, without an avowed programme—and at the 1900 Birmingham Festival Richter conducted "The Dream of Gerontius," which was translated into German by Julius Buths, performed by him at Düsseldorf and commented on in the most flattering terms by Richard Strauss.

Elgar's music is ardently admired by some and as violently disliked by others. That is the reward and the penalty of the kind of intense individuality which is one of his artistic attributes. His musical idiom is so strikingly personal that one cannot possibly mistake even a few bars of one of his representative works for any other composer's; and pronounced individuality, in music as in any other human utterance, is bound to arouse strong feelings, one way or the other, according to the hearer's temperament. What to one listener is the attraction of character is to another the irritation produced by mannerisms, and it must be admitted that Elgar is a highly manneristic composer, though one may immediately qualify this stricture by saying that he has nothing if not style, and that the style is the mark of the man— an unmistakably big man. His sequences are overdone and his brazen orchestral sounds can be all but blatant; yet he

uses the sequence in an absolutely unique way and orchestrate
with magnificent audacity.

His orchestral works surpass everything else he did, a
their best. The Variations are lovely portraiture as well a
glorious music; the two Symphonies, not perhaps perfectly
sure in design, carry a tragic yet triumphant philosophy o
life that must impress even those who think them too opulent
the Introduction and Allegro for strings has an unexcelled
perfection of form and of instrumental handling; the symphonic study of "Falstaff" surpasses any symphonic poem
by Strauss in subtlety, allusiveness, eloquent invention and
certainty of style and taste: indeed in these last two qualities
it equals Verdi's opera on the same subject—both works have
the style and taste won by mature mastery after many aberra-
tions in those respects. For indeed Elgar had often erred
though what is so often called his vulgarity is rather a kind
of creative exuberance that can stop at nothing. He was
singularly devoid of self-criticism and welcomed with an
almost childish delight any notion that would come to him
unbidden and as though simply snatched from the air, as he
thought. He had the kind of creative unaccountability we
find also in a genius contemporary with him—Sibelius
find, indeed, in a greater one not his contemporary—
Beethoven. For like Beethoven, and like Schubert, for that
matter, he did not know clearly when he had written an
inferior thing and when a masterpiece, or at any rate could
not tell at the time of writing.

On the whole the vocal works are less sure of permanence
than the instrumental, which finished with the mellow,
autumnal cello Concerto and three chamber works that were
a new departure for Elgar at the very last—almost too late,
yet their limpid tiredness is touching and unique. It is
curious that so keen a literary student should so often have
shown little discrimination in his choice of poetry. But
"Gerontius" struck a new note in oratorio, the first surprising

impact of which one can never forget, even though oft-repeated festival experiences may have made the emotionally surcharged music a little oppressive. "The Apostles" and "The Kingdom" continued in a similar vein and on so large a scale that one cannot get great refreshment from them, but they contain pages of unrepeatable originality and deal with vast structures in a way that shows a Wagnerian grasp. Otherwise, in spite of a masterly use of the *Leitmotiv* and an occasional approach to the luxuriance of "Parsifal," there is nothing in these oratorios that does not once and for all belong to English music and exclusively to this English master, who dominates the period of renascence as Byrd did that of the last Tudor sovereign and Purcell that of the Restoration.

CHAPTER XI

The Folk-Music Revival

For a thorough study of the people's songs and dance music in the British Isles (for here Scotland, Wales and Ireland are just as conspicuous as England) we should have to return to the beginnings of their musical history, indeed even beyond the period roughly fixed in the first chapter for the beginnings of music as a consciously cultivated art. But folk tunes being of unknown origin, and their dates being usually impossible to determine with any accuracy, an attempt at discussing this topic chronologically, or to link it up step by step with the history of "art music," would have been futile. It is therefore convenient to place this chapter at the end of the nineteenth century, a time when a new interest in the country's folk music led to its revival by research, publication and active cultivation as a branch of art.

That revival at least can be chronologically placed, and it is useful to do so in the year 1898, when the English Folk-song Society was founded. Its example was followed by a similar organization for Ireland in 1904 and another for Wales in 1909. All these societies have made extensive researches with the aid of experts, publishing in the journals issued by them and elsewhere large numbers of songs and dance tunes, many of which were in imminent danger of being lost for ever. For not only were they very largely unknown to musicians, most of whom up to the end of last century saw no reason why they should take any particular interest in a branch of their art they considered as being hardly artistic at all; they were about to be forgotten by the very people who had somehow or other preserved them from generation to generation, although most of them had never been written down. Those people were country folk as a rule, except in special cases such as those of the sea shanties (or chanties, a term probably derived from the French *chantez*), which belonged to merchant shipping until they went out with sail-propelled craft and to the strenuous labour connected with it, which sailors had lightened by singing rhythmically to their work.

Like the shanties, folksongs and folk dances were on the point of dying out when collectors like the Rev. S. Baring-Gould, Dr. W. Alex. Barrett, Frank Kidson, Lucy Broadwood and J. A. Fuller Maitland began to make a systematic search for them up and down the country. They and the greatest of collectors, Cecil Sharp, who began to work in Somerset in 1905, often found that a song could only be extorted with difficulty from some old crone at her wash-tub or some oldest inhabitant in a taproom, the tune being precariously remembered only after stimulation by much confidential gossip or a tankard of ale, and the words uttered almost automatically, sometimes without any clear realization of what they all meant and often in corruptions which confused their meaning all but incomprehensibly. Different variants of one and the same song that turned up in sometimes widely separated localities complicated the task enormously. Cecil Sharp and Maud Karpeles had to go as far afield as the Southern Appalachian Mountains in 1916–18 to find many of the songs in their purest and most primitive form as well as some tunes forgotten in England, preserved by the descendants of early English settlers thanks to their seclusion from the influence of modern American life. A learned authority on sources and variants is Anne Gilchrist.

Not all folk tunes, of course, are preserved to us only by oral transmission. Composers began early to use them for their work, and there are collections—some of our best— dating from round about the opening of the seventeenth century (1597, 1609, 1610, 1612). The Elizabethan virginalists, for example, liked to base variations on them: thus Byrd would have kept us the tunes of "The Carmans' Whistle" and "Sellenger's Round," for instance, and John Bull that known as "The King's Hunting Jig," even if they had otherwise disappeared, and occasionally church composers of the same period or a little earlier would use a popular tune as a *cantus firmus*, a basic melody on which to construct the polyphonic fabric of a Mass or motet, rare as the custom was in England compared with foreign practice. The Masses by Christopher Tye, John Shepherd and John Taverner on the song called "The Western Wind" are well-known cases in point. Composers at that time, aware of a general budding musicality, used familiar tunes because, like Shakespeare, they wished to allude to what people knew and understood.

In 1609 Ravenscroft issued two books of roundelays and catches, many of which are folksongs, entitled "Pammelia" and "Deuteromelia," and in 1650 Playford did for the English country dance tunes what Thoinot Arbeau had done for French dances in his "Orchésographie" of 1588 by publishing a number of them and so transferring them from the village green to the houses of the well-to-do citizens of the Commonwealth, recommending them to "young Gentlemen." If only the times and the nature of the dance had agreed better, as Playford said in his preface he could not feel they did, and if the masque, which cultivated dancing, had not just then declined, he might have begun that necessarily somewhat sophisticated yet perfectly sincere and appreciative revival of country dancing that is flourishing in many parts of England to-day, not so much among the peasantry as among townspeople, carefully organized by the experts at Cecil Sharp House in London.

The numerous song-books issued during the second half of the seventeenth century contained some old anonymous songs and ballads such as "Greensleeves," "Chevy Chase," "Sir Eglamore," etc., including some Irish tunes with new words by contemporary writers. One of these songs, "Cold and Raw," having been sung by Arabella Hunt to Queen Mary in the presence of Purcell and greatly liked by the queen, was afterwards used by that master as the bass for a song in the Ode, "Love's goddess sure was blind," for Mary's thirtieth birthday in 1692. Durfey drew upon folksongs as well as popular tunes by composers of the day for his "Wit and Mirth" and printed them in music type, and we have seen that John Gay in turn relied largely on Durfey for the tunes in "The Beggar's Opera" of 1728 and its sequel, "Polly." Later ballad operas, needless to say, also made use of folk material, although by no means exclusively or even principally. The term "ballad" in that connection was very far from suggesting ancient balladry of the type of "Lord Randal" or "The Twa Sisters of Binnorie." It has been suggested—quite plausibly in view of "Wit and Mirth"—that it derives from "bawdry" and "bawdy."

Until the end of the nineteenth century so much less was done for English folksongs than for those of the rest of the British Isles that an impression prevailed both at home and abroad that England possessed no treasury of folksong comparable with that of other countries, whereas it is quite plain now that this treasury is considerably richer and far more varied than that, for instance, of Germany, where countless square-cut and stereotyped melodies of no particular distinction are, to begin with, not genuine folk material, but songs written down and harmonized by one person, often by inferior musicians (Silcher, Kücken, etc.), and of no considerable antiquity. This is quite natural: countries that breed composers very thoroughly and extensively are apt to neglect their folk music and to give their people spurious substitutes for it. What is true of Germany has for long applied also to Italy, but real folksongs in great variety have of late been collected there in various regions.

Collecting was pursued vigorously, if without much scholarship, in Scotland and Ireland a century before England came into this field, and the Scottish amateur George Thomson included Welsh and Irish songs in his large collections, published between 1793 and 1841. He not only engaged Pleyel, Hummel, Weber, Shield and Bishop to provide new accompaniments for the songs (with "symphonies," i.e. instrumental introductions, etc.), but actually succeeded in interesting Haydn and Beethoven in this task to such an extent that the former contributed no fewer than 187 settings and the latter 126. It was a triumph for Thomson to secure the services of five foreign masters three of whom are now among the major classics, but it was not to the advantage of songs which were foreign to them to be treated as though they were material for composition in the masters' own style.

While Thomson was thus engaged, two great poets allowed themselves to be persuaded to write new words to large quantities of folksongs, thus doing even more to enrich the art of poetry than to help the repopularization of precious tunes. Burns supplied poems for "The Music of Scotland" in the 1790's and Tom Moore those for the "Irish Melodies" published in 1807. But even as early as 1765 an eager literary antiquarian, Bishop Thomas Percy, had done something to revive the ballads that go back into the dimmest antiquity of our history by publishing their words—unfortunately without their tunes—in his "Reliques of Ancient Poetry."

Ballads are narrative songs relating chivalric adventures, love stories and tales of horror. They are probably the oldest folksongs we still possess, dating back beyond the middle ages, when the people at large could not read and were supplied by minstrels with some sort of oral equivalent of the modern epic, novel or even detective story. Bards and scalds went from place to place with their harps (the most useful instrument for their purposes because it could be easily transported, was capable of producing accompanying harmony and left the singer or reciter free to use his breath for the delivery of his poem or song). The more famous among them visited the castles of the great, the humbler contented themselves with appearing at fairs and markets. But their audiences were one society and had essentially the same tastes, except that the common people liked to have their stories illustrated, just as readers of books did later. So the custom arose of showing series of pictures sectionally on large placards, each section being pointed to with a stick at the appropriate verse of the ballad. With the invention of printing in the fifteenth century this form of delivery disappeared gradually, but the ballads themselves, and accompanying pictures too sometimes, were printed on broadsheets, no longer to be sung by minstrels, but to be sold by chapmen to the multitude for its own singing. Autolycus in "The Winter's Tale" is such a pedlar ("My traffic is sheets"), and if Shakespeare makes him sing his ballads with his customers to let them sample his wares, he is doubtless showing precisely the kind of thing that happened.

Another category of folksong, the carol or nowell, benefited early from publication in book-form: Wynkyn de Worde issued a collection in 1530. But although in France, which possesses by far the richest and finest fund of these Christmas songs, many of them may claim great antiquity and have a dance origin (being mostly in triple time), while others are merely adaptations of later fashionable tunes, in England few carols can be traced back beyond the fourteenth century and many of them are known to be "composed" songs. Comparatively few are based on one or other of the modes, as "God rest you merry, gentlemen" is, for example; most of them are in major or minor keys.

Other English folksongs, so far as they are genuinely

old, are modal, and even those which appear to be in major
or minor keys may, of course, actually be in the Ionian or
Aeolian mode, in the latter case with some *musica ficta*
modifications—adjustments of accidentals before the penultimate note (the seventh) of the scale in such a way that at
a cadence a semitonal leading-note appears which the true
Aeolian mode does not possess. Irish and Welsh songs are
less often modal, probably because the harp provided a
chordal accompaniment, and the modes do not easily lend
themselves to harmonization. Scottish songs, on the other
hand, because they were only sung, not played, are often
pentatonic, i.e. built on a primitive scale of only five notes,
as represented by the black keys of the piano. (You can
play the tunes of "Auld lang syne" or "Ye banks and
braes" entirely on the black keys, for instance.) The
modes occurring most frequently in English folksong, not
counting the Ionian, which is identical with modern major,
are the Aeolian (A to A on the white keys); next come the
Dorian (D to D) and Mixolydian (G to G, with F natural).
The Phrygian (E to E) is very rare, the Lydian (F to F)
practically non-existent; but in the latter case we find am-
biguous examples with a gapped scale of six notes which
omits the augmented fourth (or tritone) that is characteristic
of the Lydian mode. Whether such tunes are to be regarded as originally pentatonic with another note added in
later versions—and there are such earlier forms to be found
in the Appalachians—or as Lydian with a gap made by the
omission of B natural, or again as modern major with a
B flat omitted, will never be determined.

Not nearly all tunes that are generally regarded as folksongs are anything of the sort. Much material appears in
modern popular song-books that is either mere valueless
sing-song stuff, like "There is a tavern in the town" or
"Clementine," quaint music-hall entertainment of bygone
days of the kind described in the last chapter or the work of

more or less forgotten, more or less distinguished composers. As to the last category, such a beautiful and deservedly remembered song as "Drink to me only with thine eyes" is not a folksong but the product of collaboration between a composer (? Dr. Harington, see p. 148) and a poet (Ben Jonson), though they missed being contemporaries; and "Cherry ripe" (by Charles Edward Horn) is decidedly a composition, even a very neatly organized composition in the form of a miniature rondo with two episodes and a coda.

Here, then, is plenty of matter for controversy for the Folksong Society, or whomsoever it pleases, to speculate on and squabble over to their hearts' content, and that, perhaps, will do as much as the beauty, variety and value of the rescued treasury to keep folksong alive. Questions of authorship and dates, of different variants of tunes and words, of the prior claim of certain localities to this or that melody and various other points will go on calling for the attention of enthusiastic research workers and yielding pleasure and interest to those whom these workers have so admirably served. And folk music will continue to inspire composers, though the best of those who have been so inspired, as for instance Vaughan Williams and Holst, have shown that it is its spirit and feeling and flavour, allowed to act upon their own individual inspiration, rather than any direct borrowing which is most fruitful.

Folksongs, it must be remembered, cannot be discussed apart from folk dances. The two are often inseparable, sometimes indistinguishable, in England. What makes the old modal songs so strikingly different from modal plainsong is their strong rhythm, which is more often than not a dance rhythm. The breezy Somerset song, "Blow away the morning dew," a wonderfully shapely tune, is only the first example that comes to mind of a song that might quite well be a country dance, and we know that "Hunt the squirrel," "The Geud Man of Ballangigh" and many similar things are both songs and country dances. No doubt the tunes of such songs were often danced to if a fiddler who played on some village green or in some hostelry happened to know them and to find that their rhythm fitted the dance desired by the company. Such a fiddler, in an amateur way, was Thomas Hardy's grandfather, who left his great descendant a manuscript book of tunes full of old songs and dances, all of which, we may imagine, were used by him for the purpose of playing at just such gatherings as the dance at Shepherd Fennel's described in the "Wessex Tales." Hardy, in fact, possessed three such books, and he too in his younger years frequently played the fiddle at such rustic functions, enjoying the artless but racy music and learning much about human beings that became distilled into great art and profound philosophy. The folk tunes must have helped him: they reach back into the well-springs of mankind.

CHAPTER XII

The Twentieth Century

Not a final chapter but another volume would be needed to bring the story of British music adequately up to date. For it is a very crowded story as we see it in our memory of the last forty-seven years. We must therefore take a more comprehensive view than hitherto and deliberately overlook many details. Dismissing individual performers and records of the appearance of separate works, we can only pass in review some of the outstanding activities of the immediate past and then conclude the survey with a brief discussion of some of the British composers of whom most are still alive and, in the majority of cases, still productive.

Among the most characteristic nineteenth-century musical activities carried into the twentieth are the great provincial festivals. The Three Choirs Festivals at Gloucester, Worcester and Hereford continued until the outbreak of war in 1939, and are now being resumed. Leeds also went on, while Norwich did so at least tentatively and Sheffield was actually revived. The competitive festivals seemed to have enough vitality to withstand even the most appalling war in history. A new one of a special kind was added to their list in 1900, when the National Brass Band Festival was founded on the basis of earlier movements of the kind. Bands consisting chiefly of workers gather annually to show their often surprisingly high skill in what is a singularly beautiful musical medium. Composers of the front rank, including Elgar, Bantock, Holst, Vaughan Williams and Ireland, did not disdain to write test pieces for these occasions.

Many provincial towns have orchestral concerts of some sort, but all the larger ones ought to have a municipal orchestra on the lines of that run by Birmingham, where Leslie Heward was conductor from 1930 to 1943, and where he was succeeded by George Weldon. Manchester has been fortunate in keeping the Hallé Orchestra alive, Liverpool, which previously had a share in the Hallé, now possesses its own Philharmonic Orchestra to occupy the magnificent modern Philharmonic Hall, and the Scottish Orchestra also continues. The Manchester orchestra, formerly under the guidance of Sir Thomas Beecham and Sir Hamilton Harty, is now in John Barbirolli's charge. It was Harty's long-term engagement which chiefly kept the Hallé Orchestra in its fine form. The Scottish Orchestra was for a time placed under Barbirolli before he went to New York. Among the seaside orchestras pre-eminence seems now to have passed from Bournemouth to Hastings, where Julius Harrison was in charge. Malcolm Sargent and Basil Cameron must here be mentioned as outstanding conductors.

London had two new great orchestras given to it, while a third, the London Symphony Orchestra, reorganized under pressure of the new competition, restored itself to its former excellence. It is run on co-operative lines, as is also the magnificent London Philharmonic Orchestra, though it was founded by Beecham in 1932, when it was merged with the Royal Philharmonic Society and used at Covent Garden during the international summer seasons of opera. Ten years earlier, when the British Broadcasting Company (now Corporation) was established, one of its first concerns was the formation of a first-class orchestra for its own purposes, though it could also be used for public concerts provided that they were broadcast at the same time. This provision, of course, made the B.B.C. Orchestra a national concern, though it functioned in the capital, except during war-time evacuation. The conductor-in-chief is Sir Adrian Boult, who was also the B.B.C.'s musical director until Arthur Bliss succeeded him in 1942, and two years later Victor Hely-Hutchinson, who, however, died in 1947.

The Promenade Concerts (always known to the huge mixed and unvaryingly enthusiastic audiences that frequent them as the "Proms") have not been suppressed even by the loss of Queen's Hall, and Sir Henry Wood remained in charge of them until his death in 1944. A later scheme, intended to offer good orchestral music not only to a wide public, but to a young one, are the Children's Concerts founded by Sir Robert Mayer. They were so successful in London that they started a movement on similar lines throughout the country. Their first conductor was Dr. Sargent, who was also concerned in the Courtauld-Sargent Club, established by Mrs. Samuel Courtauld in 1928 for the purpose of giving a hearing of the best possible orchestral programmes mainly to members of the staffs of business houses and government offices, for whom a large portion of the seats was exclusively reserved at very moderate prices. The venture was so successful that before long two performances of the same programme had to be given. Another interesting new departure were the concerts given in the beautiful staircase of the London Museum, the charge for admission being no more than the usual museum fee of sixpence.

The moving spirit of these concerts was Ernest Makower, who is also concerned in the musical interests of the British Council, established in 1925, which has done admirable work in propagating the arts of Great Britain abroad, a task that cannot be said ever to have been congenial to the national temper. While other countries have shown themselves frantically anxious that we should accept various manifestations of their arts at their own valuation, a proud "take it or leave it" has generally been Britain's attitude. The odd thing is that when the B.B.C. Orchestra or the L.P.O., the English Singers or the Fleet Street Choir are sent abroad, to mention only some outstanding instances of recent "foreign missions," audiences there make far more fuss of them than we do ourselves. Only our creative musicians they still

refuse to accept readily, keeping to the old tradition, so satisfying to national complacency, that there is no such
phenomenon as a British composer in creation. However,
we may perhaps hardly expect them to take to Elgar or
Vaughan Williams unless we more extensively cultivate
Bruckner or Roussel or Casella, and so we remain for ever
goat glerheads.

Meanwhile at home the old "exotic and irrational entertainment" continued to flourish. In 1925 Covent Garden
resumed its activities, dropped during the first world war,
and went on much as usual, though the chief interest now
centred in German rather than Italian opera and there was
a sprinkling of French works. The repertory was unenter-
prising, and when for a change a rare work was given, the
audience stayed away. Annual performances of Wagner's
"Ring," splendidly sung and after a time given an impressive
new production, were *de rigueur*, and the Italian repertory,
often lamentably sung since the marked decline of Italian
vocal art, consisted chiefly of the current Verdi and Puccini.
Anything else that was staged was done, as a rule, for the
sake of some capricious star or other; even such things as
"Martha" and "Fedora" had to be sat through for the sake
of dictatorial singers. The fine orchestral playing was
hardly noticed by many of the patrons who paid very high
prices for the pleasure of taking the best for granted. Star
conductors, however, took a secondary share in the glory.
It was all rather absurd and remote from any thorough
musical cultivation. As for the beautiful, mellow historic
theatre, there will never be anything like it for atmosphere.
A sort of nostalgia of pride and regret seized one again and
again at Covent Garden. The theatre narrowly escaped
destruction during the second world war, and it was ready
to be re-opened surprisingly soon after the declaration of
peace under a new management much more inclined to
favour a progressive policy. It was even ready to include

the first great English opera of the century, Benjamin Britten's "Peter Grimes," which had been produced by Sadler's Wells in 1945. Indeed, opera in English on a grand scale is now the policy.

Not displays of the abnormal accomplishment of stars but the perfection of team-work was aimed at by the festival performances at Glyndebourne, the private opera established in 1934 by John Christie at his Sussex country house. The singing was often first-rate, but by no means always, for the choice of artists was made, in England and abroad—for preference abroad, it seemed—among those who combined vocal gifts and suitable appearance (a rare thing in opera) with willingness to submit to perfect collaboration (a rarer one still). The Mozart performances, in the original languages, had a special virtue of beauty, cultivation and respect for the composer's intentions rather than for tradition. But still it was all alien in execution and limited as a social function. The poor could go to Glyndebourne if they had sufficient enthusiasm to save up for the adventure, but it was too easy by comparison for the rich to go merely because it was the thing to do. "And are you fond of music?" one exquisitely gowned patron was heard to say to another, whom she must have known to have spent an amount on the expedition that would have been sinfully extravagant for an unmusical person. For the truly musical Glyndebourne was an unforgettable experience. Its revival raises hopes that it will be so again.

Broadly speaking, neither of these institutions yet gives England an opera of its own. That has been done, in a much more modest way but far more fruitfully, by the old suburban theatre of Sadler's Wells, which we have already come across as a very humble contributor to London's music in earlier times. It was rebuilt into a delightful modern theatre and opened in 1931 as a branch of the Old Vic. for the alternate production of Shakespeare (with some other classics of the drama) and opera. Lilian Baylis, an autocrat in artistic matters and a large-hearted democrat where the public was concerned, was the moving spirit. She had already done admirable spade-work for opera at the old-fashioned theatre in the Waterloo Road, beginning with such things as "The Bohemian Girl" and "Maritana," for which the quaint old house somehow made the perfect setting. Later Mozart, Verdi and other masters were added to the repertory, and when the opera was finally transferred to Sadler's Wells, drama remaining at the Old Vic., almost anything could be done—and has been done—though never on a vast scale. The singing as a rule has not more than the sound competence one finds at the average German opera-house (with the difference that there it is always taken, especially by English people, as being outstandingly good) and the productions are never very lavish; but a splendid spirit of collaboration, combined with excellent taste in staging, has in recent years resulted in some performances that have remained unforgettable, such as those of Gluck's "Orpheus," Beethoven's "Fidelio," Wagner's "Mastersingers," Verdi's "Don Carlos," Rimsky-Korsakov's "Tsar Saltan," Strauss's "Rose Cavalier" and, most remarkable of all, the original version of Mussorgsky's "Boris Godunov," done here for the first time outside Russia. The "Macbeth" by Lawrance Collingwood, the theatre's chief conductor, must also be mentioned. What matters more, however, is that the performances are given in English for the ordinary English theatre-going public, at ordinary theatre prices, and most of all that Sadler's Wells has become a school, the first and only one, for operatic art cultivated by native artists. It is due to this undertaking that Dr. Johnson's countrymen have begun to think of opera as rational after all, and as exotic only in so far as it must continue to rely almost exclusively on foreign works.

It will not always be so if the school continues, but opera is a species of composition that will grow only if there is the right soil for it in which to take root. Even now, however, several good operas have been written by various composers in the course of their general work, with Vaughan Williams at their head, and some show a tendency to take to opera as a speciality, which may not be altogether a good thing for music, but may prove useful to the stage. Arthur Benjamin's outstanding works are two spirited comic operas in a witty modern vein, "The Devil take Her" and "The Prima Donna," and George Lloyd has tried his hand at romantic works in "Iernin" and "The Serf," a hand rather fettered by tradition but with a decided dramatic knack. Britten's "Peter Grimes" stands alone at present as a modern English work as capable of taking the stage abroad as Berg's "Wozzeck," and indeed a foreign critic has called it the most remarkable opera since the appearance of that work. Less than a year after its production it had been accepted for production in Swedish at Stockholm, in Dutch at Antwerp and in German at Basle and Zurich, as well as in the original in the U.S.A. By 1947 Britten had produced his third opera.

Earlier Rutland Boughton had gone so far as to establish a sort of English Bayreuth at the historic Arthurian Glastonbury in Somerset, where he produced his own stage works, some of them based on the Arthurian legends and including "The Immortal Hour," which afterwards had a surprisingly long run in London, somehow capturing the public imagination in spite of a subject wrapped up in Celtic twilight, little vitality of action and music that is curiously wan and undramatic. The Glastonbury venture failed to attract more than a passing curiosity because the presentations lacked finish and the repertory was restricted to a single composer who had a poetic gift and earnest ambition but a somewhat monotonously limited inventive range and no very compelling mastery. It was none the less a noble if wayward venture.

Returning to Sadler's Wells for a moment, we find there

a school for another branch of art, though one allied to opera whenever the latter calls for it. There is now a brilliant English ballet company there, quite capable of giving performances of its own that have had a continuous success and of devising original new productions in which music, stage designing and dancing receive the most intelligent attention on equal terms. Its success with Arthur Bliss's remarkable "Checkmate" at the Paris Exhibition of 1937 showed that it is perfectly fit to sustain an international reputation, and a number of British composers, apart from Bliss, including Lord Berners, William Walton, Constant Lambert and Gavin Gordon have written new works for it. In 1946 Covent Garden became its headquarters.

Modern English ballet may be said to have taken its departure from the Camargo Society, whose production of Vaughan Williams's sombre and impressive masque of "Job," based on William Blake's illustrations for the Book of Job, was its finest achievement; and this in turn owed its existence to the influence of Diaghilev's Russian Ballet, which was one of the outstanding features of London's artistic life for some years from 1913 onward—though it does not strictly belong to our story—and even had its headquarters there for a time. Diaghilev, whose musical insight was often instinctively penetrating, but not based on profound knowledge and detached judgment, permitted himself some sweeping condemnations of English music without taking the trouble to know much about it. He nevertheless commissioned a few English works. Constant Lambert made his first appearance as a composer under the Russian Ballet's auspices with "Romeo and Juliet" and Lord Berners wrote an entertainingly satirical score for "The Triumph of Neptune," a modern view of the old-style English panto-mime presented in the manner of the "penny plain, twopence coloured" toy theatre that had once enchanted Robert Louis Stevenson.

Before Sadler's Wells was resurrected north of the City, another old suburban home of popular melodrama was re-opened for more artistic pursuits west of the West End. This was the Lyric Theatre at Hammersmith, where in 1920 Nigel Playfair produced a revival of "The Beggar's Opera" with a score delightfully if somewhat artificially furbished up by Frederick Austin. It had such a success that Playfair not only kept it running for nearly three years, but was encouraged to stage other eighteenth-century musical pieces, including Sheridan's "Duenna" with Linley's music. Later on the Lyric brought out some modern light operas, two of which had some success and deserved more: Armstrong Gibbs's charming "Midsummer Madness," with a witty book by Clifford Bax and some haunting tunes, and Thomas Dunhill's "Tantivy Towers," a pointed satire by A. P. Herbert the music for which was rather wanting in stage effectiveness but as musicianly as Sullivan and sufficiently though never startlingly up-to-date.

Opera in English—as distinct from English opera—had engaged the attention of several travelling companies long before the new Sadler's Wells was thought of. The Carl Rosa, Moody-Manners and Quinlan companies were the best-known, and the first of these still exists. On a much higher artistic level, however, were Beecham's several ventures into opera at various times, in and after 1909. He gave memorable performances of many great or interesting works, including Strauss's "Elektra" and "Feuersnot," Verdi's "Othello" and "Falstaff," Mozart and Wagner, several Russian works and two English operas which had both been originally written to foreign librettos: Ethel Smyth's "The Wreckers" and Delius's "A Village Romeo and Juliet." Beecham at first worked with artists chosen *ad hoc*, but later formed what was intended to be a more permanent company. This became the British National Opera Company in 1922, which did some admirable work in many of the larger towns. Unfortunately it was self-supporting, and no opera can support itself for long. The B.N.O.C. was eventually forced into liquidation by the want of official help such as opera has never yet been adequately granted in this country. This has undoubtedly been an artistic loss to England; on the other hand this country has sufficiently proved that to be non-operatic is not to be non-musical, and it has at least saved itself from the extravagant expenditure in money and artistic energy which operatic countries lavish on one unsuccessful or ephemeral work after another in order to throw up a success once a year and perhaps one masterpiece every decade or so.

The provinces have had their own operatic enterprises in some places. Nothing has been done systematically, but the occasional outbursts have been all the more surprising. The Glasgow Grand Opera Company, consisting of amateurs, performed almost incredible feats under Erik Chisholm by staging, of all things, the operas of Berlioz, not only "Benvenuto Cellini" and "Beatrice and Benedick," but even "The Trojans," complete in two parts. A similar undertaking at Falmouth earned much praise by doing, among other things, such Mozartian curiosities as "Idomeneus" and "The Clemency of Titus."

The most interesting operatic revivals, generally of little-known and sometimes of historically important works, have been given by the Oxford University Opera Club and the Cambridge University Musical Society. The former's greatest service to music were the performances of Monteverdi's "Orfeo" and "L'incoronazione di Poppea," edited by J. A. Westrup, then still an undergraduate, but now one of the outstanding younger musical scholars and author of a book on Purcell. At Oxford, too, such works as Rameau's "Castor and Pollux," Gluck's "Iphigenia in Aulis," Weber's "Freischütz," Rimsky-Korsakov's "Night in May," Dvořák's "The Devil and Kate" and Vaughan Williams's "Sir John in Love" were given. Cambridge has been notable for its Purcell performances, especially "The Fairy Queen" and "King Arthur," under the direction of Cyril Rootham and the scholarly supervision of Professor Edward J. Dent; also for some stage performances of Handel oratorios, translated versions of Mozart's "Idomeneus" and "The Impresario," and first productions of Vaughan Williams's "The Poisoned Kiss" and "Riders to the Sea," the latter a setting of Synge's drama.

The Royal Academy and Royal College of Music have given students' performances of opera which at times revealed excellent new talent, the latter at the Parry theatre specially constructed for the purpose at the College. Both these institutions have flourished under their recent heads. At the Academy Sir John McEwen succeeded Mackenzie as principal and was in turn followed by Sir Stanley Marchant, who is also Professor of Music at London University; at the College Sir Hugh Allen came after Parry, and the present director is Sir George Dyson. One special feature of London's scholastic musical life must not be forgotten: the Patron's Fund established by the munificence of Lord Palmer of Reading, which makes it possible for rehearsals of orchestral and other works to be held for the purpose of trying them out before they reach the public. If they ever do reach it, that is; but their chances of doing so have been increased by the Patron's Fund.

A recent pedagogic institution that deserves attention is the School of English Church Music, founded in 1927, established in St. Nicholas's College at Chislehurst two years later under the direction of Sir Sydney Nicholson, and now removed to Canterbury. Much has been done for the improvement of the music in the Anglican church in recent years, not least by some of the cathedral organists, who are invariably musicians of the highest specialist qualifications and among the readiest recipients of musical knighthoods. It is in the peculiar nature of their functions that they should have enormous influence within their dioceses and be little known except by name beyond, unless they happen to have distinguished themselves as composers for their church, in which case their fame may be bounded only by the frontiers of that church's sphere of influence. Modern services and anthems, however, though produced in huge quantities, seldom represent modern English music in a way the old masters of ecclesiastical composition represent their own periods in the eyes of historians. The explanation is simple: the great composers were once bred by the church, whereas nowadays they are much more likely to come from the schools of music and the universities.

If modern Anglicanism has done little to add to the treasury of musical settings of the services, it has made splendid efforts to improve its hymnody. The "English Hymnal" of 1906 and its second, revised edition of 1933 exclude the maudlin tunes of the Sankey and Moody type, revive folk and plain-song melodies and add some fine new hymns by composers of repute. Even broader in its choice, because intended to lay stress on good musical quality, is the collection of "Songs of Praise," first published in 1925, the musical editors of which are Vaughan Williams and Martin Shaw.

Musical scholarship, though not nearly widespread enough, is in good hands where its opportunities are adequate. The late Oxford Professor of Music, Sir Hugh Allen, never published a book, but he devoted much time to organiza-tion and administrative work that has been invaluably useful to others. His successor, J. A. Westrup, is a productive scholar, however, and the general editor of the projected *New Oxford History of Music*. Another Oxford scholar who has done fine work is Ernest Walker, who is also known more widely as a cultivated composer writing rarely but sensitively. At Cambridge Dent, who succeeded Charles Wood, a fine scholar and sensitive composer, stimulated more than one generation by his alertness of mind and profound learning, and innumerable musicians beyond are indebted to him for his literary work, including his books on Alessandro Scarlatti, Mozart's operas and English opera. He holds the view that the standard classics, whom he knows as well as anybody, should not be revered as a matter of course or allowed to obscure one's interest in other music of importance, however old or modern. His sympathy with the latter, together with his tact and great linguistic gifts, made him the ideal chairman for the International Society for Contemporary Music, which has held three of its festivals in England so far, at Oxford and London in 1931 and London in 1938 and 1946. In 1939 Dent's office went to another Englishman, Edwin Evans, the most cosmopolitan of London's critics, whose interest in modern movements is well known, but whose death in 1945 left the office vacant before he had a chance to exercise his gifts in it. At Cambridge Dent was succeeded by Patrick Hadley.

The other universities now all have well-staffed music departments. Birmingham, for instance, with J. A. Westrup and later Anthony Lewis as professor, Sheffield with Frank Shera in the chair, and so on. The great professor of the recent past outside Oxford and Cambridge was, of course, Sir Donald Tovey, who occupied the Reid chair at Edinburgh from 1914 until his death in 1940. He might almost be said to have made reverence for the classics his exclusive musical concern, if he had not occasionally shown surprising insight into other matters and a knowledge that seemed inexhaustible. His books remain as a monument to classical scholarship. As a composer he had unlimited skill and ease, but was too much under the spell of the great masters to pursue an original line. Such works as the opera, "The Bride of Dionysus" or the cello Concerto written for Casals have all the attributes of greatness except that of spontaneous invention.

Many other scholars ought to be mentioned; it is lack of

I

space, not invidious preference, that may lead to the omission of some who deserve inclusion as much as anyone named here, among whom Sir Henry Hadow must be recalled and Sir Percy Buck introduced. The following at least should also be remembered:—Edmund H. Fellowes, a canon at Windsor and Mus. D., whose new editions of Elizabethan music, including the complete works of the madrigalists, are beyond estimation; Charles Sanford Terry, notable for his research into matters concerning Bach's biography and musical practice; William Gillies Whittaker, the late Professor of Music at Glasgow, who did fine work, some of a more practical nature, for the same master and others; R. O. Morris (sixteenth-century counterpoint); F. T. Arnold (thorough-bass); Marion Scott (Haydn); C. B. Oldman (Mozart); Ernest Newman (Wagner and Wolf); and H. C. Colles, who brought the *Oxford History of Music* down to the year 1900 and edited the third and fourth editions of *Grove's Dictionary*.

Colles was also the chief music critic of *The Times*, where he had two admirable lieutenants in Frank Howes and Dyneley Hussey, who have written books, the former on Byrd, the musician's psychology and opera, the latter on Mozart and Verdi. Howes succeeded Colles as chief critic on the latter's death in 1943. Criticism has also been well cultivated by A. H. Fox Strangways, the founder of the quarterly *Music & Letters*, in *The Observer*, where he was succeeded by William Glock, Ernest Newman in *The Sunday Times*, Richard Capell in *The Daily Telegraph*, to which F. Bonavia has also long been attached, and several others. Percy Scholes, formerly among London's critics, has for some years devoted himself to the production of books that have profitably spread musical knowledge among the general public. Excellent critics not attached to daily papers are William McNaught, Gerald Abraham (now professor at Liverpool), Constant Lambert, Cecil Gray, Scott Goddard and Edward Lockspeiser, to mention only a few. *The Musical Times* and several other specialist journals keep up a high standard.

The Sunday papers still have their weekly articles on music, and after the war they were resumed by *The Daily Telegraph*, where Capell's essays are always worth attention for their exceptional literary distinction. A few of the provincial dailies have kept weekly musical essays going, including *The Birmingham Post*, *The Glasgow Herald* and *The Liverpool Post*. *The Manchester Guardian* has long been famous for musical criticism of the finest literary quality: Samuel Langford was worthily succeeded there by Neville Cardus. Liverpool has a discerning critic in A. K. Holland. *The Yorkshire Post* formerly did good work, its critic for many years being Herbert Thompson and later A. H. Ashworth.

Among specialist writers must be mentioned Walter Willson Cobbett, a keen amateur patron of chamber music whose *Cyclopedic Survey*, to which many British and foreign authors contributed, is a notable work of reference. Authorities on instruments are the late F. W. Galpin and Kathleen Schlesinger. So, in a more practical way, was Arnold Dolmetsch, whose workshop at Haslemere turned out fine reproductions of old instruments such as recorders, harpsichords and clavichords, on which as well as on viols and lutes he and his gifted family played old music, much of which he rediscovered and edited. Festivals at which such music was to be heard were started at the pleasant little Surrey town in 1925, and Dolmetsch's descendants and disciples still keep them going.

At the other end of instrumental evolution is the invention of electrical recording for the gramophone, which has resulted in much more realistic and musically satisfying reproductions, so that the gramophone has become a more valuable means of studying music at home. It has the advantage over the radio that the music may be chosen at will, but the disadvantage that records are still far too expensive to offer the average music-lover anything like a comprehensive collection. Radio music, on the other hand greatly deteriorated because of war conditions, though it was difficult to see why they should make any difference. Peace conditions at first showed few signs of improvement and the chief fault of the B.B.C. seemed to be that it strove to be democratic at all costs. But the new Third Programme, started in 1946, offers an amazing variety of interesting work of quality and cleared the B.B.C. of the reproach of wishing to please the majority; a mistake because in questions of art it is the intelligent minority which should be given every consideration.

This brings us to the popular aspects of music in our days. They are not pleasing. Operetta has steadily degenerated since Sullivan's time, and although Lionel Monckton, Howard Talbot and others—we must disregard the vogue of Viennese purveyors like Lehár, Leo Fall and Oscar Straus— still managed to whip up some pleasant froth, the English modern musical comedy now falls quite flat. When it has some spirit left it takes it from Americans like George Gershwin or Jerome Kern, and even then it is very palpably second-hand. Most of its writers are no longer even craftsmen: the "composer" whistles a tune or plays it with one finger on the piano to a musician of sorts, who writes it down; a musician of another sort (or the same) harmonizes it according to all the new conventions; a third scores it in the only recognized way, which is that of crudity and blatancy.

Much more refreshing than the musical comedies are the revues, which at their best can be both pretty and witty and even now and then carry wit into their music. Walter Leigh was a gifted composer who could turn parody as good as Sullivan's—which could even parody Sullivan—to admirable account in some of the more devastatingly clever revues, and he also wrote a delightful light opera, "The Jolly Roger," which the musical-comedy public decided to turn down as not conforming to the latest rules of the game. These rules are dictated by jazz, so far as the music is concerned. But jazz is not part of our story. The experts say that there is no English jazz worth talking about, and they ought to know. The musician neither knows nor cares.

To come down to the lowest reaches of popular music and the latest days, one may just add that the second world war produced no English songs even as good as "Tipperary." The pity is that some composer with a gift for that kind of thing did not write a really good tune to topical words which, without pretending to be poetry, do not descend to twaddle. One can imagine Thomas Wood doing this, for instance, for he is a musician with an ear for the people's melodies and with the broadest human sympathies, as his capital autobiographical books have shown, books matched only by the very different but no less delightful ones in which Dame Ethel Smyth recorded her life's experiences.

Of the outstanding British composers still to be briefly discussed as belonging to the twentieth century, from the point of view of their art, several are no longer among us. The oldest as well as the most important of them were Frederick Delius, Gustav Holst and Frank Bridge. Delius, of German (some say Dutch) descent and in some ways antagonistic to the country of his birth, though in the end he asked to be buried in a quiet English country churchyard, is nevertheless an English artist and now valued in Britain alone, for all his initial German and Scandinavian successes, which anyway were never more than local and personal. His work is the ideal counterpart of English lyric poetry, poetry of a special kind in which no country has ever excelled in the same way, poetry that truly "aspires to the condition of music." One never thinks of Delius as a musician in a technical sense and somehow wonders how he ever managed to set that elusive, shifting, dream-like music of his down on paper at all. He is a great poet among musicians, and in another way his work may also be said to aspire to the condition of painting. Colour, both instrumental and harmonic, predominates in it over texture and form, and even over melody, to an extent found in no other composer, not even in Debussy. It is all as transient as a sunset, and his mood too is usually that of a man facing darkness. If one may not hope that it will last for future generations, it is so poignantly lovely at its best that one cannot help fervently wishing that fear to be wrong.

Holst, Swedish by ancestry but born on the edge of the Cotswolds and as English as Hardy or Housman, was a far more robust musical personality and a master of all the technical resources. One of his virtues was his passionate love of folk music, often reflected in his own art; another an open-mindedness that led him to try his hand at all manner of new problems without ever allowing him to dabble in experiment merely for experiment's sake. The trouble was, all the same, that he often made one feel that certain passages in his works were the result of deliberate premeditation, always interesting and sometimes arresting, but not vitalized by immediate inspiration. At other times his vitality seemed to be purely physical, so that one was smitten at a first hearing—of "The Planets," for instance—only to feel later that the experience could not be often repeated. Much of his work resembles magnificent frescoes one must not expect to endure for ever. What will endure, though, is his integrity and his influence. Revivals of his works will always re-awaken interest and astonishment.

Frank Bridge's genius was much more withdrawn and self-sufficing, which is the reason why it found its finest expression in chamber music. He too had an alert and inquiring mind, for he began comparatively conventionally, in the Brahmsian manner that was cultivated for preference by chamber musicians early in the century and finished with a series of works that show a serious endeavour, almost an anxiety, to find a new mode of expression indebted to no other master. It was not quite convincing, but Bridge's sincere and restless quest after an ideal of beauty made his work lovable even where reason would not allow full approval.

More than one composer was lost to England too young. George Butterworth, who fell in the war of 1914-18, had great talent, but as in the case of Rupert Brooke's poetry it is difficult to decide whether it would have come to as much as regret at his early loss not unnaturally suggests. His actual work is slight but, so far as it goes, beautiful, sensitive and finished. He belonged to the school that is English for the English only. But that was not only his limitation; it also made him a character.

A musician of much the same sort was Ivor Gurney, a gifted poet as well as a composer of many exquisite songs who was a sadder casualty than Butterworth, for war, not depriving him immediately of life, robbed him for long years of his reason. An even richer contribution to the finest modern treasury of English song was made by Peter Warlock, who was also a first-rate scholar, critic and editor of old music under his real name of Philip Heseltine. Warlock's very large collection of songs, set to a choice from the finest English poetry, shows three distinct aspects: in one he captures the tone and feeling of the Elizabethan masters with extraordinary felicity without falling into mere archaism, in another he shows a melancholy, nostalgic vein that owes something to the influence of Delius, but is also most intimately his own, and in a third, which is more crabbed and self-conscious, he obviously but not very successfully followed Bernard van Dieren. That brilliantly gifted but rather over-intellectual artist, though Dutch by birth, belongs decidedly to the English scene, for he did not take to composition until he had settled in London for good. Van Dieren was never at his best as a song-writer, for he handled words arbitrarily; but as an instrumental composer he was far more important than either the public or criticism has so far been willing to recognize. Gifted with technical facility as great as that of the most cunning fifteenth-century contrapuntists, he did not make things easy for his listeners, and a certain emotional aridity in his writing is not to be denied. But he will have to be given a more prominent place if injustice is not to be done to his memory, and he was a master of so many styles that there should be something for most musicians in his work.

We now come to living composers. The oldest among those to be discussed here is Sir John McEwen, a master especially of the string quartet, whose fine works in that form ought to be far better known than they are. The greatest is Ralph Vaughan Williams, whom it is neither national pride nor national prejudice to rank among the pre-eminent contemporary composers. He began, like Holst, as a folksong enthusiast and cultivator of an art that seemed to aim at nothing more than the satisfaction of adding to the English heritage. Perhaps that aim has remained his only one, but he has far outstripped it, intentionally or not. He has continued to take English poetry, English drama and the grand prose of the English Bible as sources for his inspiration, but except for the handicap of language there is nothing about his recent work, and indeed about the greater examples of his earlier work, to prevent any musician in any country from understanding it and appreciating its imaginative range and technical power and originality. *if* the flavour remains English, it does so in the same way that the flavour of Bartók's work remained Hungarian, which did not prevent that master from being universally acclaimed by progressive music-lovers. Progressive they will have to be, indeed, if they are to do justice to the later Vaughan Williams, who, now over seventy, seems to be more enterprising than ever. He has never tried out innovations, any more than the great masters of the past, for the mere pleasure of seeing what will happen, first to tentative compositions as such and then to the public that hears them for the first time. It is the smaller people who have always done this (very usefully, it may be said), and Vaughan Williams is one of those who have always calmly let them, absorbing all the time such suggestions as could serve their own purpose. In the end, indeed long before the end, he was capable of sometimes turning out works of an audacity that must have astonished even himself, at the same time sharpening his wits and schooling his emotion by the study of other people's work, as Bach did with that of Buxtehude or Vivaldi and Handel with that of the elder Scarlatti or Purcell.

There is far more to be said, and separate works ought to be singled out for discussion, in Vaughan Williams's case as in that of others; but a term must be set to this survey.

Josef Holbrooke wrote innumerable works of all kinds, some of them of the most ambitious dimensions and requiring the most extravagant means. Their chief fault is inconsistency of style, their chief merit fertility of invention. Cyril Scott, like Delius, had some personal successes in Germany, with the result that these two are still sometimes named as the only modern English composers in perfunctory works by German historians. Actually Scott has been greatly neglected here in recent years and in recent years he became less productive. One would not care to say whether the fault lay more with the public or with him, but it is certain that he had the kind of originality which is so startling at first that it is subsequently exploited to excess and so hardens into mannerisms. Well, one feels at times that even a man like Grieg had that fault. Let us assign to Cyril Scott the place of an English Grieg and leave it to others to say, if they wish, that this is too generous.

More in the public eye still is Sir Arnold Bax, who also has some personal characteristics that show a tendency to become manneristic, but at the same time possesses a great and versatile creative imagination. Beginning mainly as a miniaturist with piano pieces and songs, he steadily grew, through the discipline of chamber music, to the stature of a symphonist. His symphonies, and any other works approximating to the sonata form, have a tendency to sag into slow music at the second subject of an animated first movement, and indeed anywhere in his music energy is liable to become dreamy and clean melody to be swamped in decorative detail. But then the slow music is full of rich poetry, the dreams have a seizing, regretful loveliness and the decorations often show a life of their own. And after all the energetic music can be splendidly bracing and adventurous while it lasts. There are Celtic and Russian influences at work in Bax, sometimes very evidently; yet he is one of the big, original personalities in modern music.

Akin to him in some ways, but more austere, sometimes more simple and often more consistent in mood, is John Ireland. When he does not deliberately aim at simplicity, as he has admirably succeeded in doing occasionally, he is not an easy composer to come to terms with, yet one with whom one feels that it would be more than pleasant to do so. There is something that strikes one as genuinely warmhearted about his work, yet something too to keep one at arm's length, perhaps merely because the composer is determined not to sacrifice artistic integrity to the extent of becoming gushing. Thus things that are essentially unaffected expressions of feeling become overlaid with complicated harmonies of auxiliary notes which make discordant frictions, agreeable to the modern ear but disconcerting to the open mind. Such ambiguity is resented by many hearers, which is a pity, for it becomes plain soon enough that Ireland, far from wishing to be evasive, honestly confronts his hearers with difficulties in order to make their affection the more lasting once he has won it. Whatever the discouragements, his music is worth the effort of overcoming them.

Arthur Bliss is much more direct. Whether we like his music or not is a matter of indifference to him, or at any rate to the artist in him. He says categorically what he has to say, and there is an end to it. Really an end, once he has finished a work, for he will make the next one an entirely different task. He likes setting new problems for himself over and over again and then solving them by finding a new style suited to them. This does not mean that he is inconsistent; indeed he has progressed, from almost freakishly enterprising though never tentative beginnings, with remarkable single-mindedness. Not all his works appeal to any one hearer. Some have been repellent, some almost enchantingly attractive; but each one has been, whether a work of art or only an *objet d'art*, shaped with unfailing skill and determination.

Although eight years older than Bliss, Sir George Dyson, much occupied with educational duties, came forward later as a composer, but he has been steadily productive in recent years, mainly at the Three Choirs Festival. He is astonishingly accomplished: one feels that no technical feat would be beyond him, and in setting words—usually in large-scale choral works—he infallibly finds the right tone-picture to illustrate any passage. But he does, one cannot help feeling, illustrate rather than imaginatively illuminate. One comes away from a performance feeling disappointed that he has impressed only the poet's image vividly upon one's mind, not his own; but also pleased that such a thing can be so well done.

An illustrator who works on a smaller scale but in his limited way with a well-trained hand is Roger Quilter. His songs add music to poems as Arthur Rackham used to put pictures to books. They are always in the same manner, whatever the subject may be, but the manner is personal and tasteful.

Among the composers born in the last decade of the nineteenth century is Herbert Howells, who has written comparatively little and never tried to catch the inattentive ear, but whose music at its best, without showing anything very striking in any particular way, has the virtue of quality in all its aspects. Eugene Goossens, born in England, of Belgian descent and long settled in the U.S.A., perhaps hardly belongs to the English school any longer; but he wrote and produced his early works in London. They were, however, strongly impregnated with the French influences of some twenty years ago. His luxurious and evanescent music has changed little since. The Indian Kaikhosru Shapurji Sorabji belongs still less to England, although he has lived in London all his life, for his art, though not literally Eastern, is exotic so far as the British school is concerned. Elaborately decorative compositions on an enormous scale, which by turns become even more elaborately polyphonic, are patiently evolved by Sorabji as though he were weaving immense tapestries. Nobody knows where to put them when they are done, but the tremendous labour that goes into them as well as their austerity and technical ingenuity command respect. Ernest John Moeran, on the other hand, is an entirely home-bred composer who has done some folksong research and writes music that speaks a familiar language with a touch of dialect, but with a rough beauty and honest truthfulness, and lately with a new kind of subtlety.

We have now reached the composers born in this century who, hardly in mid-career as yet—or so we hope—must not be judged with any finality and will therefore be dealt with in few words—and not by any means all of them.

The personality among them of whom one feels most sure is William Walton. His is that rare gift of being able to create a musical work that is not only all of a piece, but remains unique and unrepeatable, for each time he tackles a new composition it turns out to be entirely different from the last, though certain marks of individuality remain, as they do in the work of all composers of character, not least the greatest among them. Walton not only shapes music well; he has creative passion, humour when humour is called for, poetry, tragic pathos, drive and fantasy. He has been reproached abroad with having no settled "system" or aesthetic. Does it matter? He has what is worth more: style and maturity.

Constant Lambert is less single-minded as a composer, having been busy as a brilliant critic and author as well as an excellent conductor. But he has turned out more than one work modern music would be the poorer for having missed. The youngest of those who can now be said to be established—the Benjamin in fact is Britten. As late as 1942, in the first edition of this book, it was said that "his is a brilliantly versatile and witty gift that only needs to be deepened by experience to produce incontrovertible evidence of exceptional genius. Meanwhile it is easy enough to believe without evidence." Now, by 1947, the evidence has arrived, and it is incontrovertible. A musician rather similarly endowed, though producing more quiet and intimate work, is Alan Rawsthorne. The largest composition he has turned out so far is a piano Concerto; he may turn out a larger one at any moment, and the point is that his smaller works all shape themselves admirably to their size. Edmund Rubbra, on the other hand, has reached his fifth Symphony. Developing rather slowly under the influence of Holst, he has lately found himself and is likely to remain the big English symphonist of his generation. His belief in long-phrased melody and in its intricately polyphonic application would alone indicate a disposition for work on a large scale, but he has all the other requirements to turn belief into fact.

Two composers devoted mainly to song-writing, worthy followers of Gurney, Warlock and Armstrong Gibbs, and as discerning in their choice of poetry, are Gerald Finzi and Charles Wilfred Orr. Both live in the country and write music that could have come from nowhere, one almost feels, but the Berkshire Downs and the Cotswolds. Two others conceal rather than reveal their Englishness: Lennox Berkeley, who was a pupil of Nadia Boulanger's in Paris and shows strong French influences, but has become increasingly independent and sensitive lately, and Alan Bush, who devotes much of his time and talent to the service of communism; but there is no reason why one's liking or dislike of Bush's music should have anything to do with politics.

Patrick Hadley, Gordon Jacob and Robin Milford are adherents of musical Englishry and write good, healthy music that can be assigned to that school at a first hearing; Herbert Murrill and Hugh Bradford just write attractive music without professing any special adherence; Howard Ferguson is a more passionate artist tending towards spacious works, still somewhat diffuse in form and not always without tributes to composers whose modernism is beginning to wear out, but having the merit of verve and enthusiasm; Stanley Bate, Arnold Cooke and Norman Demuth are given more to quests after new modes of expression.

A very gifted composer who went his own way from the first has by this time asserted himself as a considerable figure. He is Michael Tippett, perhaps the only one among the outstanding modern creative musical Englishmen who shows none of the leaning towards romanticism or nostalgia for the past discernible more or less clearly in others of similar artistic standing, even in Britten, when all is said. But although Tippett is in a sense the most progressive, one also feels in him, more strongly than in others, a feeling for tradition, and a purely English tradition at that, which is

probably precisely what saves him from any kind of sentimentality, but lets him express true sentiment.

There are several women composers, three of whom at
least must be mentioned. Freda Swain's music somewhat
resembles John Ireland's, but is without his emotional and
technical complications. She can write a neatly finished small
piece or song, but is also capable of designing a large work
that hangs admirably together. Elizabeth Maconchy is more
enterprisingly, sometimes aggressively up-to-date. She, too,
has the gift of shaping a composition, which she does wilfully
and yet convincingly. Elizabeth Lutyens, the youngest of
them, is so far the only English composer before the public
who has turned Schoenberg's twelve-note system to account.
As the daughter of a great architect she will doubtless
discover sooner or later that it does not make structures
which are easily convincing in performance, but may produce
only blue-prints which look well on paper; but much of her
work shows that she is as much interested in past traditions.

Among the youngest creative musicians now coming
forward might be mentioned another woman composer,
Priaulx Rainier, as well as Benjamin Frankel, Inglis Gundry,
Antony Hopkins, Wilfrid Mellers, Bernard Stevens, William
Wordsworth and an even larger number of gifted people.
It is difficult to draw a rigid line between inclusion and
exclusion where so many musicians are concerned in whose
hands lies the making of a new chapter in the history of
British music. That chapter will form part of a later book
than this, and there is no doubt that some of those discussed
here, together with others who should not have been omitted,
will take their place in future works written on the present
subject.

Index

*Dates of birth and death, and in some cases titles,
are shown with the names of musicians only.*